KIPA Case Study Series 1

2016 KIPA Collection Volume 03

Korean Cases in Public Administration for Training and Practice

Korea Institute of Public Administration

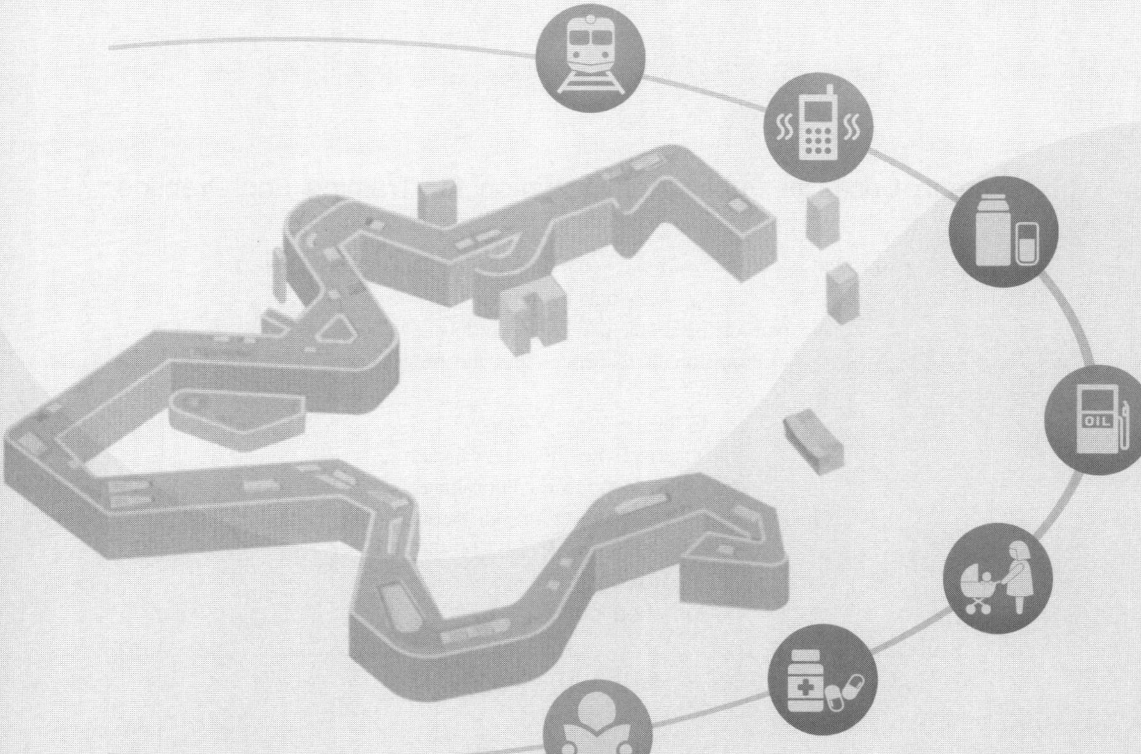

Daeyoung Moonhwasa

Korean Cases in Public Administration for Training and Practice

ISBN 978-89-7644-595-7
Published by Choon Hwan Lim
Daeyoung Moonhwasa Publishing Co.
5, Cheongpa-ro 61-gil, Yongsan-gu, Seoul, 04308, Korea
TEL (02) 716-3883, (02) 714-3062
FAX (02) 703-3839
Published on 30 Dec, 2016

Price ₩15,000

Foreword

Under the change of global environment, the importance of national policy is growing. Also, needs for the research through systematic case study on various policy are increasing.

Significant research on policy cases in South Korea are following. First, the Korea Institute of Public Administration (KIPA) published *Cases in Administration and Policy* in 1995. In 2014, the Korean Association of Public Administration (KAPA) published *Research in Policy Case Studies*, and KAPA hosted the 2016 Administrative and Policy Case Study Contest. These publications and events were for facilitating basic learning of policy cases, and contributed to the development of public administration and policy studies.

As importance and needs to policy cases increase, interest in the collection of policy cases and their quantitative and qualitative improvement is increasing. It is necessary to discover and develop meaningful and important policy cases and to share and spread the policy cases and administrative experience of South Korea as well. In particular, cases in public management, conflict management, public leadership, regulation, leadership, governance, and other policies are drawing attention of scholars, public officials, and the public.

Therefore, this research, which seeks to identify the relevant cases, analyze their implications and ascertain solutions to specific problems, is necessary today. For example, institutions such as the Evans School at University of Washington and the Kennedy School at Harvard University are independently identifying and accumulating case studies base on the importance of policy case study. In this context, it is a task of supreme importance to develop policy cases in English and to distribute to academic institutions and governments in developing countries.

With this background, this research seeks to identify meaningful and applicable cases in South Korea, and systematically analyze the dynamics in overall policy making process. In addition, we have constantly kept in contact with the distinguished scholars in the world to identify cases in English and to improve the quality of the research. The cases, seven in total, are classified into three categories: public administration, public policy, and governance. Each case is accompanied by teaching note in order to satisfy the needs of various reader groups.

This research presents the analysis as well as its implications in a multi-faceted and comprehensive manner through systematic analysis of each case study. It analyzed existing literature, policy documentation, field research notes, and other documentation, and carried out in-depth interviews in order to reach policy proposals relevant to each case as well.

To sustain this research and to disseminate its findings, we are planning to establish and operate an online system to upload and manage policy cases through the KIPA website based on the benchmarking systems in place at the University of Washington and Harvard University.

Hopefully, this research contributes to the development of Korean policy case studies, improves the capacity of students and public officials regarding policy studies, and helps globally spread awareness regarding Korea's best practices in public administration. I would like to commend the efforts of Dr. Su Jae Yoon, who was the chief researcher on this project. I also would like to thank Professor M. Jae Moon at Yonsei University and members of the Section on Korean Public Administration in the American Society for Public Administration, who were fully supportive in the crafting of this report. Finally, I would like to thank Professor Ha Zoong Song at Kyunghee University, Professor Gyun Soo Yoon at Korea University, and Professor Stephen Page at the University of Washington for their counsel on this research.

December 2016
Yoon Soo Jung
President, Korea Institute of Public Administration

Contents

01

Chapter

Introduction

M. Jae Moon

This is a collection of case studies conducted for the purpose of being utilized in various training programs or academic courses in the area of public administration, public policy, and governance. Selected case studies were compiled by seven faculty members who are currently teaching in either public administration or health administration programs in the U.S. In addition to the case studies, additional teaching notes are prepared as a teaching guideline. As indicated in the following table, the seven cases are largely categorized into three groups: public administration, public policy, and governance.

Professor Kim Younhee of Pennsylvania State University analyzed a public administration case entitled "Performance Evaluation Systems for the Korean Central Government Agencies: Self and Specific Evaluations." The Korean government performance evaluation system has been evolving since the Government Performance Evaluation Act of 2001 was revamped in 2006. A significant change to the existing evaluation system was the adoption of self-evaluation along with specific evaluation systems for central government agencies. Self-evaluation is a mandatory evaluation conducted by each agency's evaluation committee, while specific evaluation is a top-down evaluation to coordinate individual agencies' key policies with overall national government agendas. Specific evaluation is conducted by the Government Performance Evaluation Committee under the Prime Minister's Office and focuses

Types	Authors	Themes
Public administration cases	Younhee Kim	Performance Evaluation Systems for the Korean Central Government Agencies: Self and Specific Evaluations
	Eunju Rho	Contracting Out or Contracting Back In: School Foodservice Contracts in South Korea
Public policy cases	Taehee Kim	Work-Life Balance for Working Mom and Dad in South Korea
	Chul-Young Roh	Stakeholders in the Public Policy-Making Process: The Case of the Separation of Prescription and Dispensing in South Korea
Governance cases	Hee Soun Jang & Jung Wook Kim	Transforming Seoul: Rethinking Neighborhood
	Kyujin Jung	Critical Assessment of the 2012 Gumi Chemical Spill: An Adaptive Governance Approach
	Dohyeong Kim	Public Health Crisis in South Korea: Policy Failure or Social Distrust?

on five target areas: national affairs tasks, regulatory reform, policy publicity, normality tasks to modify anomalies, and agency-wide common matters. Self-evaluation as annual internal evaluation focuses on three target areas: prioritized policies, consolidated financial projects, and administrative management capacity.

Both self-evaluation and specific evaluation use a quantitative ranking system and qualitative analysis to evaluate target subjects and identify causes of underperformance. Since the evaluation system is tightly linked to results-based management, the evaluation results should be reflected in the next year's budget proposal, organizational operations, personnel, and incentive pay practices. The evaluation systems for central government agencies tend to integrate various evaluation activities and authorities with the intention of leading and supervising evaluation operations, but the systems are still fragmented, duplicated, and unrealistic in certain aspects. Many questions have to be addressed to make the evaluation systems acceptable to internal and external stakeholders.

This case provides an overview of the performance evaluation system of Korean central government agencies to understand the types, operations, procedures, evaluation methods, and use of evaluation results. This case will be especially useful for: teaching how to evaluate the structure of the performance evaluation system, explaining the types, processes, methods and indicators and implementation plans; discussing the advantages and disadvantages of self-evaluation and specific evaluation; articulating the responsibilities of evaluation committees, individual agencies, supervising ministries, and other stakeholders; redefining evaluation target areas for self-evaluation and specific evaluation; redesigning evaluation methods and indicators; and discussing the use of evaluation results.

This case will clarify how and what performances of central government agencies should be assessed for better evaluation with reasonable evaluation techniques and criteria. This case also offers students of Public administration ways to consider the dynamic relationships between key players in the performance evaluation process and how to implement the results of evaluation to maintain or improve agencies' commitment to the evaluation system. Although this case somewhat simplifies the complicated government evaluation systems in South Korea, it has important implications for how the performance evaluation system itself can direct individual agencies' goals and shape their operations. It provides practical insights to improve the performance evaluation system and the use of evaluation results in other countries.

Professor Rho Eunju of the University of Akron wrote "Contracting Out or Contracting Back In: School Foodservice Contracts in South Korea." Over the last two decades, the South Korean government has implemented several policy initiatives and interventions designed to improve student health and education. In order to enhance the efficacy of school foodservice delivery and student health outcomes, a variety of school food management methods have been piloted and implemented. This case illustrates changes in the school foodservice policies in South Korea, focusing on the decision of the Ministry of Education to contract back in foodservices for public schools in South Korea as a key tool to address the problem of contracted foodservice management.

The School Meals Act of 1981 was enacted to improve the health and well-being of the nation's children. In accordance with this Act, the Korean government has expanded school foodservices. In particular, since the Act was amended in 1996, contract foodservice management companies have been allowed to operate school meal services, and the contract foodservice system contributed to the rapid expansion of nationwide school foodservices.

However, after several massive foodborne disease outbreaks, the School Meals Act was significantly revised to introduce stringent safety guidelines and strict regulations. The Act also required elementary and middle schools to set up self-operated foodservices, and many schools that had adopted contracted foodservice management switched to self-operation based on these legal requirements.

By examining the different steps of school foodservice management policies in South Korea, this case highlights potential benefits and challenges to contracting-related issues with an approach that involves a diverse set of stakeholders. The various issues of cost saving, better service quality, and accountability are important elements in the debate over contracting out. This case is designed to help readers examine the debate surrounding contracting for services and empirical evidence on school foodservice contracts in South Korea.

Since the difficulties of the agency that oversaw service delivery are readily identifiable, it is a fairly simple case to teach and provides students an opportunity to diagnose problems of privatization and understand various actors that impact the policymaking process and implementation process. This case also introduces a series of changes in public service delivery methods and helps students to develop solutions targeted at the specific problems they have identified. This case can be utilized in many different academic settings, including courses on public management, organizational theory, leadership, collaboration, and policy process.

There are two public policy cases. "Stakeholders in the Public Policy-Making Process: The Case of the Separation of Prescription and Dispensing in South Korea" was prepared by Chul-Young Roh of Lehman College. The case study examines how policy stakeholders have behaved in the changing public policy context specifically in the separation of prescription and dispensation (SPD) of drugs in South Korea. Roh conducts stakeholder analysis to figure out the key stakeholders in SPD reform. This case study also identifies the power, position, and commitment of each key stakeholder and investigates which opposition groups could be convinced to change their position and how power and influence of supporter be increased.

The most powerful stakeholder is the Korean Medical Association (KMA), which represents physicians. The KMA is well-organized and has substantial organization resources and credibility. In this case, the KMA used their resources to stop SPD reform. Another opposition group against SPD reform was Korean Pharmaceutical Association (KPA), which represented pharmacists. After the KPA recognized that several conflicts related to SPD reform existed between the KMA and themselves, the KPA turned to support SPD reform.

The government is the key actor in the SPD reform, but the position of the government was passive compared with that of other major stakeholders. In particular, civic organizations were organized and led by progressive academics. These civic organizations in general strongly supported SPD reform based on their analyses of the existing system. Civic organizations hold a critical position in SPD reform. They were experienced in advocating for democracy and savvy about working with media.

Professor Kim Taehee wrote a public personnel policy case entitled "Work–Life Balance for Working Mom and Dad in South Korea." The increasing participation of non–traditional employees (e.g., women, the disabled, the elderly, dual–career couples, and contingent workers) has been a compelling reason for creating and building an inclusive work environment where this heterogeneous group of people work together. However, it has been noted that these non–traditional employees may have greater difficulties balancing their work roles with their personal or family roles. To accommodate diversified work–life balance needs in the workforce, government agencies as model employers have implemented work–life balance–promoting policies and programs including childcare, alternative work schedules, telework, and wellness programs.

Differently from Western countries, it appears that the Korean government has created policies and programs which appear to be narrowly tailored to addressing the needs of employees with family obligations. The Korean government tends to pay more attention to addressing the needs of working parents; organizations help employees fulfill the obligations they may have outside of the workplace, whereas less attention is given to creating work–life balance policies and programs that aim to enhance employees' well–being and work motivation.

In the U.S., however, the federal government in the U.S.A. has implemented health and wellness program as well as employee assistance programs as part of work–life balance programs which are intended for employee capacity development, leisure or stress management (e.g., providing a free counseling services so that employees can develop competency in managing workplace stress).

Moreover, despite governmental efforts to address the gender equality, there is still a gap between policy rhetoric and reality. Subtle forms of bias, prejudice and discrimination against women hinder achieving family-friendly workplaces. This might be attributable to long-held Confucian influences that have constrained the participation of women in the workforce and reinforced the traditional gender division of labor. Moreover, the "ideal-worker norm" of workers who prioritize their career over family and are willing to work overtime has been a major impediment to employees' use of work-life policies. The hypothetical case provided in this report along with descriptive information about work-life policies and programs in South Korea provides an introduction to the topic of work-life balance and illustrates the issues involved in implementing work-life balance policies and programs. Specifically, this report aims to facilitate an understanding of the importance of cultural changes in materializing the benefits of work-life policies.

Work-life balance policies and programs exist as measures to both address past gender inequality and improve organizational performance. In the Korean context, the focus of work-life balance policies appears to be on achieving gender equality. It should be noted, however, that work-life balance policies are part of practical measures of managing a diversified workforce by helping them address their non-work needs and in turn improve performance. The hypothetical case and its related descriptive information about work-life balance policies in South Korea may help initiate a dialogue in class about the role of understanding gender issues in designing and implementing work-life balance policies and facilitate classroom discussion about the necessity of creating a comprehensive policy that cover employees who might not have any family obligations but still need work-life balance. That is, considering that different employees have different needs in relation to balancing their work and life, a one-size fits all approach to designing and implementing work-life balance policies is flawed and cannot work. This case may also help direct more attention to the importance of having a supportive/inclusive culture in order to effectively implement work-life balance practices and achieve the benefits of helping employees to balance their multiple needs.

There are three governance-related cases which mainly demonstrate the significance of inter-sectoral collaboration. The first is written by Professor Kim Dohyeong of the University of Texas at Dallas and reviews three major infectious disease outbreaks in South Korea since 2000 (SARS, H1N1 and MERS). The case presents how the country addressed each of the epidemics, focusing on three sources of the public health crises: governmental system failure, poor communication and social distrust. Most of the literature, including media reports and journal articles, reported those three issues as keys to explain various social phenomena observed during the outbreaks in South Korea. The detailed discussion on these issues will help students think about the most critical problems in handling public health crises in the Korean context and understand how these issues are related to each other. It will also assist students as they deliberate on policy questions related to what issues should be prioritized when a country with limited resources faces an unexpected disease outbreak. Although a direct comparison among the outbreaks is limited considering their intrinsic distinctions such as pathologic and epidemiologic characteristics of each disease, a comparative review of these experiences will help policymakers, stakeholders, scholars and students obtain a clear and broad picture of the problems and generate wisdom for the Korean government and society about how to avoid repeating the same mistakes and challenges when the next public health crisis comes.

This case consists of a case study document, a role play exercise, and teaching resources to engage students in discussion about three recent outbreaks of infectious diseases in South Korea. These will offer comprehensive policy analytic perspectives and allow students the opportunity to discuss critical public health issues such as: (1) key factors of the nationwide social panic during the MERS crisis in South Korea in comparison with the two previous outbreaks of SARS and H1N1; (2) the Korean government's preparedness for and response to SARS, H1N1 and MERS; (3) the capacity and organizational structure of the KCDC in controlling the unprecedented disease in comparison to the U.S. CDC; (4) the government's strategy for information sharing about diseases and patients during the outbreaks; (5) the roles and responsibilities of the central government and local governments in handling a public health crisis; (6) the mechanism of trust and distrust formation among the government, news media, and citizens within their complex relationships and interactions; and (7) the negative impact of social distrust and poor communication processes on public health crises. The lessons from this case study on these controversial but critical issues are a valuable contribution to the design of informed public health policy that will improve the government's disease control and prevention system, facilitate an open and unbiased communication process and decrease the level of social distrust in South Korea.

The second governance case deals with new initiatives for community building in the Seoul Metropolitan City. The case is prepared by Jang Hee Soun & Kim Jung Wook of the University of North Texas. The Seoul Metropolitan Government launched a progressive community-building effort called Community Building Policy (CBP) to shape the social and human values of citizen life in Seoul in vital ways. The foundational mechanisms of CBP are *citizen leads* and *government supports*. CBP strongly encourages ordinary citizens to take the initiative to build their own community programs and adopt grassroots approaches to engage public and private partnership. The success stories in the case demonstrate that CBP contributes to civic culture development, community capacity building, and democratic practices at a community level. The case also illustrates vital conditions for effective community development practices: leadership commitment, government support, community space, and a sense of belonging. In many local governments, community-building policy has been challenged due to citizens' lack of interest, knowledge and time, along with broken trust in the community.

The primary focus of this case study is to understand social capital as a key component of CBP and how CBP may support community-building processes in Seoul's neighborhoods. The case helps students understand theory-driven public policy practices and analyzes the real applications of policy intentions in a diverse urban context. The political goals of the newly elected activist mayor Park Won-soon, who emphasized local initiatives and self-help (or self-governance), seem opportune and timely, but the notion of community building is less likely to be addressed in short-term policy investment for a global city that is economically segregated and whose communities have been disintegrating over the past few decades. In furthering community building today, high priority should be given to addressing immediate obstacles in an effort to recognize effective community-building practices.

The last case is written by Professor Jung Kyujin of Korea University. "Critical Assessment of the 2012 Gumi Chemical Spill: An Adaptive Governance Approach" follows the 2012 Gumi chemical spill and investigates key stakeholders affiliated with public agencies, nonprofits, media, and affected communities. On September 27, 2012, a toxic chemical leak in Gumi's National Industrial Complex, located 124 miles of southeast Seoul, released hydrofluoric acid. The accident occurred when two Hube Globe Chemical Corporation workers working on a tanker attempted to unload hydrofluoric acid into a storage tank. About 8 tons of hydrofluoric acid escaped into the atmosphere, spreading across a 4-km radius, killing 5 workers, affecting 12,243 residents, and damaging 212 hectares of agricultural land and 3,944 livestock. More than 11,000 people received treatment for nausea, chest pain, rashes, or sore eyes after inhaling fumes from the chemical leak. More than 300 residents including elderly people were evacuated to public-run facilities in Bongsan-ri, Incheon-ri, and Baekhyeon-ri.

This case study includes two critical issues: (1) crisis management as conceptual background; and (2) an adaptive governance approach as an analytic tool to help the instructor guide students' group discussion of the case. In the first section on crisis management, a conceptual basis is discussed to define a crisis and the roles of various stakeholders in coping with unanticipated events within a society. In the second section on the adaptive governance approach, a general view of the analytic tool is used to identify multiple stakeholders in deliberative mechanisms responding to an unexpected situation. Since crisis response manuals in general and response activities in the case of chemical spill might not fully present an opportunity for responders to be adaptive to a veiled event, the case helps to discuss challenges and future opportunities of (1) responsiveness; (2) public and scientific learning; and (3) deliberation process.

The adaptive governance perspective provides the following implications. First, the hierarchical structure embedded in crisis management imposes inefficiency as decisions by one specialized agency may impose negative externalities on others. Second, the chemical spill crisis was induced by organizational failures and human errors. Lastly, the crisis was exacerbated further by media coverage about human suffering and environmental consequences. Since the crisis management system's reliance on a leading agency may not be effective when initially responding to a crisis, the principal control tower should have sufficient authority to secure timely information to allocate resources and to coordinate the first-responding organizations.

The seven selected Korean cases not only offer us great managerial and policy lessons but also leave us compelling challenges that we continue to face in governments at different levels. The cases suggest that governments are always dealing with multiple stakeholder who often demand for better, faster, and more efficient and effective services while they are making managerial and policy decision in the lieu of more complex and complicated environment. We hope that the selected cases help both current and future government officials to understand and prepare for future administrative, policy, and governance challenges.

Chapter 02

Performance Evaluation Systems for the Korean Central Government Agencies: Self and Specific Evaluations

Younhee Kim

The Korean government has acted to embed performance-based evaluation systems across all levels of public agencies and public institutions after enacting the Government Performance Evaluation Act (GPEA) of 2001. Paralleling the Government Performance and Results Act of 1993 in the United States, the GPEA 2001 intended to reform Korean government agencies' capacities and operations in order to improve their efficiency, effectiveness, and responsibility at the national and local levels. Individual central government agency were required to set a 5-year strategic plan and an annual performance plan, evaluate performance based on indicators, report evaluation results, and implement feedback on evaluation. Since individual ministries ran own evaluation standards to assess their performance, it was hard to apply consistent and interconnected implications from results of performance evaluations across central government agencies.

The Korean government substantially revamped the Act of 2001 to integrate various performance evaluation systems in 2006. Thereafter the Act of 2006 has been revised several times, but its foundation framework and contents have remained the same. The Korean government performance evaluation system has been tightly linked to results-based management in order to utilize evaluation results for policy improvement, budget allocations, organizational management, and so on. Although the Korean government performance evaluation system has become much more realistic by integrating and evolving performance management and evaluation systems since 2006, its operations and implementations are still fragmented, duplicated, and overlapping.

The overall evaluation system of the Korean government is divided into three types of evaluations based on different levels of public provisions depicted in Figure 2–1: central government evaluation, local government evaluation, and public institution evaluation. This case study focuses on the self–evaluation and specific evaluation systems at the central government level newly proposed in 2016. Self–evaluation is a mandatory performance evaluation to be conducted by individual central government agency evaluation committees, while specific evaluation is a supplemental tool of self–evaluation to be prepared by the Government Performance Evaluation Committee (GPEC) co–chaired by the Prime Minister's Office. Self–evaluation focuses on each agency's performance activities in relation to short–term policies or programs. Specific evaluation assesses each individual agency's performance on mid–term to long–term strategies directly linked with prioritized national policies.

Figure 2–1. The Korean Government Performance Evaluation System

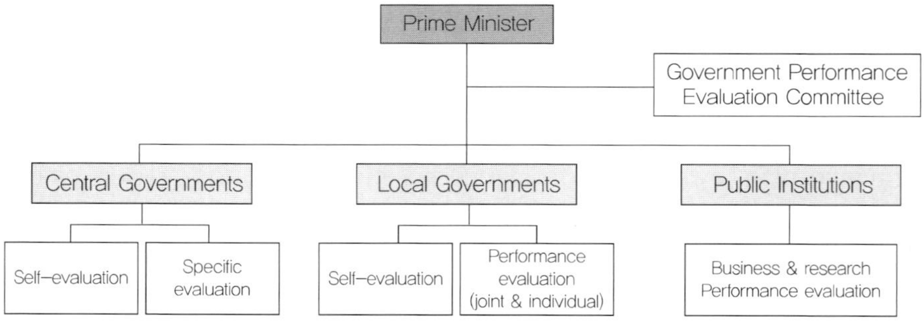

Source: Government Performance Evaluation Committee (2016).

Self–evaluation System

The purpose of self–evaluation as annual internal evaluation is to improve efficiency and accountability of government operations by reflecting evaluation results in policy, budget, organization, personnel, and administrative management. Since self–evaluation aims at policy and program improvement, the results of self-evaluation directly affect decision making to update the agency's existing goals. Practically, each agency's self-evaluation results are integrated into national performance management.

The target subjects in policy, finance, and organizational and administrative management have remained the same, but the categories and names of the subject areas have been slightly changed depending on government priorities overtime. For example, the target areas of self-evaluation in 2015 were subjected in prioritized policies, financial projects, R&D projects, and administrative management capacity, while its target areas in 2016 were prioritized policies, consolidated financial projects, and administrative management capacity. The major change between two time periods was merging the R&D project field into the consolidated financial projects area in 2016.

As Table 2-1 shows, the prioritized policies area evaluates all major policies identified by each agency's annual implementation plan of performance management. The consolidated financial projects area includes target projects in general finance, R&D, and local development fields. The administrative management capacity area focuses on management in personnel, organization, and information technology. Unlike the other two areas, financial projects were evaluated at every three-years between 2006 and 2015, but the consolidated financial evaluation will be performed annually from 2016.

Table 2-1. Target Areas of the Self-evaluation System in 2016

Target Area	Direction in Evaluation
Prioritized policies	Major projects designated by the 2016 performance management implementation plan
Consolidated financial projects	General targeted financial projects, R&D projects, local development projects
Administrative management capacity	Organization, human resources, information technology

Source: Prime Minister's Office (2016).

Before 2016, only one-third of national financial projects were subject to evaluation, so that target financial projects were selectively determined based on consultation between each agency and the Ministry of Strategy and Finance. Newly reformed evaluation operations of financial projects are scheduled to evaluate all financial projects incrementally by 2018. Major reforms intend to unify operating evaluation systems and simplify procedures, which are expected to reduce the individual agencies' burden and strengthen agencies' own evaluation of their financial projects. Therefore, the consolidated financial self-evaluation is conducted in two evaluation phases: regular self-evaluation by individual central agencies and meta-evaluation by the Ministry of Strategy and Finance. The meta-evaluation was introduced to improve quality of the self-evaluation method by reevaluating the results of regular self-evaluations that were prepared by individual central government agencies. In other words, meta-evaluation enables to validate relatability of the self-evaluation process and appropriateness of the self-evaluation results. Projects in each upper 10% and lower 10% after combining all self-evaluation results are only subject to meta-analysis. Then, the Ministry of Strategy and Finance determines either good or unsatisfactory agencies based on the results of meta-analysis. If central government agencies are evaluated as good by meta-analysis, they will get incentives in in next year's budget and vice versa. In 2016, six agencies were rated as good, while four agencies were rated as unsatisfactory among the 47 target agencies.

In response to the GPEC's self-evaluation guidelines, central government agencies have to use a set of self-evaluation indicators developed by the GPEC. Each agency is eligible to revise the GPEC's suggested common indicators for the target areas in both financial projects and administrative management capacity. Each agency also constructs its own evaluation criteria to evaluate the prioritized policy area that reflects agency-level goals and organizational environments in consultation with a self-evaluation committee.

Specific Evaluation System

Specific evaluation intends to align individual agencies' key policies and organizational capacities in order to manage national government affairs under the direction of the Prime Minister. It is much more centralized than the self-evaluation type because GPEC is responsible to develop all specific evaluation procedures and construct a set of evaluation indicators. The target areas for specific evaluation change constantly over time, depending on the emphases of each presidential administration (e.g., economic development or innovation). The authority for evaluation of target areas is largely given to the Prime Minister's Office along with other five supervising ministries that initially assess performance of given projects in the specific areas described in Table 2-2.

Table 2-2. Target Areas of Specific Evaluation System in 2016

Target Area	Direction in Evaluation	Supervising Agency	Num. of Agencies Evaluated
National affairs tasks	Core reform projects, interagency collaboration	Prime Minister's Office	42
Regulatory reform	Outcomes of regulatory reform	Prime Minister's Office	27
Policy publicity	Promotional efforts and results for policy publicity	Ministry of Culture, Sports and Tourism	42
Normalization to repair anomalies	Project selection and implementation, impacts of normalization efforts to modify anomalies, dissemination of normalization outcomes	Prime Minister's Office	39
Agency-wide common matters	Government 3.0	Ministry of the Interior	42
	Performance management	Prime Minister's Office	
	Specific policies in disability employment and products, small and medium business products, R&D projects	Ministry of Employment and Labor, Ministry of Health and Welfare, Ministry of Small and Medium Business Administration	

Source: Prime Minister's Office (2016).

There were five target are as for specific evaluationas external evaluation in 2016: national affairs tasks, regulatory reform, policy publicity, normalization tasks to modify anomalies, and agency-wide common matters. Compared to the target areas in 2015, minor changes were made in the area of agency-wide common matters. In place of the interagency collaboration field, which moved to prioritized policies, performance management was newly included in agency-wide common matters.

The first area, national affairs tasks, is directed to analyze the 140 national government projects from 42 agencies objectively in order to support the successful implementation of national affairs. The national affairs propose five goals that consist of several strategies. Evaluations in core reform projects and interagency collaboration are weighted to improve performance outcomes of national affairs tasks. Table 2-3 presents details of the national affairs tasks with examples. In the regulatory reform area, the reform outcomes of 27

Table 2-3. Projects of National Affairs Tasks for Specific Evaluation in 2016

Goal	Strategy	Num. of Projects	Example and Lead Agency
Economic growth	Creative economy	22	Business start-up stimulation (Min. of Small and Medium Business Administration)
	Fair economy	6	Consumer protection (Fair Trade Commission)
	Welfare economy	14	Reduced communication cost burden (Min. of Science, ICT and Future Planning)
Citizen happiness	Customized employment service	15	Promotion of youth employment (Min. of Employment and Labor)
	Creative education	8	Simplified university entrance examination (Min. of Education)
	Citizen safety	32	Sexual violence prevention (Min. of Gender Equality and Family & Min. of Justice)
	Social integration	10	Promoting balanced regional development (Min. of Land, Infrastructure and Transportation & Min. of Trade, Industry and Energy)
Culture promotion	Enhancing cultural participation	4	Expansion of cultural participation opportunity and reduce of cultural gap (Min. of Culture, Sports and Tourism [MCST])
	Cultural art promotion	3	Preservation and utilization of cultural heritage (MCST)
	Culture and industry integration	3	Supporting Korean contents industry (MCST)
Unification	Strong national security	7	Strengthening future-oriented defense capacity (Min. of National Defense)
	Korean Peninsula Trust Process	3	Preparation for peaceful reunification (Min. of Unification)
	Trust diplomacy	5	Promotion of Northeast East Peace Collaboration and Eurasia Collaboration (Min. of Foreign Affairs)
Government	Trusted government	8	Reforming the public sector (Min. of Strategy and Finance)

Source: Prime Minister's Office (2016). http://pmo.go.kr/pmo/inform/inform01_02a.jsp

ministries with more than 30 regulations are subject to be evaluated. The policy publicity area evaluates ways to promote citizens' understanding of public policy by dissemination and response activities in 42 agencies. In evaluating the normalization tasks to repair anomalies, 100 core national government projects from 39 agencies are included to correct erroneous practices and corruption. The final area, agency-wide common matters, evaluates the three fields of government 3.0, performance management, and specific policies in 42 agencies.

Leading Committees of the Performance Evaluation System

Government performance evaluation committee (GPEC)

The GPEC is the key organization to implement all national performance evaluations. The primary responsibilities of the GPEC are supervising individual agencies' self-evaluation and conducting specific evaluation. With regard to both types, the GPEC develops general guidelines and measurement standards assisted by the Policy Analysis and Evaluation Office under the Prime Minister's Office. Each agency is entitled to customize the GPEC's set of the original measurement indicators aligning with the agency's performance goals and strategies. The GPEC is also responsible to reevaluate and reapprove the results of agencies' self-evaluation if there is concern about the objectivity and reliability of self-evaluation results.

The GPEC consists of 15 committee members from both inside and outside central governments, and the group is co-chaired by the Prime Minister and a university professor. The three members in central government are the Minister of Strategy and Finance, the Minister of the Interior, and the Minister of the Office for Government Policy Coordination. In 2016, the remaining 10 seats were assigned to eight university professors and two professionals at central and local government-funded research institutions. Excluding the four heads of central government agencies, the 11 representatives appointed due to their knowledge of target areas serve a two-year term and can be reappointed for one more consecutive term. In regard to their professional expertise, about one-third of the 11 committee members are in the field of public administration.

Self-evaluation Committee

Each agency determines its own self-evaluation committee's structure, functions, and operating rules independently, in compliance with the GPEC's self-evaluation guideline and annual evaluation schedule. A self-evaluation committee appointed by a head of the agency consists of ten to thirty members who typically serve a two-year term and can be reappointed for a consecutive term. The committee members are divided into three functional areas: policies, financial performance, and administrative capacities. Within a self-evaluation committee, several sub-committees are often organized depending on the need for particular expertise. Sub-committees and their responsibilities are also determined during the first committee meeting. In addition, each agency has to arrange a self-evaluation support team internally in order to assist the self-evaluation committee.

The GPEC and the Prime Minister's Office broadly require agencies to follow basic structural rules of self-committees that are at least one internal member and no more than 60% of external experts from one profession. For example, the number of university faculty cannot be over 60% of the total external experts to avoid a dominated opinion from one group. The majority of committee members tend to be external experts in order to validate the objectivity and expertise of evaluations. External experts primarily participate in policy process evaluation, while internal public administrators mainly take a liaison role between the agency and the self-evaluation committee. A proportion of internal and external members is determined autonomously by each agency, so the formation of self-evaluation looks quite different across agencies. For example, the Rural Development Administration appointed 26 members (9 internal and 17 external members), while the South Korea Meteorological Administration assigned 30 members (2 internal and 28 external members) in 2016. The largest group of external committee members are college or university faculty and the next largest is researchers. A small number of committee members (about 10%) are selected from nonprofit and private sectors. One or two journalists are included in both self-evaluation and specific evaluation committees.

Self-evaluation at an agency level must follow the GPEC guidelines for performance evaluation plans and operations, but the relationship between the

GPEC and a self-evaluation committee is not formally hierarchical. However, the GPEC can ask an agency to conduct a re-evaluation of the agency's self-evaluation if the Prime Minister's Office finds that the agency's self-evaluation is not satisfactory in terms of objectivity and credibility of evaluation results.

Operations of Self and Specific Evaluations

The evaluation operation of self-evaluation is administered by both GPEC and central agencies as presented in Figure 2-2. As the study conducted by Hur in 2013 detailed, the evaluation cycle is highly routinized. On the GPEC and Prime Minister's Office end, an entire evaluation cycle takes one and a half years to complete, from January to June of the next year. Their evaluation responsibilities can be divided into two parts: (1) preparation of guidelines for an annual performance plan and an operational performance evaluation plan during January to March, and (2) evaluation of each agency's self-evaluation activities from January to June of the next year.

In the first step of self-evaluation, the GPEC works with the Policy Analysis and Evaluation Office to prepare guidelines for both annual performance and performance evaluation plans in the beginning of the fiscal year. Their second task is to review and refine each agency's annual performance plan by March, once each agency has submitted a draft of the performance plan to the Prime Minister's Office. The next task is to prepare operational guidelines for self-evaluation by March. After the first round of tasks, the GPEC evaluates each agency's self-evaluation results from February to May of the next year depending on target areas. In June, high-performing central agencies receive rewards from the Prime Minister's Office and budget incentives in the following year from the Ministry of Strategy and Finance.

On the agency and its self-evaluation committee end, the evaluation procedures are grouped into three stages: (1) planning self-evaluation by July, (2) evaluating mid-point progress in July, and (3) evaluating the agency's performance by January of the next year as presented in Figure 2-2. After self-evaluation, an initial reporting process begins with individual public officials who prepare their self-evaluation reports and submit them to their division or subdivision managers. Thereafter, the division managers are responsible to report the collected individual evaluation reports to the self-evaluation task force that submits those reports to the self-evaluation committee.

Figure 2–2. Procedures of Self-evaluation

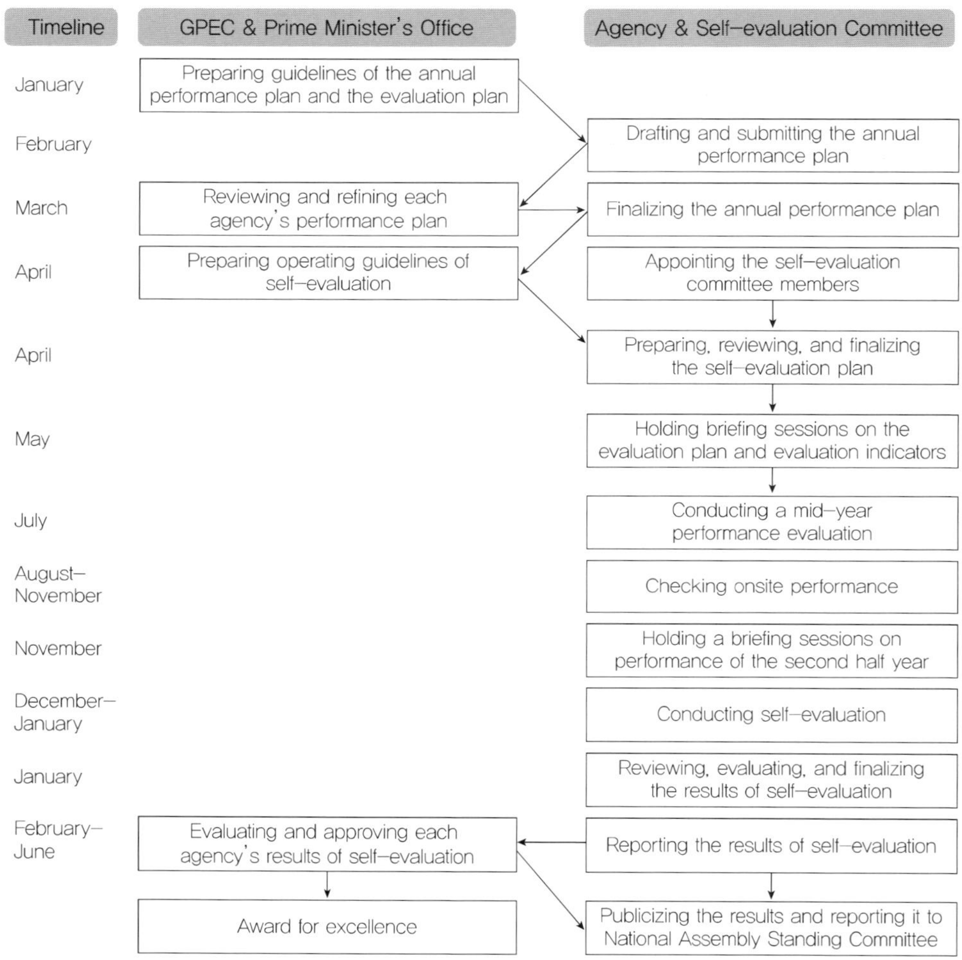

The members of the self-evaluation committee assign evaluation scores to individual programs and the sub-committees review and revise the scores, if necessary. After confirming the evaluation scores by the sub-committees, the self-evaluation committee finalizes the scores as a whole. Submission schedules for the self-evaluation results to the GPEC are different depending on target areas. In 2016, the evaluation results of the prioritized policies area were due at the end of January, while the results for the administration management capacity area were to be submitted by March. For the financial projects, the report of each agency's self-evaluation was due in May. After submitting the results of self-evaluation to the GPEC, the results are also reported to the National Assembly Standing Committee and publicized on the agency's website within one month.

Figure 2-3 presents the specific evaluation process classified into two phases. Specific evaluation as top-down evaluation is directly operated by the GPEC to conduct evaluation of national policies in the target areas and approve the results of the performance evaluations. However, projects in one target area and four subfields are initially evaluated by the five supervising ministries noted in Table 2-2. The GPEC organizes several task forces to

Figure 2–3. Procedures of Specific Evaluation

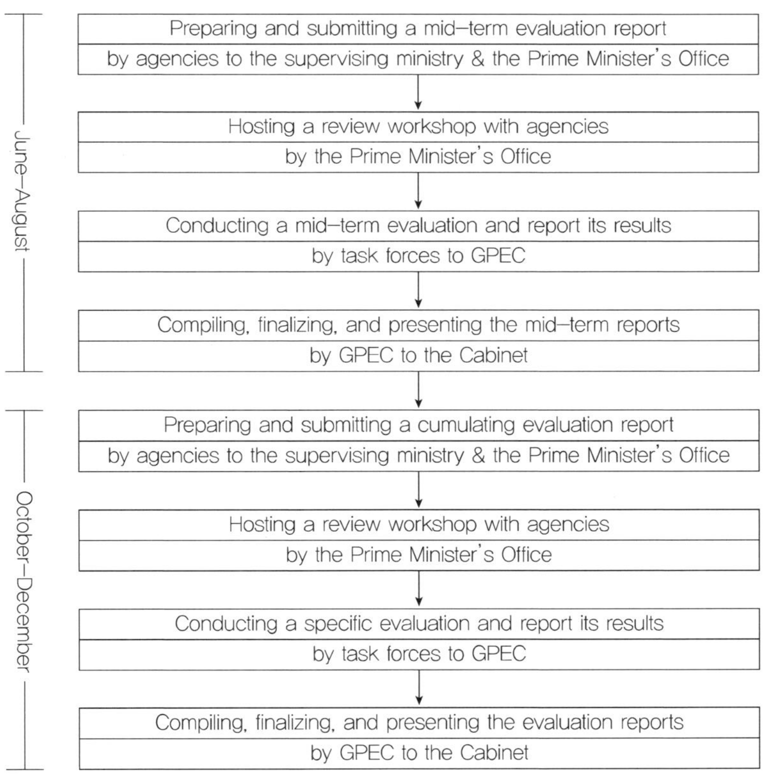

initially evaluate central agencies' projects in each target area except policy publicity, which is supervised by task forces created by the Ministry of Culture, Sports and Tourism. A task force consists of members of the supervising ministries and experts from non-governmental sectors such as academia, research institutes, and private organizations.

Methods and Indicators for Self-evaluation

The self-evaluation committee first assigns evaluation scores to individual programs based on the 100-point system and then coverts the results of the evaluations into a percentile ranking in order to make different programs comparable as a whole within each central government agency. This comparative ranking system is applied to promote usability of evaluation results for other purposes, such as policy improvement, organizational management, and individual performance evaluation. Although the evaluation scores of individual programs are slightly diverse across central government agencies, this relative ranking approach makes variability of raw scores even. Self-evaluation uses different evaluation ranking systems depending on the target areas. For example, the prioritized policies area uses the seven tiers of a relative rating system to compare the results of individual programs. In addition to the quantitative evaluation, narrative analysis as a qualitative approach is also required to justify the causes of underperformance and suggest alternatives to improve performance in prioritized policies.

For prioritized policies, the Prime Minister's Office provides a distribution standard of evaluation ranking: 1st tier (excellent) within top 5%, 2nd tier (good) ranging from top 5% to 20%, 3rd tier (somewhat good) ranging from 20% to 35%, 4th tier (average) ranging from top 35% to 65%, 5th tier (somewhat unsatisfactory) ranging from top 65% to 80%, 6th tier (dissatisfied) ranging from 80% to 95%, and 7th tier (extremely unsatisfactory) ranging from below 95%. If 20 programs are self-evaluated in a central government agency, only the first place program is included in the first tier. This forced ranking technique has benefits to make individual programs comparable across different agencies, but also has drawbacks to place excellent or mediocre agencies into normalized categories of percentiles for performance.

Table 2-4. Self-evaluation Indicators for Prioritized Policies

<table>
<tr><th>Fields</th><th>Indicators</th><th>Sub-indicators</th><th>Points</th></tr>
<tr><td rowspan="3">Performance achievement</td><td>Goal accomplishment of performance indicator</td><td>• goal achievement of performance indicators</td><td>20</td></tr>
<tr><td>Relevance of performance indicator</td><td>• a level of representation level of setting target values</td><td>5</td></tr>
<tr><td>Characteristics of a task</td><td>• difficulty, importance, creativity</td><td>5</td></tr>
<tr><td rowspan="2">Policy planning</td><td>Reliability of pre-survey and consulting</td><td>• reviewing statistical data and cases and consulting with experts</td><td>5</td></tr>
<tr><td>Appropriateness of policy analysis</td><td>• analysis of policy effects and pros and cons and preparation of complementary issues</td><td>5</td></tr>
<tr><td rowspan="4">Policy implementation</td><td>On-time progress and timely response</td><td>• timely progress of evaluation schedules
• timely, appropriate response to situational change</td><td>5</td></tr>
<tr><td>Linkage with relevant agencies' policies</td><td>• collaborative system-building with relevant other agencies for collaborative tasks
*extra points for the best collaborative project</td><td>5
(+2)</td></tr>
<tr><td>Efforts to participate in self-evaluation</td><td>• agency's active involvement in the overall evaluation process</td><td>5</td></tr>
<tr><td>Communication for policy improvement and implementation of feedback</td><td>• necessary information provided, on-site visit offer, and explanation by the self-evaluation committee
• implementation of last year's feedback for policy improvement</td><td>5</td></tr>
<tr><td>Policy effect</td><td>Degree of policy impact</td><td>• desirable outcome
• long-term impact
• major public values and indirect outcome
• citizen satisfaction</td><td>20
5
5
5</td></tr>
<tr><td colspan="3">Total</td><td>100
*(+2)</td></tr>
</table>

Source: Rural Development Administration (2016).

Individual agencies decide their own evaluation techniques with in-house developed indicators and rating scales to fit with their organizational characteristics and the nature of their tasks. Based on 100 points, each agency assigns points differently on evaluation indicators. In other word, same or similar indicators can be weighted differently depending on agencies' decisions. When individual agencies develop their own evaluation indicators, they consult with the self-evaluation committee and external experts. Agencies have to construct a valid measurement method to avoid generous self-evaluation and reserve discriminating power of evaluation results. Agencies can also use a weighting approach that reflects the difficulty and importance of projects.

A set of evaluation indicators strongly reflects four major aspects (i.e., performance achievement, appropriateness of policy planning, appropriateness of policy implementation, and policy effect) in a majority of central government agencies. In 2016, the Rural Development Administration developed self-evaluation indicators referring to the four fields detailed in Table 2-4. The performance achievement and policy effect fields took equally large portions (35%) of the evaluation. In particular, the aspect of policy effect has been continuously increased to measure prioritized policies across central government agencies.

For the consolidated financial evaluation in 2016, individual agencies evaluated their projects based on a relative rating system in three categories: good, average, and poor. The number of the self-evaluation indicators is also reduced from 11 in the three stages of planning, management and feedback to 4 in two stages of management and results. While some customized indicators developed by individual agencies have been unified under the new operational direction of self-evaluation in 2016, agencies are encouraged to use their own specialized indicators.

After individual agencies' self-evaluation of financial fields, both meta-evaluations per field and per agency are conducted by the meta-evaluation committee that consists of the Ministry of Strategy and Finance, the Ministry of Science, ICT and Future Planning, the Presidential Committee on Regional Development, the Korea Institute of Public Finance, and the National Information Society Agency. For meta-evaluation, there are six indicators in three categories of relevance of evaluation processes, appropriateness of evaluation results, and appropriateness of spending structures (see Table 2-5). In addition to the six indicators, one additional indicator is used only for the R&D subject.

Table 2–5. Meta–evaluation Indicators for Financial Projects

Fields	Indicators
Evaluation process	• relevance of organizing self–evaluation committee and operational planning • relevance of the self–evaluation committee's operations
Evaluation result	• implementation of evaluation based on the performance plan • compliance of with a relative rating evaluation • validity of the best project selection (only for R&D projects)
Adjustment of spending structure	• achievement of adjusting spending structures • appropriateness of contents of adjusting spending structures

Source: Ministry of Science, ICT and Future Planning (2016).

The last self–evaluation of administrative management capacity assesses performance in organization, personnel, and information technology management, using five standardized indicators across agencies. Table 2–6 shows the self–evaluation indicators of administrative capacity developed by the Rural Development Administration for 2016 evaluation. All three fields are equally weighted. Each indicator is detailed with three or four sub–indicators to assess each management capacity.

Table 2–6. Self–evaluation Indicators for Administrative Management Capacity

Fields	Indicators	Points
Organization	efficient uses of organizational and human resources (3 sub–indicators)	18
	collaboration with other agencies and communication with citizens (4 sub–indicators)	17
Personnel	efficient operation of personnel (5 sub–indicators)	30
Information technology	accessible e–government (3 sub–indicators)	18
	cyber security (3 sub–indicators)	17
Total		100

Source: Rural Development Administration (2016).

The GPEC oversees the operational practice of agencies' self–evaluation activities to minimize evaluation bias and make self–evaluation results realistic in February of the next year after completing each agency's evaluation. The typical monitoring tools are on–site visit, interview with agents in charge, and document evaluation. Before conducting reviews of an operational practice of agencies' self-evaluation activities, the Prime Minister's Office provides guidelines with review indicators to individual agencies. The review focuses on two fields scheduled in 2017: operational relevance and appropriate feedback. The operational relevance field has two indicators that assess the agency's efforts to improve organizational capacity and validity of the evaluation analysis. The appropriate feedback field estimates whether evaluation results are likely to improve existing policy and projects. Detailed sub-indicators will be developed after consulting with external experts and individual agencies during 2016. The results of the review are used for selecting and publicizing the best practice. Agencies with severe problems in relevance of operation and validity of evaluation results will be re-evaluated.

Use of the Evaluation Results

The evaluation results of both self-evaluation and specific evaluation are used at the institutional and individual levels. The heads of central government agencies have to reflect the results of self-evaluation in their organizational operations, budget, personnel, and incentive pay practices. The evaluation results should be also incorporate in the next year's budget proposal prepared by the Minister of Strategy and Finance.

At the institutional level, the evaluation results are used to improve policy, allocate budget, and manage the organization. If a prioritized policy is evaluated unsatisfactory by self-evaluation and reviews of the self-evaluation results, a head of the agency requests to take corrective action or to have a policy audit until the status of the policy is improved. The results of complementary action should be reported to the GPEC. For an excellent policy case, the agency and public officials associated with the specific policy will receive awards, incentive pay, or a promotion. With regard to the results of administrative management capacity, best practice cases will be shared with all central agencies for benchmarking. Like other target areas, an agency that has made unsatisfactory progress has to prepare an action plan to improve its evaluations.

However, the interviews with central government officials and experts, which were conducted by the Korea Institute of Public Administration in 2015, reported that individual agencies were often difficult to prepare a reform plan because recommendations from the GPEC were broad and abstract. For example, a recommendation after self-evaluation is expressed in a simple sentence like improving a citizen complaint procedure. Without specific standards suggested by the GPEC, performance of reforming actions for improving a citizen complaint procedure may be not much changed in consequent years. Public officials also addressed that the results of qualitative evaluation were not often provided to individual agencies and the justifications of the qualitative results were not sufficiently explained to correct unsatisfactory progress.

For linking evaluation results with budget allocation, a project will be rewarded or penalized based on the compiled results of both the agency's self-evaluation and oversight review by the Minister of Strategy and Finance. A project with an excellent rating will be given a budget increase next year, while a project that is unsatisfactory or below will have its budget reduced by 10% or be abolished. The unsatisfactory project has to provide corrective efforts and ongoing oversight review until its evaluation rating is upgraded. If a budget cut is not feasible due to the nature of the project, alternatives to reform its operations should be implemented. If a project is not under-performing but has not objectively proved sufficient performance, no budget increase is allowed in the next budget cycle. In addition, agencies can be granted differently to manage their organization in new hiring or adjusting the number of personnel per rank. An agency awarded for best practice will get incentives that lower a percentage of the unsatisfying category next year. On the other hand, an underperforming agency will be penalized that raises a percentage of the unsatisfying category and cut its next year operating budget.

The link between evaluation results and budget allocation makes agencies being highly sensitive to evaluation itself. As a result, agencies tend to set a low threshold for goal achievement, which takes the highest point among the evaluation indicators shown in Table 2-4, so they can have a better chance to receive a high evaluation score. With regard to goal achievement, the interviews with individual agencies in 2015 aforementioned were also likely to assign high weights to sub-indicators that were relatively easy to be accomplished. The interviewees pointed out that raising the bar for goal achievement at 90% is somewhat difficult since 90% of goal achievement is already high enough to delivery their services. Nevertheless, the current evaluation system placed those agencies with 90% at a low-tier ranking. No matter how well agencies are satisfied, the fact remains that the agencies do not reach 100% of goal achievement. In addition, mandating a number of percentage increase compared to last year may not be realistic to set an achievable threshold for agencies.

At the individual level, the self-evaluation results are supposed to influence promotions and incentive pay in conjunction with individual performance. The report conducted by Yoo and his colleagues in 2012 summarized that public officials in central government highly agreed with the direct use of the evaluation results for either a pay raise or incentive pay by 88.7% or 80.6% relatively. 77.5% of the interviewees responded that the evaluation results were timely released to be rewarded for incentive pay. While individual agencies had reflected the evaluation results in the personnel management system, it is not clear to what extent each agency actually reflects the results in its incentive system. In contrast, the interviewees disagreed with the direct use of the evaluation results for personnel management or promotion by 41.9% or 43.5% respectively. Overall, the interviewees perceived a positive impact of the evaluation results on pay but not much on promotion.

Another interesting survey, which focused on the use of the self-evaluation results of administrative management capacity conducted by Lee in 2014, reported that incentive pay was not consistently applied across individual agencies, unlike the case of the prioritized policies field that was directly corresponded to a pay raise or incentive pay. The interviewees addressed that a kind of monetary incentives for those who were in charge of preparing evaluation of administrative management capacity should be guaranteed to motivate them. They also pointed out that 65% of the self-evaluation results in the administrative management capacity field was incorporated to evaluate individual performance. The survey report informed that the self-evaluation results of administrative management capacity were somewhat helpful for the internal performance evaluation.

Potential Implications and Issues

Korean performance evaluation systems for central agencies have been evolving to improve their structures and operations by reflecting lessons from prior practice. The evaluation systems are structured to conduct evaluation throughout the entire process of policy activities and thus provide detailed information to the National Assembly and external stakeholders of government about the agency's goals, objectives, and results. Its operations and evaluation methods can also be internally utilized for the agency's own purposes. The evaluation systems include interest in collaboration across agencies, which is expected to stimulate desirable outcomes of national policies.

The evaluation systems are not exclusively focused on the evaluation of agencies' activities but also on giving effective feedback for learning to move the next level. Thus, individual public officials can train themselves to identify problematic issues related to their tasks and search for alternatives to resolve the issues. However, there is not a practical opportunity for public officials to be part of conducting evaluations, which isolates them from the actual evaluation. Public officials are overwhelmed by the amount of work the evaluations require but their roles are limited to conduct actual evaluations. In this context, are public officials being responsive to the self-evaluation committee? Are the public officials accountable for the evaluation results? To what extent are agencies complying with the evaluation results? The current feedback mechanism of performance evaluation is tightly linked with the incentive scheme, so this relationship somewhat misleads critical roles of evaluation as learning opportunities and skews agency time toward the tasks covered on the target fields and indicators to avoid penalties. This is similar to "teaching to the test." How well do the evaluation indicators represent the nature of the agency's tasks and unique characteristics? Meaningful use and implications of the evaluation results seem to be limited for resolving problems and improving the quality of the agency's tasks.

The evaluation systems for central government agencies tend to integrate various evaluation activities and authorities with the intention of leading and supervising evaluation operations, but the systems are still fragmented and unrealistic in certain aspects. In the case of self-evaluation, three target areas are supervised by different authorities such as the Prime Minister's Office and the Ministry of Strategy and Finance. Specific evaluation is much more complicated than self-evaluation, although the GPEC in conjunction with the Prime Minister's Office is responsible to direct the operations of specific evaluations. Supervising ministries in the five target areas conduct evaluation activities independently with their own committees and schedules. The GPEC is the leading institution for both self-evaluation and specific evaluation but does not have the enumerated power to connect the evaluation results with the budget. The GPEC is also run by part-time members with a two-year term, so their understanding of the systems and projects may be limited. Have meaningful consultations been given to direct agencies in these contexts? How can the members of the GPEC be effectively involved in the evaluation process? Are the self-evaluation committee and its agency consulting effectively with the GPEC and the supervising ministries? There are still questions that have to be addressed to make the evaluation systems feasible and approachable to internal and external stakeholders.

References

Cultural Heritage Administration(2016). *2016 Self-evaluation Plan*. Retrieved from http://www.cha.go.kr/cop/bbs/selectBoardArticle.do?nttId=31544&bbsId=BBSMSTR_1029&pageIndex=1&pageUnit=10&searchCnd=&searchWrd=&ctgryLrcls=&ctgryMdcls=&ctgrySmcls=&ntcStartDt=&ntcEndDt=&searchUseYn=&mn=NS_05_03_03.

Government Performance Evaluation Committee(2016). *Korean Government Performance Evaluation System*. Retrieved from http://www.evaluation.go.kr/psec/institution/sub01_01.jsp.

Hur, Mann Hyung(2013). 2012 Modularization of Korea's Development Experience: Korea's Government Performance Evaluation System and Operating Experience. *Knowledge Sharing Program: KSP Modularization*.

Kang, Jeong Seok & Lee, Hwan-seong(2011). A Study on the Improvement of Self-Evaluation Indicators in the Government Evaluation System. *KIPA Research Report 2011-09*. Seoul, Korea: Korea Institute of Public Administration.

Kellogg, W. K.(2004). *Logic Model Development Guide*. Michigan: WK Kellogg Foundation. Retrieved from https://www.aacu.org/sites/default/files/LogicModel.pdf.

Korea Institute of Public Finance(2016a). *Consolidated Financial Projects Evaluation System*. Retrieved from http://www.kipf.re.kr/TaxFiscalPubInfo/Fiscal-PerformanceMg.

_____(2016b). *Results of Consolidated Financial Projects Evaluation in 2016*. Retrieved from http://www.kipf.re.kr/TaxFiscalPubInfo/TaxFiscalPubTrends_DomTrends-View/2016%EB%85%84-%ED%86%B5%ED%95%A9-%EC%9E%AC%EC%A0%95%EC%82%AC%EC%97%85-%ED%8F%89%EA%B0%80-%EA%B2%B0%EA%B3%BC/523929

Korean Intellectual Property Office(2016). *2016 Self-evaluation Plan*. Retrieved from http://www.kipo.go.kr/kpo/user.tdf;jsessionid=9863ca6b30d5c3b0efd87fa848f3b649bc61adf0352d.www?a=user.ip_info.estimate.BoardApp&board_id=estimate&cp=1&pg=1

&npp=10&catmenu=m05_01_04&sdate=&edate=&searchKey=&searchVal=&bunryu=&st=&c=1003&seq=55.

Korea Meteorological Administration(2016). *2016 Self-evaluation Plan.* Retrieved from http://web.kma.go.kr/notify/information/publication_policy_list.jsp?bid=publication&mode=view&num=100.

Lee, Kwang Hee(2014). A Study on the Administrative Management Capacity Evaluation. *KIPA Research Report 2014-05.* Seoul, Korea: Korea Institute of Public Administration.

______(2015). A Study on the Development of a Manual for Performance Measurement to Improve Performance Validity. *KIPA Research Report 2015-06.* Seoul, Korea: Korea Institute of Public Administration.

Lee, Hwan Sung & Yang, Hong Seok(2015). Improvements to the Government Performance Evaluation Act of 2006. *KIPA Research Report 2015-08.* Seoul, Korea: Korea Institute of Public Administration.

Lee, Wonhee(2016). Budget and Financial Management. In *Understanding Korean Public Administration: Lessons Learned from Practice*, Park, Kwang-Kook Park, Wonhee Lee, & Seok-Hwan Lee (eds.): 100-119. New York, N.Y.: Routledge.

Ministry of Science, ICT and Future Planning(2016). *2015 Result Report of Self-evaluation.* Retrieved from http://www.msip.go.kr/web/msipContents/contentsView.do?cateId=mssw11231&artId=1301490.

Ministry of Strategy and Finance(2016a). *Implementation of Consolidated Financial Evaluation in 2016.* Retrieved from http://www.mosf.go.kr/nw/nes/detailNesDtaView.do?menuNo=4010100&searchNttId1=MOSF_000000000001602&searchBbsId1=MOSFBBS_000000000028.

_____(2016b). *The Results of the First Consolidated Financial Evaluation in 2016.* Retrieved from http://www.mosf.go.kr/nw/mosfnw/neslistDetail.do?menuNo=4030000&searchNttId1=MOSF_000000000003933&searchBbsId1=MOSFBBS_000000000023

Prime Minister's Office(2015). *2015 Government Performance Evaluation Enforcement Plan.* Retrieved from http://www.evaluation.go.kr/psec/sub04/sub01.jsp?mode=view&article_no=48107&board_wrapper=%2Fpsec%2Fsub04%2Fsub01.jsp&pager.offset=0&board_no=50.

_____(2016a). *2016 Government Performance Evaluation Enforcement Plan.* Retrieved from http://www.evaluation.go.kr/psec/sub04/sub01.jsp?mode=view&article_no=48556&board_wrapper=%2Fpsec%2Fsub04%2Fsub01.jsp&pager.offset=0&board_no=50.

_____(2016b). *2016 Self-evaluation Enforcement Plan for Central Government Agencies.* Retrieved from http://www.evaluation.go.kr/psec/sub04/sub01.jsp?mode=view&article_no=48557&board_wrapper=%2Fpsec%2Fsub04%2Fsub01.jsp&pager.offset=0&board_no=50.

Rural Development Administration(2016). *Introduction to the 2016 Government Performance self-evaluation.* Retrieved from http://rda.go.kr/board/board.do?mode=html&prgId=

eva_gvmtbizevlinfoQuery&html_page=eva_gvmtbizevlinfoQuery_04.

Yoo, Keum-Rok, et al.(2012). *A Study on the Diagnosis of Operation of Government Performance Evaluation System and the Improvement Plan*. Seoul, Korea: Office for Government Policy Coordination, Prime Minister's Secretariat. Retrieved from http://www.prism.go.kr/homepage/entire/retrieveEntireDetail.do;jsessionid=E599590F637445D446963AC832A58A78.node02?cond_research_name=&cond_research_start_date=&cond_research_end_date=&research_id=1101000-201200020&pageIndex=1156&leftMenuLevel=160.

Yoon, Soo Jae(2012). *A Study on the Meta-evaluation of the Government Performance Evaluation*. KIPA Research Report 2012-15. Seoul, Korea: Korea Institute of Public Administration. Retrieved from http://www.kipa.re.kr/public/basic_report/basic_report_view.jsp?typeID=75&boardid=68&seqno=893.

Teaching Note

Performance Evaluation Systems for the Korean Central Government Agencies: Self and Specific Evaluations

Performance Evaluation Systems for the Korean Central Government Agencies: Self and Specific Evaluations is a descriptive case explaining the structures, types, procedures, and evaluation methods of the central government performance evaluation system. This case aims to introduce students to self-evaluation and specific evaluation systems for central government in South Korea and to allow students to deliberate on its applicability to other countries. This case provides a snapshot of fragmented, overlapping operational practices, a series of relationships between supervising agencies and individual agencies, and implementations of evaluation results which can be viewed as challenges and dilemmas facing all central government agencies and evaluation committees. Although the complicated self-evaluation and specific evaluation mechanisms may not be fully understood within limited class time, students can observe operational and implementation issues to make the evaluation systems improved.

This case can be used in any public performance management or policy analysis course at a graduate level. Students can straightforwardly grasp the evaluation approaches for measuring agencies' performance. This case is useful for many types of class activities such as in-class discussions, group work for analyzing the current evaluation system and developing new action plans, stakeholder analysis, conceptualizing performance evaluation criteria, written homework assignments, and so on.

Case Synopsis

The Korean central government is responsible for evaluating public agencies' performance in central, local, and public institutions. The government performance evaluation system has been evolving since 1961 and was substantially changed after enacting the Government Performance Evaluation Act (GPEA) of 2001 that intended to reform Korean government agencies' capacities and operations in order to improve their efficiency, effectiveness, and responsibility at the national and local levels. An especially meaningful change of the evaluation system was the adoption of self-evaluation. The Act was revamped in 2006 to outline two types of evaluation for central government agencies: self-evaluation and specific evaluation.

Self-evaluation is a mandatory performance evaluation conducted by each agency's evaluation committee. Self-evaluation aims at policy and program improvement, so its results have to directly guide decision making about updating the agency's existing goals. Self-evaluation as annual internal evaluation focused on three target areas in 2016: prioritized policies, consolidated financial projects, and administrative management capacity. The prioritized policies area is evaluated in terms of all major policies identified by each agency's annual performance management implementation plan. The administrative management capacity area focuses on management in personnel, organization, and information technology. The consolidated financial projects area includes target projects in general finance, R&D, and local development fields. The financial area is included in the self-evaluation along with an additional step: meta-analysis performed by the Ministry of Strategy and Finance.

Specific evaluation, also called top-down evaluation, coordinates individual agencies' key policies with overall national government affairs by the Prime Minister. The target areas for specific evaluation have changed constantly to reflect the emphases of each presidential administration, such as economic development and innovation. The evaluation for each specific areas is led by six supervising ministries, even though the Prime Minister's Office is the primary agency for the entire specific evaluation. In 2016, specific evaluation focused on five target areas: national affairs tasks, regulatory reform, policy publicity, normality tasks to modify anomalies, and agency-wide common matters.

The Government Performance Evaluation Committee (GPEC) under the Prime Minister's Office operates all national evaluations by supervising individual agencies' self-evaluations and conducting specific evaluations. The GPEC develops general guidelines and measurement standards, and each agency can modify these original measurement indicators based on its unique work characteristics. For a self-evaluation committee, each agency determines its structural rules, following the GPEC's self-evaluation guideline and annual evaluation schedule. Within a self-evaluation committee, several sub-committees are organized to make use of particular expertise. The majority of committee members are external experts who can validate the objectivity and expertise of evaluations. External experts mainly participate in policy process evaluation, while internal public administrators mainly act as liaisons between the agency and the self-evaluation committee.

Self-evaluation uses a relative ranking system, following a distribution standard of ranking to avoid generous evaluation scores from an agency's self-evaluation committee and have variation across evaluation results. In addition, narrative analysis is also required to justify causes of underperformance and suggest alternative actions to improve performance. Individual agencies determine their own evaluation techniques with indicators and rating scales to fit with its organizational characteristics and nature of tasks. A set of evaluation indicators focuses on four major aspects: performance achievement, appropriateness of policy planning, appropriateness of policy implementation, and policy effect in a majority of central government agencies. Self-evaluation activities are overseen by the GPEC to minimize evaluation bias, so the GPEC conducts on-site visit, interview with agents in charge, and document evaluation.

The heads of central government agencies have to reflect the results of self-evaluation in their organizational operations, budget, personnel, and incentive pay practices. Furthermore, the evaluation results should be reflected in the next year's budget proposal prepared by the Minister of Strategy and Finance. Budget allocation for a project will be rewarded or penalized based on the results of both the agency's self-evaluation and the oversight review by the Minister of Strategy and Finance. A project with excellent ratings will be given a budget increase the next year, while an unsatisfactory project will have its next year's budget reduced by 10% or even be abolished. The evaluation systems for central government agencies tend to integrate various evaluation activities and authorities with the intention of leading and supervising evaluation operations, but the systems are still fragmented, duplicated, and unrealistic in certain aspects. There are still remaining questions that have to be addressed to make the evaluation systems acceptable to internal and external stakeholders.

Teaching Objectives

This case presents an overview of the performance evaluation system of central governments in South Korea. This case intends to fulfill the following teaching objectives:

- Evaluating the relevance of the target areas of self-evaluation and specific evaluation that should be assessed to meet the goals of evaluation;
- Prioritizing the areas and levels of performance that should be evaluated;
- Conceptualizing performance evaluation criteria in terms of formality, types of process focus, types of product focus, stakeholders, and units of analysis;
- Evaluating the appropriateness of evaluation methods and validity of indicators;
- Articulating and analyzing roles of evaluation committees, individual agencies, supervising ministries, and other stakeholders;
- Developing a feasible, practical evaluation system for central government agencies.

This case will help students to clarify how and what performances of central government agencies should be assessed for better evaluation with reasonable evaluation techniques and criteria. Students will also consider how to implement the results of evaluation to maintain or improve agencies' commitment to the evaluation system.

Teaching Strategies

This case can be delivered in various ways to teach the key issues in public management and performance management and taught in one or two 90–minute courses. All case–related activities are very effective in a group format.

Suggested Discussion Questions

The instructor briefly summarizes this case to students in 5~10 minutes and asks them to read the entire case themselves in 10 minutes. After this individual session, students can gather in groups of 4~5 to discuss aspects of the performance evaluation system in terms of structures, operations, primary responsibilities of committees and individual agencies, evaluation procedures, evaluation methods and indicators, and the use of evaluation results. After group discussion, each group will present their findings and solutions.

The following questions may be used to facilitate discussions of the case:

- To what extent are self–evaluation and specific evaluation valuable to individual agencies and the central government as a whole?
- Can a relative rating approach with a distribution standard be objective by minimizing generous grading practices by the self–evaluation committee?
- What are the benefits of operating two evaluation systems (i.e., self–evaluation and specific evaluation) for central government agencies? Any advantages and disadvantage of having two evaluations? Any duplicated aspects between two evaluations?
- Why is the consolidated financial project area required to conduct both self–evaluation and meta–evaluation? Is there any duplication in this method?
- Are three target areas good enough to measure an agency's performance?
- To what extent are onsite performance checks by the self–evaluation committee valuable to assess the agency's performance within a limited time?
- Are there any conflicts between GPEC and the self–evaluation committee? If so, how can the identified conflicts be resolved?

- What are the roles of individual agencies for self–evaluation and specific evaluation?
- Can the self–evaluation committee or GPEC conduct accurate and sophisticated evaluation within a relatively short time frame or a limited 2–year term or on a part–time basis?
- How can the members of GPEC be involved effectively in the self–evaluation processes?
- How well can the evaluation indicators represent the nature of an agency's characteristics?
- Are the indicators of self–evaluation in prioritized policies relevant and sufficient?
- Should the performance achievement indicator field be getting along with other three policy–related indicator fields?
- To what extent are agencies complying with the evaluation results by either the self–committee or GPEC?
- To what extent does an agency reflect the results of evaluation in its incentive system?

Based on these discussions, the instructor can ask students to write a brief memorandum (no more than one page) that recommends strategies to redesign the performance evaluation system. This one–page written memo will be suitable for a take–home assignment.

SWOT Analysis with Group Work

At the beginning of the case, conducting a SWOT (strengths, weaknesses, opportunities, threats) analysis will guide students to understand an overview of the central government performance evaluation system in South Korea. A SWOT analysis can situate students to learn quickly about the status of the Korean performance evaluation system. Students are expected to determine these conditions, grouping them into internal and external contexts based on the given case situation. By exploring these factors, students can clarify directions of the evaluation systems for central government agencies.

The instructor may also use a SWOT analysis again at the end of the case to discuss where changes are possible with a newly reformed evaluation system. Students can refine new opportunities and threats.

A SWOT analysis can be arranged as either in–class discussion or a group homework assignment. It should be thorough, considering all related issues of the Korean performance evaluation systems and operations. With other students' perspectives, a SWOT analysis practice can be far more objective and comprehensive. The instructor can arrange the students in groups of 3 or 4 and then ask them to address key factors of the four areas related to accomplishing the goals of the performance evaluation system, using a SWOT analysis matrix (see Table 2–7). Strengths and weaknesses as internal elements can be identified in operating structures, evaluation processes, leading agencies, evaluators, professionalism, methods and indicators, the implementations of the evaluation results, feedback and so on. Opportunities and threats as external elements may be related to the use of the evaluation results, the impact of the evaluation results on individual agencies, relationships with primary stakeholders, connections with other evaluation systems for local government and public intuitions, public awareness of prospects, changing policy trends, and other outside factors.

Table 2–7. SWOT Analysis

Internal Factors	
Strengths	Weaknesses
External Factors	
Opportunities	Threats

Once students complete a SWOT analysis, the instructor asks them to develop strategies and action plans for minimizing negative factors while maximizing positive factors. For example, if a student group identifies a lack of full–time committee members as a weakness, they should work together to link these negative factors with further actions to overcome the weakness.

PRINCE (Prove, Interact, Calculate, Execute) Analysis

This case offers students a way to consider the dynamic relationships between key players in the performance evaluation process. Understanding a stakeholder's power to respond to the evaluation system is critical to propose solutions, if changes are necessary. Since this case study does not fully describe institutional background of individual central government agencies, the instructor can apply a simple, modified version of PRINCE (Prove, Interact, Calculate, Execute) analysis. PRINCE analysis as one of stakeholder analysis is not a complicated technique. Rather, it intends to identify stake-holder acceptability or political viability on specific issues by measuring the position a stakeholder holds on issues, the power a stakeholder has to get what they want, and the importance of issues to a stakeholder. Although this case is limited to apply a rigorous PRINCE analysis, students can identify stakeholders' acceptability to the evaluation system with given case information.

Student groups first list all primary stakeholders who have direct influences and interests on the evaluation system and select a manageable number of the stakeholder groups for PRINCE analysis. Students will discuss stakeholders' position, power, and salience to bot self-evaluations, using a blank sample of Table 1. Position is whether one favors or opposes a particular solution to an issue and is measured with a scale of −3 (strongly against) to 3 (strongly prefer). Power is the stakeholder's ability to make his or her preference on an issue happen and is measured on a scale of 0 (not powerful) to 3 (very powerful). Salience is the level of strength to which a stakeholder supports or opposes any particular idea and is measured on a scale of 0 (not important) to 3 (very important). Position and salience tend to be similar, but is not always the case. For example, the National Assembly is highly interested in the evaluation system (high position) but may not be willing to do about the system (low salience).

After assigning values for position, power, and salience, each stakeholder's position, power, and salience in each evaluation type are multiplied by all three values and then total scores for each stakeholder are added together to determine the overall strength of the coalition among the stakeholders. The total score is used to represent the stakeholder's acceptance of the evaluation system. After conducting PRINCE analysis for about 30 minutes, each group presents their results and discusses them with the entire class.

Examples of primary stakeholders:

- Prime Minister's Office
- Government Performance Evaluation Committee (GPEC)
- Agency's self-evaluation committee
- Central government agencies
- Ministry of Strategy and Finance
- Meta-evaluation committee: Ministry of Science, ICT and Future Planning, Presidential Committee on Regional Development, Korea Institute of Public Finance
- Supervising agencies: Ministry of Culture, Sports and Tourism, Ministry of Interior, Ministry of Employment and Labor, Ministry of Health and Welfare, Ministry of Small and Medium Business Administration
- Policy Analysis and Evaluation Office

Table 2-8 shows five stakeholders' power and influence to estimate their support and opposition on the evaluations. Listed stakeholders should be the same on both sides. In case of self-evaluation, the Prime Minister's Office is a lead organization to plan and direct an annual performance evaluation plan, so the Office with high power holds high favor to both evaluations and is willing to deal with evaluation issues. GPEC has the most power and influence on self-evaluation. GPEC is responsible to develop detailed measurement standards and conduct actual evaluation, so GPEC holds much stronger power than Prime Minister's Office. On the other hand, individual central government agencies acknowledge the importance of the evaluations to their agencies, but do not much favor ways to operate the evaluations with little influence over the decision on self-evaluation. Central government agencies, indeed, lack the ability to affect change to the self-evaluation system, which assigns them to a score of 0 under power. One of interesting results is that central government agencies can be persuaded for or against self-evaluation since their position and salience are opposite. Based on total scores of self- evaluation and specific evaluation, self-evaluation is more likely to be politically viable than specific evaluation.

Table 2-8. PRINCE Analysis

Position: −3 = strongly against; −2 = against; −1 = somewhat against; 0 = neutral; 1 = somewhat prefer; 2 = prefer; 3 = strongly prefer
Power: 0 = not powerful; 1 = somewhat powerful; 2 = powerful; 3 = very powerful
Salience: 0 = not important; 1 = somewhat important; 2 = important; 3 = very important

	Stakeholders	Position	Power	Salience	Total (A×B×C)
Self-evaluation	1. Prime Minister's Office	3	2	3	18
	2. GPEC	3	3	3	27
	3. Self-evaluation committee	3	2	1	6
	4. Government agencies	−1	0	1	0
	5. Ministry of Strategy and Finance	1	1	1	1
					52
Specific evaluation	1. Prime Minister's Office	3	2	3	18
	2. GPEC	3	3	3	27
	3. Self-evaluation committee	3	0	0	0
	4. Government agencies	−2	1	1	−2
	5. Ministry of Strategy and Finance	1	1	1	1
					44

Redesigning Evaluation Fields, Methods and Criteria

This case provides opportunities to redesign the measurement method and criteria. Currently, self-evaluation uses a relative rating system with a distribution standard of evaluation ranking. The instructor asks students to evaluate whether the current evaluation method is appropriate across all agencies and to redesign better approaches to reform the system. With the given examples of the self-evaluation indicators (see Tables 2-4, 2-5, 2-6), students can rebuild the indicator tables with their own ideas to upgrade the evaluation system by changing fields, scales and so on.

The instructor can introduce a logic model to develop indicators as an in-class group activity. A logic model enables students to build indicators based on a reasonable conceptual framework since it presents sequential relationships among resources, activities, and results. The basic components of the logic model include five steps: inputs, activities, outputs, outcomes, and impacts. Inputs refer to any resources in human, financial, and institutional forms, while activities are processes, tools, and actions during project implementation. Outputs are activities and services delivered by the program. Outcomes refer to the expected changes in services, activities, and behaviors, while impacts represent the intended or unintended changes in the long term. Since measuring impact is difficult, the Korean government uses the first four components to identify key indicators. The instructor first asks students to come up with specific indicators related to one of the three target areas for a specific central government agency, using the logic model exampled in Table 2-9. Then, each student group will develop a complete set of the self-evaluation indicators for the agency. Students can also discuss to what extent the logic model helps them to finalize the full set of the self-evaluation indicators, once they develop the indicators.

Table 2-9. Examples of Indicators by the Logic Model

Type	Indicators
Inputs	Budget execution rate, number of personnel
Activities	Level of program process, a degree of progress
Outputs	Number of offered training, training completion rate
Outcomes	Percentage of citizen satisfaction, citizen recognition

Source: Lee (2015: 295).

03

Chapter

Contracting Out or Contracting Back In: School Foodservice Contracts in South Korea

Eunju Rho

Over the last two decades, the South Korean government has implemented several policy initiatives and interventions designed to improve student health and education. With so many school-age children getting about half of their daily calories from school meals, it is critical to appropriately manage school foodservices and ensure safe food practices to prevent massive foodborne illness. Since 1970s, the Korean Ministry of Education has promulgated and implemented a variety of school meal programs for enhancing the efficacy of school foodservice delivery and student health outcomes.

While nation-wide policies are being built and set by the Ministry of Education, the Office of Education in each metropolitan area and province implements and administers school meal and nutrition programs. Public officials working in the metropolitan and provincial offices of education have set rules, standards, and procedures regarding the regional school foodservice systems. In addition, school principals in local schools are also a key stakeholder group because school principals have discretion to select and implement a certain school foodservice system regardless of changes in nation-wide school meal policies. However, they also have to follow the guidance set by the Ministry of Education and the Office of Education in each metropolitan area and province, and they are responsible for any incident and foodborne illness outbreak occurred in their schools. These key stakeholders play a critical role in establishing and expanding school meal programs.

Among various issues related to the school meal program in South Korea, this case particularly discusses the contracting experiences of the school foodservice management systems. The next session illustrates the historical review of school foodservice operation policies that provides insights and lessons regarding what factors induce the adoption of contracting strategies, what issues stimulate the changes in service delivery methods, what are (dis)advantages of contracting out, and why government returned to self-operation or in-house production of public services.

Case Overview

Early Stage of School Meal Programs: 1953~1980

School foodservice was first introduced to South Korea right after the Korean War in 1953 with the aid of the United Nations Children's Fund (UNICEF). In 1957, CARE (Cooperation for American Relief Everywhere) inherited the Milk Feeding Program from UNICEF, and modified it to a School Lunch Program that continued to 1966. The UNICEF-CARE program assisted more than 1.1 million children every year.

From 1967 to 1972, more than 1.6 million Korean children have benefited directly from U.S. food assistance, named the Food for Peace program. In 1969, the Public Law 480 agreements between USAID (United States Agency for International Development) and the Korean government included national interventions to expand school meal programs. South Korea first specified a system of school foodservice under the School Health Act of 1967, and the Korean school meal program started in 1973 as part of the trial project in accordance with the P.L. 480 agreement. From the beginning, the Ministry of Education became a key agency undertaking national school meal policies. In May 1973 the Ministry of Education first launched the workshop and council for school meal programs, including school principals, superintendents, parent group leaders, and nutrition teachers.

On 14 January 1977, the Korean Ministry of Education[1] enacted funda-

1) Since its establishment in 1948, the Ministry of Education (MOE) has undergone several major large-scale organizational changes. In 2001, MOE was renamed as the Ministry of Education and Human Resource Development and tasked to establish, oversee, and coordinate human resource

mental policies for the implementation of the school meal program, simply titled Rules of the School Lunch Program (Ordinance No. 401 of the Ministry of Education). The 1977 Rules described the purposes of the school lunch program as follows:[2)]

a) To promote the correct understanding of nutrition and inculcate good eating habits in the daily diet.
b) To build good human relationships and create a spirit of collaboration by improving children's school lives.
c) To promote rational eating, nutritional improvement, and health enhancement.
d) To contribute to the implementation of state policies on food consumption by giving pupils an appreciation of the production and distribution of food resources.
e) To run it as a part of Saemaul Undong[3)] with the cooperation of parents and local communities in order to achieve a self-supported school lunch system [rather than relying on the government support].

---

development policies on a national level. In 2008, the Government Organization Act was revised, and the Ministry of Education, Science, and Technology was established to integrate the functions of the Ministry of Science and Technology (nurturing S&T manpower, basic science policy, nuclear safety and research) and the Ministry of Commerce, Industry and Energy (nurturing industry workforce) into the function of human resources development. In 2013, based on the revised Government Organization Act, preliminary research on policy and research development, nuclear research/development/production, and work related to science and technology, previously delegated to the Ministry of Education, Science and Technology, was transferred to the Ministry of Science, ICT and Future Planning to restructure the divisions and functions of the Ministry of Education (For more information, see http://english.moe.go.kr/sub/info.do?m=0104&page=0104&s=english). In this case study, the term "Ministry of Education" (MOE) is used to indicate the central government agency that is in charge of educational programs, regardless of timeline and different organizational names.

2) Park, K. (2013). State and Food in South Korea: The National Diet in Wartime and Beyond. Retrieved from https://openaccess.leidenuniv.nl/bitstream/handle/1887/20552/Chapter7%20KHPark.pdf?sequence=16. Accessed 15 Jan. 2017.

3) United Nations Development Programme (UNDP) describes Saemaul Undong ('new village movement' in Korean) as "a movement of sustainable development in the Republic of Korea that transformed that nation from a developing to a developed country in a single generation" (For more information, see http://www.undp.org/content/undp/en/home/ourwork/development-impact/south-south-cooperation/saemaul-initiative-towards-inclusive-and-sustainable-new-communi.html).

In September of 1977, more than 200 elementary school students reported symptoms of food poisoning, later traced to the cream bun served for school lunch. This was only the beginning of the outbreak. At that time, 263 public elementary schools in Seoul provided school meals through contracted foodservices with Hankook Food Manufacturing, which had an exclusive contract with the Seoul Education Committee. On September 16, Hankook Food Manufacturing delivered 82,388 contaminated cream buns to 173 schools. The foodborne illness outbreak affected 7,872 elementary students, resulting in 948 hospitalizations and one death. After an in-depth investigation, the company was slapped with misdemeanor criminal violations of agriculture, health, and safety guidelines (laws). Following the outbreak, the Korean government announced discontinuation of school foodservices. As a result, of 1,456 schools that had provided free lunches to children, 1,244 schools no longer did so. Only 288 elementary schools in the nation were permitted to provide free school meals.

From 1978 to 1981, the Korean government set the rule details to better establish and expand the school meal programs. For instance, the Ministry of Education published the School Foodservice Report in June 1978, and revised the Rules of the School Lunch Program in November 1978. The 1977 Rules set the overall tone for school meal policies and became the foundation for the School Meals Act of 1981.

Expansion of the School Lunch Program: 1981~2005

The School Meals Act,[4] an independent and comprehensive legal basis for the school meal program in South Korea, was enacted on 29 January 1981 to improve the health and well-being of the nation's children and to encourage and promote healthy diet. It outlined the nutritional standards for school meals, required schools to prepare facilities for maintenance and operation of school meal programs, encouraged schools to hire qualified professionals for service operation and management, and listed the roles of local, provincial, and central governments concerning school meal programs. The School Meals Act was amended a total of 24 times in the nearly 36 years since its first

4) The following information about the School Meals Act and its amendments was obtained from Korea Legislation Research Institute. For more information, see elaw.klri.re.kr/kor_service/lawView.do?hseq=29851&lang=ENG.

enactment in 1981.

After 1981, the Korean government expanded school meal services. From 1982 to 1989, the school meal programs were primarily administered by the Ministry of Sports with support from the Ministry of Education. In particular, the Ministry of Sports initiated a Five-Year Plan for School Meal Program Expansion for 1985~1989 to expand and develop school foodservices. In 1990, the school meal programs were transferred back to the Ministry of Education, and the government tried to seek a broad expansion of the school meal programs starting with all elementary schools in the nation. As a result, the government started providing school meal programs for all special-education schools in 1992, for all elementary schools in 1998, for all high schools in 1999, and for all middle schools in 2003.

In order to efficiently implement school meal services and raise the necessary funds, the 4th amendment of the School Meals Act (Act No. 4593, Dec. 10, 1993) allowed the involvement of supporters' association that consist of parent groups, juristic persons or individuals who support a school's meal service program. It also allowed the superintendents of the boards of education and educational superintendents to employ nutrition specialists who should be responsible exclusively for school meal service programs.

The 5th amendment of the School Meals Act (Act No. 5236, Dec. 30, 1996) first indicated that the superintendents of the boards of education or educational superintendents may set up group meal service facilities and equipment for schools meal services within their jurisdictional areas. In addition, it allowed the "externally managed meal service" for schools that fail to be furnished with the facilities and equipment for self-operated school meal services. Thus, contract foodservice management companies were allowed to operate school meal services to promote effective expansion of the school meal programs. The newly adopted contract foodservice system contributed to the rapid expansion of nationwide school meal programs in spite of insufficient government budgets. According to the Act, the principals of the schools can implement contracted foodservices in consideration of the opinions of the school management committees or parents (limited to the cases where school management committees are not organized) only for the students wishing to participate in the externally managed meal service. Thus, this amendment alleviated the conditions for contracting by allowing school principals to choose which foodservice companies to contract with based on opinions from school management committee members and parent groups.

According to an investigation of middle schools serving contract-managed school meals, conducted by the Seoul Metropolitan Office of Education in March of 2001, of 193 middle schools in Seoul (54.5% of total middle schools in Seoul), 192 contracted with foodservice companies. The number of schools contracting their meal services with management companies continued to increase; in 2004, about 17% of all schools contracted their meal services with management companies.[5] However, student and parent surveys revealed a lower satisfaction level for contracted services than for self-operated services (e.g., Shin, 1999).

Transition from Contracted to Mandatory Self-operated Foodservice: 2006~Present

On June 23, 2006, the Korean government ordered dozens of schools to suspend their school meal programs after another outbreak of food poisoning. Specifically, the Ministry of Education took this measure for 68 schools in Seoul and the surrounding Gyeonggi Province, which received lunch catering services from one company, CJ Food System, after 1,709 students from 25 of the schools showed food poisoning symptoms, including stomach pain, diarrhea, and vomiting. A total of 3,613 students in 46 middle/high schools were affected, and among these schools, 31 schools had contracted directly with CJ Food System. An investigation found that the main cause of the outbreak was contaminated food provided by CJ Food System.

After this large-scale foodborne outbreak occurred in schools with the contracted foodservices in 2006, the Education Committee of the National Assembly of the Republic of Korea significantly revised the School Meals Act to introduce stringent safety guidelines and strict regulations such as penalty systems. As a result, the School Meals Act was wholly amended by Act No. 7962, July 19, 2006 in the 25 years since its enactment.

In terms of the operation mode of school meal services, the School Meals Act of 2006 required that a school principal should directly manage and operate the school meal services, and under this Act, elementary and middle schools were required to set up self-operated foodservices within three years

5) The Ministry of Education (2004). *The 2004 Status of School Foodservice*. Seoul.

of the 2006 amendment (before January 19, 2010). As a result, many schools that had adopted contracted foodservice management switched to self-operation based on these legal requirements.

This Act concretized the responsibility of state and local governments. Before its amendment in 2006, the Act stated, "the State and local governments shall devise the policies necessary for improvement of eating habits through nutritional education and the efficient implementation of school meal plans." However, the wholly amended Act of 2006 refined their duty as follows:

- The State and local governments shall provide administrative and financial support to make the school meal services of good quality safely offered, and devise the policies necessary for the cultivation of students' capability to manage correct eating habits through nutrition education, and for the succession and development of traditional eating culture.
- The superintendent of the Offices of Education of the Special Metropolitan City, Metropolitan City, Do, and special autonomous DO (referred to as the 'educational superintendents') shall establish and execute plans for school meal service every year.

Under the contracting system, the superintendents of the local/state education offices and related administrators reviewed the procurement procedures between local schools and foodservice management companies, and provided procurement updates and training. However, under the revised School Meal Act of 2006, additional work duties were imposed on them. Superintendents should also establish a school meal services committee under their jurisdictions in order to deliberate plans for school meal services and supports of expenses for meal services. Furthermore, as the number of temporary workers under the supervision of the Office has increased due to the transition to self-operation, the political power of labor unions for temporary and outsourced workers has intensified. In this context, superintendents of the Office of Education and public officials related to school meal programs have often suffered from an influx of additional duties to manage labor relations. In addition, like school administrators, they are also responsible for any accident or foodborne illness.

The School Meals Act of 2006 specified the responsibilities of school principals. In addition to their role to directly manage and operate the school meal services, principals should provide the proper guidance of eating habits for students and pupils (Article 13) and conduct a nutrition consultation and required guidance (Article 14). School principals and school personnel related to the school meal services should abide by quality control criteria, nutrition management criteria, sanitation and safety control criteria, and other matters necessary for quality and safety of school meals services (Article 16). Therefore, compared to the contracted management system, principals often perceived that self-operation might put a heavy additional burden on their routine services because of newly imposed responsibilities to directly manage the school meal operations. In addition, the Act also required the schools to place the nutrition teachers under the provisions of Article 21(2) of the Elementary and Secondary Education Act and the cooks under the provisions of Article 36 of the Food Sanitation Act (Article 7). In accordance with this new requirement, in March of 2007 1,700 nutrition teachers were appointed and another 2,386 nutrition teachers have been posted since September 2007. Their main duties include both providing meal services and educating students by developing nutrition education materials. In this situation, for school principals, the transition to self-operation also brought additional labor relations with nutrition teachers and in-house cooks, and human resource management adds another burden, while nutrition teachers and cooks were generally satisfied with self-operated school meal services due to better work environment and salaries.

Under the contracting system, school staffs were required to plan, research, send invitations for the bidding process, and award contracts every other year. Compared to their duties under the contracting system, the self-operation system required more work duties, such as managing the foodservice environment, planning and monitoring the process of food purchasing, and supervising hourly employees. Like the principals, other school administrators related to school meal services are also responsible for any accident or foodborne illness. In this sense, school administrators generally opposed the mandatory transition to self-operation systems. For instance, the president of the Korean National Association of Elementary, Middle, and High School Principals, Principal Kibong Lee (Seould Bongeun Middle School) argued, "If the self-operated foodservice is adopted, the quality of school meals will be sacrificed due to increased costs. In particular, the rise of labor costs will cause the increased costs for meals that will lead to the increased financial burden on parents."[6] Likewise, some of Seoul private school principals issued a joint statement for revising the School Meal Acts, arguing that the mandatory transition to the self-operated system is not acceptable.

On the other hand, parent groups, students, and local communities asserted to the Ministry of Education or local education offices that food and nutrition services could be significantly improved through the transition to self-operation because the in-house foodservice can purchase high-quality food ingredients, provide nutritious meals, and increase participation among students and parents. Previous studies found that most middle and high school students were not satisfied with contract-managed foodservice in terms of food quality, menu variety, and sanitary conditions compared with self-operated foodservice systems (Cha et al., 2004; Kim et al., 2003). After the transition to self-operated meal services, parents and students argued that most school foodservice environments have been improved, and students and parents were satisfied with the improvement. In this regard, some community nonprofit organizations brought an accusation against 40 school principals who did not switch their foodservice systems to self-operation in 2010.[7]

In 2006, the South Korea Contracted Foodservice Association lodged a constitutional complaint, arguing that the fundamental rights of occupational freedom and equity were violated by Article 2, Article 7, and Article 15 Section 3 of the amended School Meal Act, which stipulated that schools should restrict the use of contracted foodservice operations. The contractors argued that the improved sanitation and facility management under the self-operated system were not guaranteed, and that while the transition to self-operation was caused by massive foodborne outbreaks, the numbers of foodborne illness outbreaks and cases under the self-operated system were not significantly lower than those under the contracted system. Moreover, they argued that the freedom of school foodservice contractors was violated by the restriction of contracted foodservices only in schools, compared to others who provided contracted foodservices in other industries, such as hospitals and

6) Han, J. (2010, January 8). School Principals Oppose Self-Operated Foodservices. Retrieved from http://v.media.daum.net/v/20100108023509243. Accessed 15 Jan. 2016.

7) Ibid.

companies. However, the Constitutional Court dismissed the constitutional complaint on its merits, holding that the provision at issue in this case is not in violation of the Constitution.

In response to contractors' constitutional complaints, the Minister of the Ministry of Education argued that the revised Act was not intended to fully restrict the activities of contracted foodservice management companies; rather it restricted the case that contractors would be fully in charge of the school meal programs. In addition, the main purpose of the self-operated management of foodservices in schools was to improve student health and nutrition status through quality control of meal programs and appropriate monitoring systems to ensure food safety. He argued that such goals of the revised Act contained the consideration of public interests and public health concerns and that self-operated foodservices are more likely to attain such goals than contracted foodservices.

Since 2006, the School Meals Act was partially amended 13 times but the operation mode of school meal services still remains as self-operated school meal services. Table 3-1 presents the key differences between the School Meal Act of 1996 that allowed the contracted management and the School Meal Act of 2006 that restricted it.

Table 3-1. Summary of Key Differences between 1996 and 2006 Amendments of School Meals Act[8)]

	School Meals Act of 1996 (Act No. 5236, Dec. 30, 1996)	School Meals Act of 2006 (Act No. 7962, Jul. 19, 2006)
Purpose	To contribute to the sound development of students' mind and body through school meal service programs and, furthermore, to the improvement of the public's eating habits by prescribing the matters concerning the school meal service.	To elevate the quality of school meal services and to contribute to the sound mental and physical development of students and the improvement of the nation's diet by prescribing matters on school meal services, etc.
Definitions	"School meal service" means the meal service which is provided for students of a school or of its neighboring schools, in order to achieve the purpose under Article 1, with the installation of meal	The term "school meal services" means meal services provided by school principals to students and pupils of schools or classes under the provisions of Article 4, in order to achieve the

8) Korea Legislation Research Institute. https://elaw.klri.re.kr/kor_service/lawView.do?lang=ENG&hseq=18889. Accessed 15 Jan. 2017.

	service facilities and equipment within the school concerned and the meal service provided for students of various school levels within the jurisdictional areas of superintendent of the boards of education and educational superintendents of the Seoul Special Metropolitan City, other Metropolitan Cities, and Dos (hereinafter referred to as the "City/Do") through group meal service facilities and equipment installed by them; "Externally managed meal service" means a meal service operated by or implemented through transporting of prepared or processed food by school meal service providers upon being entrusted with the school meal service by school principals; "School meal service provider" means any person who conducts the externally managed meal service as referred to in subparagraph 2; "Meal service expenses" means food costs, meal service operation costs, and expenses for meal service equipment and installation necessary for a school meal service.	purpose under Article 1. The term "school meal service providers" means persons executing the business of school meal services upon entrustment according to contracts with school principals, pursuant to Article 15; The term "expenses for meal services" means food costs, meal services operation costs and other expenses for meal service facilities and equipment, which are necessary for school meal services.
Operation Mode of School Meal Services	Article 10 (Externally Managed Meal Service) (1) In case of a school that fails to be furnished with the facilities and equipment for school meal service within the school, the installation and operation of the facilities for the school meal service may be entrusted to, or an externally managed meal service program may be implemented through transporting of prepared and processed food by, school meal service providers under contract. (2) Externally managed meal service programs shall be implemented by the principals of the schools intending to implement the externally managed meal service program in consideration of the opinions of the school management committees referred to in Article 44 (2) of the Local Education Autonomy Act or	Article 15 (Operation Mode of School Meal Services) (1) A school principal shall directly manage and operate the school meal services, but may make the person equipped with specific requirements execute the affairs of school meal services by entrusting him/her therewith subject to the deliberation of the school operation committee under the provisions of Article 31 of the Elementary and Secondary Education Act: Provided, That he/she shall not entrust such person with the business of the selection, purchase and inspection of food materials, with the exception of inevitable cases for the given conditions of school meal services. (2) Where the compulsory education agency intends to entrust the business

	parents (limited to the cases where school management committees are not organized) only for the students wishing to participate in the externally managed meal service; (3) The meal service costs for externally managed meal service program shall be borne by the parents, but the State or local governments may support part of the meal service costs, if necessary, under the conditions as prescribed by the Presidential Decree. (4) Necessary matters concerning the standards for the school meal service providers and methods of the contract for external management referred to in paragraph (1) shall be determined by the Presidential Decree. [This Article Wholly Amended by Act No. 5236, Dec. 30, 1996]	under the provisions of paragraph (1), it shall obtain in advance approval of the competent authority. (3) The scope of business entrustment for school meal services under the provisions of paragraph (1), the requirements to be met by school meal service providers, and other matters necessary for business entrustment shall be prescribed by the Presidential Decree.
Duty of State and Local Governments	The State and local governments shall devise the policies necessary for improvement of eating habits through nutritional education and the efficient implementation of school meal plans.	(1) The State and local governments shall provide administrative and financial support to make the school meal services of good quality safely offered, and devise the policies necessary for the cultivation of students' capability to manage correct diet and eating habits through nutrition education, and for the succession and development of traditional eating culture. (2) The Superintendents of the Offices of Education of the Special Metropolitan City, Metropolitan City, Do and Special Self-Governing Province (hereinafter referred to as "Superintendent of the Office of Education") shall establish and execute plans for school meal services every year.
Penalty	None	Article 23 (Penal Provisions) (1) The school meal service provider who has violated the provisions of Article 16(1) 1 shall be punished by imprisonment for not more than seven years or by a fine not exceeding 100 million won. (2) The school meal service provider who has violated the provisions of Art-

		icle 16(1) 2 or 3 shall be punished by imprisonment for not more than five years or by a fine now exceeding 50 millions won. (3) The person failing under any one of the following subparagraphs shall be punished by imprisonment for not more than three years or by a fine nor exceeding 30 million won: 1. The school meal service provider who has violated the provision of Article 16(1) 4; and 2. The person who has refused or obstructed or avoided without any justifiable reason the entry, inspection, perusal or removal under the provision of Article 19(1). Article 24 (Joint Panel Provisions) Article 25 (Fine for Negligence)

Status of School Foodservices in South Korea

The proportion of schools providing foodservices grew from 17.6% in 1992 to 99.2% in 1998 for elementary schools; from 8.6% in 1997 to 83.1% in 2002 for middle schools; and from 9.8% in 1997 to 94.7% in 2000 for high schools. The percentage of elementary, middle, high, and special education schools serving school meal services reached almost 100% in 2003, from only 13.3% in 1991. More schools have developed lunch programs, and as of 2015, 1,326 out of 1,330 schools in Seoul provide school meal services. Currently students with family income below 80% of the poverty level are eligible for a free school lunch, and 99% of schools have adopted a self-operated foodservice system.

Table 3-2 and Figure 3-1 show the development and expansion of school foodservices in South Korea. Data for student participation rates across multiple school years were obtained directly through the Korean Educational Development Institute database. Due to the discontinuation of school foodservices caused by massive foodborne illness outbreaks in 1977, the percentage of students who participated in the school meal programs dropped from 22% in 1977 to 2.3% in 1978. In 1996 when contract foodservice management companies were allowed to operate school lunch services, 51.5% of students participated in the school meal programs, and the percentage grew consistently up to 98.5% in 2009.

Table 3-2. Status of School Foodservices Participants (schools and students) by Year[9)]

Year	No. of Schools	No. of Students (thousands)	% of Students	Year	No. of Schools	No. of Students (thousands)	% of Students
1954	4,024	1,250	44.0	1982	432	152	2.8
1955	4,171	1,250	43.0	1983	439	162	3.0
1956	4,334	1,250	39.0	1984	464	171	3.4
1957	4,350	1,100	34.0	1985	541	200	4.1
1958	4,425	1,200	36.0	1986	569	213	4.4
1959	4,500	1,236	33.0	1987	616	237	5.0
1960	4,509	1,238	32.0	1988	660	254	5.3
1961	4,552	1,276	33.0	1989	701	264	5.4
1962	4,648	1,358	33.0	1990	854	289	6.0
1963	4,762	1,779	42.0	1991	998	372	7.7
1964	4,897	1,812	41.0	1992	1,298	513	11.2
1965	5,215	1,861	39.0	1993	1,654	661	15.2
1966	5,552	1,912	37.0	1994	2,291	931	22.6
1967	5,892	2,000	37.0	1995	3,512	1,543	38.9
1968	5,495	2,000	36.0	1996	4,487	1,963	51.5
1969	5,705	2,000	36.0	1997	6,100	3,205	38.5
1970	5,717	2,164	38.0	1998	7,256	3,782	46.1
1971	5,983	1,771	31.0	1999	8,071	4,762	58.0
1972	6,097	2,184	38.0	2000	8,807	5,533	68.8
1973	5,820	1,476	26.0	2001	9,394	6,011	76.7
1974	6,208	1,402	25.0	2002	9,275	5,989	76.6
1975	5,980	1,384	25.0	2003	9,860	6,523	83.9
1976	6,010	1,172	21.0	2004	10,213	7,012	90.0
1977	6,265	1,200	22.0	2005	10,453	7,206	92.5
1978	360	129	2.3	2006	10,645	7,330	93.8
1979	382	142	2.5	2007	10,850	7,414	95.6
1980	412	155	2.7	2008	11,225	7,456	97.7
1981	425	160	2.8	2009	11,303	7,339	98.5

9) Yang, S. (2010). Evaluation of School Foodservices in South Korea and OECD Countries. Korean Educational Development Institute (CR2010-19). Data Combined from the Korean Educational Development Institute.

Figure 3–1. Status of School Foodservices Participants by Year[10)]

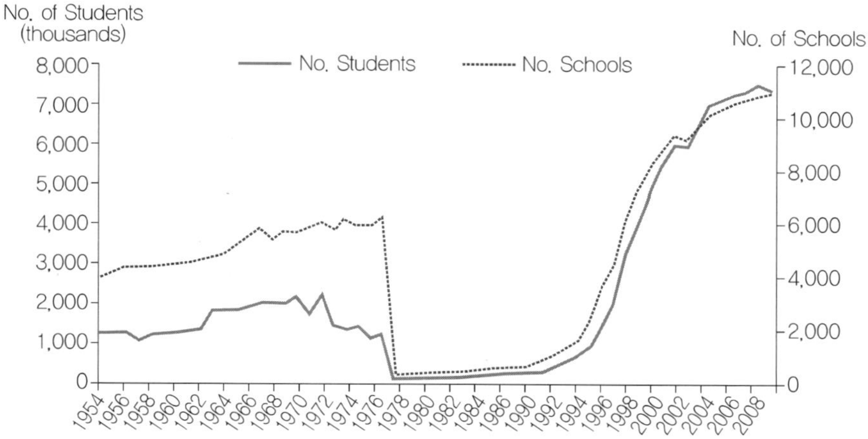

As aforementioned, the operation mode of school meal services can be broadly categorized into self-operated foodservice management and contracted foodservice management. The Ministry of Education provides a description of each management type as shown in Table 3-3. While the Ministry of Education and the Office of Education in each metropolitan area and province set the guidance and policies, the decision to determine whether foodservice management is "self-operated" or "contracted" is determined by school principals.

Table 3–3. Types of School Foodservice Management[11)]

Management Types		Description
Self-operated foodservice		School employees (nutrition education teachers, cooks) manage all food preparation procedures, serve the food, and clean up the facilities.
Contracted foodservice	Partial contracts	Nutrition education teachers (school employees) are involved in food ingredient purchasing, storage, and management. The contractor is responsible for cooking, serving, and cleanup.

10) Ibid., 52.

11) Ministry of Education (2008). *Manual for Transferring Contracted Foodservices to Self-Operated Foodservices*. Seoul.

	Full Contracts	School foodservice contracts	For schools equipped with foodservice facilities, the contractor and their employees prepare and serve the food. The contractor is expected to directly manage all aspects of foodservices.
		Vended meals	The contractor acts as a vender only. For schools without foodservice facilities, the contractor provides prepackaged or pre-plated meals.

In 2008, the nationwide statistics provided by the Ministry of Education indicate that about 99.7% of schools provided school meal programs, and among them, about 88.5% of schools chose the self-operated foodservice management system. Among schools with contracted meal services, only 1% of schools adopted vended meals; the majority used foodservice contracts as shown in the nationwide statistics of the status of school foodservice operation in South Korea as of 2008.

Table 3-4. Korean Schools that Participated in School Meal Programs: By Types of School Foodservice Management (2008)[12]

Management Types			Number of Schools	Percentage of Schools
Self-operated foodservice			9,827	88.5%
Contracted foodservice	Partial contracts		1	0.0%
	Full Contracts	School foodservice contracts	1,165	10.5%
		Vended meals	113	1.0%
Total			11,106	100%

The percentage of schools that contracted with foodservice management systems varies according to the school types. Self-operated management occurs in about 99.7% of elementary schools, while 66.1% of high school foodservices were directly managed by each school (See Table 3-5).

Table 3-6 presents the 2015 data from the Seoul Metropolitan Office of Education. In elementary and middle schools, 100% of schools provided meal programs using self-operated foodservice management systems. However, among high schools, only 53.5% of school foodservices were self-operated,

12) Ibid.

Table 3-5. Korean Schools that Participated in School Meal Programs: By School Types (2008)[13]

	Number of Schools			Number of Students (1,000)			Operation Types	
	Total	School meals	%	Total	School meals	%	Self-operated (%)	Contracted (%)
Elementary	5,791	5,791	100	3,826	3,738	97.7	5,775 (99.7)	16 (0.3)
Middle	3,035	3,021	99.5	2,068	2,049	99.1	2,491 (82.5)	530 (17.5)
High	2,166	2,155	99.5	1,858	1,794	96.6	1,424 (66.1)	731 (33.9)
Special Education	144	139	96.5	23	22	95.7	137 (98.6)	2 (1.4)
Total	11,136	11,106	99.7	7,775	7,603	97.8	9,827 (88.5)	1,279 (11.5)

Table 3-6. Seoul Metropolitan Schools with School Meal Programs: By School & Management Types (2015)[14]

Category		School Types					Total
		Elementary	Middle	High	Special Educ.	Kinder-garten[15]	
School Meal Program Participants: Total	schools	598	384	318	26	192	1,518
	students	451,026	262,525	297,817	4,302	14,414	1,030,084
Self-operated: Total	schools	598	384	166	26	191	1,365
	students	451,026	262,525	148,610	4,302	14,188	880,651
Contracted: Total	schools	-	-	152	-	1	153
	students	-	-	149,207	-	226	149,433

while other 46.5% were operated using contracts.

13) Ibid.

14) Seoul Metropolitan Office of Education (2015). School Foodservice Improvement Medium-Term Plan. Seoul.

15) Kindergarten annexed elementary schools are only counted.

Issues Related to School Foodservices

Better Service Quality Arguments

As illustrated in the previous sections, after the amendment of the School Meals Act of 1996, contract foodservice systems contributed to the rapid expansion of nationwide school lunch services. However, after several massive foodborne disease outbreaks, the School Meals Act was significantly revised to require elementary and middle schools to set up self-operated foodservice management systems. Since the school meal program was established to improve the health and well-being of the nation's children, the safety and nutritional quality of school meals remained the biggest issue. Regarding government contracting, issues related to service quality are highly controversial. Proponents argue improved effectiveness and better quality of services as the advantages of contracting, while opponents posit sacrificed service quality and accountability issues as the biggest problems of contracting out. This section provides information regarding the service quality of school lunch programs, particularly focusing on safety issues and foodborne disease outbreaks in order to provide opportunities to evaluate contracting performance in terms of service quality.

Food Safety[16)]

In 2007, The Ministry of Education conducted the safety and hygiene inspections according to the School Meal Act Article 19 and Enforcement Rule Article 6 and Article 8 paragraph 1. The results in Table 3-7 show that 1.8% of schools with contracted foodservice systems received a grade D or lower, meaning that they failed to meet the minimum requirements, and 0.4% of schools with self-operated foodservice systems received the grade D.

In 2006 (June 27~July 10), the Ministry of Education inspected the school foodservice systems of a total of 9,186 elementary, middle, and high schools in South Korea. The main purpose of this special inspection was to investigate the risk factors affecting the quality of school meal services. For this nationwide inspection, 16 metropolitan/province-level and 182 local-level inspection teams were arranged, with a total of 7,282 public employees re-

16) Ministry of Education (2008). *Manual for Transition from Contracted to Mandatory Self-Operated Foodservice*. Seoul.

Table 3-7. Safety and Hygiene Inspection Grade by Foodservice Operation System[17)]

			Inspected Schools	Grade A	Grade B	Grade C	Grade D	Grade E
2007 Spring	Self-operated	Number (%)	8,296 (100.0)	5,550 (66.9)	2,517 (30.3)	207 (2.5)	22 (0.3)	- -
	Contracted	Number (%)	1,086 (100.0)	405 (37.3)	609 (56.1)	60 (5.5)	11 (1.0)	1 (0.1)
2007 Fall	Self-operated	Number (%)	8,446 (100.0)	6,467 (76.6)	1,857 (22.0)	111 (1.3)	10 (0.1)	1 (0.0)
	Contracted	Number (%)	1,097 (100.0)	512 (46.7)	522 (47.7)	54 (4.9)	7 (0.6)	1 (0.1)

quired to find whether each school's foodservice system met a total of 46 standards, including 11 criteria concerning foodservice facilities and 8 criteria for food purchasing and storage processes.

School foodservice facility and equipment: Overall, due to limited physical space in the school facility for foodservice systems, 76% of schools did not have enough space to set up walls and doors to separate prep, cooking, and washing areas, and 57.7% of schools did not have a prep area. The inspection teams found that many schools had no air conditioning (A/C) systems in the kitchen (85.5%), no coolers (77.7%), no heated cabinet (89.2%), and no combi oven (88.8%). The A/C installation rate was higher among self-operated schools (25.9%) compared to the contracted schools (14.9%); however, coolers, heated cabinets, and dishwashers were installed more often in contracted schools (95.2%) than in self-operated schools (68.2%). The inspection teams concluded that the quality of overall facilities and equipment of schools with contracted foodservices was better than those with self-operated foodservices.

Food selection, purchasing, and storage: During the inspection period, the inspection teams found five schools that violated the requirements in terms of unlicensed vendors and expiration dates. Two of them employed contracted foodservices while three schools had the self-operated foodservice system. Overall, the quality of food selection, purchasing, and storage is quite good in general, though schools with self-operated foodservice systems have

17) Ibid.

Table 3-8. Self-op vs. Contract: School Foodservice Facility and Equipment[18)]

Criteria	Total		Self-operated		Contracted	
	Yes	No	Yes	No	Yes	No
1. Are food preparation area, cooking area, and washing area divided by walls or doors?	24.0	76.0	24.2	75.8	22.8	77.2
2. Are food preparation areas separated from other areas?	42.3	57.7	42.1	57.9	43.3	56.7
3. Is A/C installed in the cooking area?	24.5	75.5	25.9	74.1	14.9	85.1
4. Are ventilation systems proper in the cooking area?	90.2	9.8	91.5	8.5	81.0	19.0
5. Is lighting proper in the cooking area?	88.6	11.4	88.9	11.1	87.0	13.0
6. Are there refrigerators and freezers for ingredients?	98.1	1.9	97.9	2.1	99.1	0.9
7. Are there coolers for cooked food?	22.3	77.7	20.5	79.5	34.5	65.5
8. Are there heated cabinet for cooked food?	10.8	89.2	9.2	90.8	21.9	78.1
9. Is a combi-oven installed?	11.2	88.8	11.1	89.0	12.7	87.3
10. Is a dishwasher installed?	71.6	28.4	68.2	31.8	95.2	4.8
11. Is a hand washing sink installed in the cooking area?	94.6	5.4	94.2	5.8	97.2	2.8

* Note: Total number of schools inspected: 9,186 (Contracted 1,161; Self-operated 8,025)

Table 3-9. Self-op vs. Contract: Food selection, purchasing, and storage[19)]

Criteria	Total		Self-operated		Contracted	
	Yes	No	Yes	No	Yes	No
1. Does this school restrict the use of foods from unlicensed vendors?	99.9	0.01	100	0	99.9	0.09
2. Does this school restrict the use of foods that exceed the expiration date?	99.9	0.03	99.9	0.02	99.9	0.09
3. Does this school use meat, poultry, and fish products cured at a food processing plant regulated by HACCP?	92.3	7.7	93.6	6.4	83.0	17.0
4. Does this school properly daily record the inspection results concerning food temperature, expiration date, place of origin, etc.?	96.9	3.1	97.1	2.9	95.2	4.8
5. Does this school use processed foods?	55.0	45.0	54.5	45.5	58.2	41.8
6. Does this school properly store foods?	98.2	1.8	98.6	1.4	95.3	4.7
7. Are food storage areas (cabinets, refrigerators, freezers) clean?	97.9	2.1	98.4	1.6	94.7	5.3
8. Do parents participate in food inspection?	88.1	11.9	88.5	11.5	85.4	14.6

* Note: Total number of schools inspected: 9,186 (Contracted 1,161; Self-operated 8,025)

18) Ibid.

19) Ibid.

higher rates of the standards than those with contracted systems.

Food hygiene (sanitation): Food hygiene and sanitation are the conditions and measures necessary to ensure food safety from production to consumption. Food can become contaminated at any point during slaughtering or harvesting, processing, storage, distribution, transportation, and preparation. Lack of adequate food hygiene can lead to foodborne diseases and death. For all seven criteria, more than 97% of schools met the standards, though schools with contracted services show a higher rate of violations than schools with self-operated foodservice systems.

Table 3-10. Self-op vs. Contract: Food hygiene (Sanitation)[20]

Criteria	Total		Self-operated		Contracted	
	Yes	No	Yes	No	Yes	No
1. Are cooking and washing areas clean?	97.2	2.8	98.3	1.7	89.5	10.5
2. Do they use separate machinery and equipment, such as vacuum packing machines, slicers and mincers, for raw and ready-to-eat food?	98.9	1.1	99.3	0.7	96.8	3.2
3. Do they store food and nonfood items at least 24 inches (60 centimeters) off the floor?	98.9	1.1	99.3	0.7	96.6	3.4
4. Do they check and record whether meat, poultry, seafood, and other cooked foods reach a safe minimum internal temperature (74°C)?	98.4	1.6	98.6	1.4	97.2	2.8
5. Do they use proper serving equipment?	99.0	1.0	99.1	0.9	98.8	1.2
6. Do they clean and disinfect food areas and equipment?	99.2	0.8	99.5	0.5	97.2	2.8
7. Do their staff wash and dry their hands thoroughly between different tasks, especially after handling raw food?	97.3	2.7	97.7	2.3	94.6	5.4

* Note: Total number of schools inspected: 9,186 (Contracted 1,161; Self-operated 8,025)

Foodborne Disease Outbreaks

As shown in Table 3-11, 614, or about 16.5%, of the total 3,730 foodborne outbreaks that were reported nationwide between 2002 and 2016 occurred in schools. These outbreaks affected about 48,113 students. School is the second largest location where food was provided, followed by public restaurants

20) Ibid.

(1,186, 31.8%). Information on these outbreaks at schools shows that for last 15 years, 454 cases, or about 73.9%, occurred at schools with self-operated foodservice systems, and the remaining 160 cases occurred at schools with contracted foodservice systems. Such large outbreaks resulted from improper food preparation and handling practices in school kitchens. Most commonly, foods involved in the outbreaks were contaminated with Norwalk-like viruses, which cause a mild gastrointestinal illness.

Table 3-11. Number of reported foodborne disease outbreaks and cases by dining place[21)]

Place		2002	2003	2004	2005	2006	2007	2008	2009	2010	2011	2012	2013	2014	2015	2016	Total
School: Self-operated	Outbreaks	7	16	42	12	24	36	33	27	30	27	51	42	49	38	20	454
	Cases	497	1,230	4,952	1,412	1,994	2,308	2,533	1,496	2,770	1,648	2,851	2,161	4,058	1,980	880	32,770
School: Contracted	Outbreaks	2	33	15	7	46	21	6	12	8	3	3	2	2	-	-	160
	Cases	309	3,391	1,760	892	4,998	793	450	1,220	620	413	334	86	77	-	-	15,343
Other food service	Outbreaks	7	18	15	11	23	41	22	20	15	10	9	14	15	26	10	256
	Cases	586	1,509	1,026	1,447	1,081	1,432	633	719	799	460	246	608	380	802	375	12,103
Public restaurant	Outbreaks	31	46	34	53	108	289	208	98	133	117	95	134	213	199	128	1,886
	Cases	624	1,441	1,049	1,021	1,971	3,476	2,392	1,132	1,704	1,753	1,139	1,297	1,761	1,506	1,129	23,395
Household	Outbreaks	7	7	7	9	15	30	24	11	3	8	14	5	7	9	2	158
	Cases	117	81	44	111	119	151	176	89	11	51	54	22	28	34	11	1,099
Others	Outbreaks	23	15	39	13	33	82	48	24	25	33	22	24	50	54	29	514
	Cases	734	257	1,206	729	515	1,320	1,108	664	774	2,217	758	502	1,078	1,641	322	13,825
Not detected	Outbreaks	1	0	13	4	10	11	13	36	57	51	72	14	13	4	3	302
	Cases	113	0	351	99	155	206	195	679	540	563	676	282	84	18	101	4,062
Total	Outbreaks	78	135	165	109	259	510	354	228	271	249	266	235	349	330	192	3,730
	Cases	2,980	7,909	10,388	5,711	10,833	9,686	7,487	5,999	7,218	7,105	6,058	4,958	7,466	5,981	2,818	102,597

Based on the data from the Ministry of Food and Drug Safety, Table 3-12 presents a comparison of foodborne disease outbreaks and cases by the management types of school meal programs. According to the Ministry of Education report (2008), the analysis of data on the total number of schools

21) Ministry of Food and Drug Safety (2017). Foodborne Illness Statistics. http://www.foodsafetykorea.go.kr/portal/healthyfoodlife/foodPoisoningStat.do?menu_no=519. Accessed 15 Jan. 2017.

by foodservice operation systems and the foodborne outbreaks in Korean schools shows that the percentage of foodborne outbreak cases in self-operated foodservice schools in 2007 was 0.0021% of the total number of schools with self-operated foodservice, while the percentage of outbreaks in schools with the contracted foodservice system was 0.0082%. Figure 3-2 provides an annual summary of foodborne outbreaks and illnesses by school foodservice management types for South Korea from 2002 to 2016.

Table 3-12. Self-op vs. Contract: Foodborne Disease Outbreaks and Cases[22)]

	Number of Schools offering School Meal Program (Number of Students)			Foodborne Disease Outbreaks (Cases)		
	Self-operated	Contracted	Total	Self-operated	Contracted	Total
2000	6,688 (4,289,856)	1,780 (898,921)	8,468 (5,188,777)	8 (1,482)	7 (2,549)	15 (4,076)
2001	7,248 (4,534,131)	1,850 (1,419,924)	9,098 (5,954,055)	17 (1,990)	19 (2,899)	36 (4,889)
2002	8,115 (5,093,571)	1,874 (1,451,449)	9,989 (6,545,020)	7 (497)	2 (309)	9 (806)
2003	8,300 (5,358,613)	1,942 (1,639,860)	10,242 (6,998,473)	16 (1,230)	33 (3,391)	49 (4,621)
2004	8,413 (5,408,259)	1,930 (1,625,983)	10,343 (7,034,242)	42 (4,952)	15 (1,760)	57 (6,712)
2005	8,793 (5,647,512)	1,793 (1,579,915)	10,586 (7,227,427)	12 (1,412)	7 (892)	19 (2,304)
2006	9,125 (5,830,121)	1,655 (1,521,022)	10,780 (7,351,143)	24 (1,994)	46 (4,998)	70 (6,992)
2007	9,556 (6,050,286)	1,430 (1,385,441)	10,986 (7,435,727)	36 (2,308)	21 (793)	57 (3,101)

22) Data were combined from the Ministry of Food and Drug Safety and Ministry of Education, Science, and Technology. For more information, see http://www.foodsafetykorea.go.kr/portal/healthyfoodlife/foodPoisoningStat.do?menu_no=519

Figure 3-2. Self-op vs. Contract: Foodborne Disease Outbreaks and Cases[23)]

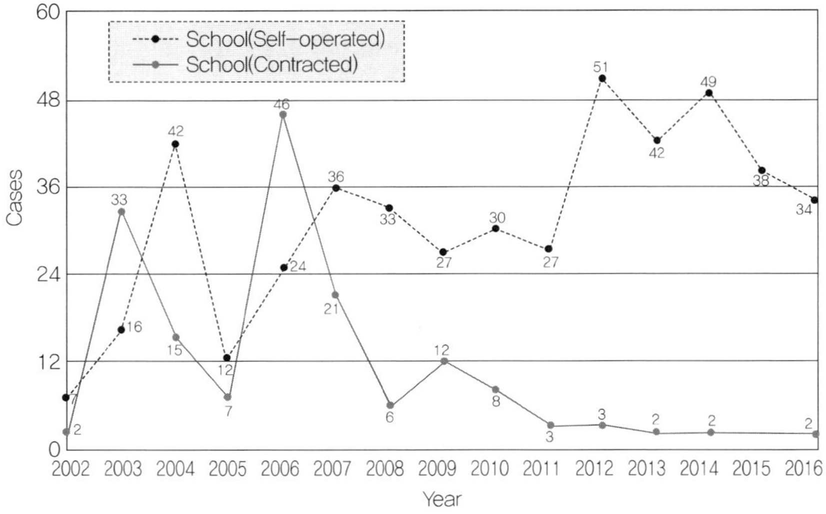

Foodservice Cost

The relationship between service contracting and total government expenditure has been tested in various empirical studies; however, it is still debatable whether contracting out is associated with lower spending. From 1992 through 2002, over 1.3 trillion won were spent to expand foodservices and related facilities for 8,254 schools in South Korea. During the seven-year period of the transition from contract-managed to self-operated foodservice (2003~2009), a total of 1,707 schools switched their foodservice operation systems, and the government spent more than 417.5 billion won to support this transition. Table 3-13 shows the number of schools that changed their operation system and the related budget to support them.

To examine the costs related to school meal programs, this section focuses on one specific region, the Seoul metropolitan area. Seoul is the capital and largest metropolis of South Korea. The Seoul metropolitan area has 588 elementary schools, about 10% of the total number of elementary schools in South Korea, 381 middle schools and 325 high schools, about 14% (see Table 3-14). Considering the size and scope of this system, a case study of school meal programs in Seoul would be beneficial to understand Korean school meal programs.

23) Ibid.

Table 3-13. Budget Support for Korean Schools that Switched to Self-operation[24]

	No. of Schools: from Contracted to Self-operated Foodservices	Budget Support (unit: 100 million won)			Budget Support per School
		Ministry of Education	Metropolitan and Provincial Offices of Education	Total	
Before the revised School Meals Act of 2006 (2003~2006)	681	252	1,243	1,495	220 million won per school
After the revised School Meals Act of 2006 (2007~2009)	1,026	327	2,353	2,680	260 million won per school
Total	1,707	579	3,596	4,175	240 million won per school

Table 3-14. 2016 Schools and Students in the Seoul Metropolitan Area[25]

	Elementary Schools		Middle Schools		High School	
	Schools	Students	Schools	Students	Schools	Students
Seoul	5,885	3,299,113	3,144	1,979,656	2,313	1,496,227
Nationwide Total	588 (9.99%)	566,168 (17.16%)	381 (12.12%)	348,375 (17.60%)	325 (14.05%)	303,609 (20.29%)

Reported costs include those costs that are related to school meal programs, such as school meals for low-income students, the free meal program, and meal production systems including facilities, cafeterias, equipment, administrative costs, and so on. As shown in Figure 3-3, the Seoul Metropolitan Office of Education has proposed approximately 389.2 billion won per year for school meal programs in its fiscal year 2016 budget. The eco-friendly free meal program has taken about 73% of the total budget since its implementation in 2012. Before this program began, one of the biggest portions of the budget was allocated to the school meal subsidies for low-

24) Yang, S. (2010). Evaluation of School Foodservices in South Korea and OECD Countries. Korean Educational Development Institute (CR2010-19). 43.

25) Ministry of Education (2017). For More Information, see http://english.moe.go.kr/sub/info.do?m=050101&page=050101&num=1&s=english.

income students. Since the transition from contracted to mandatory self-operated foodservices, about 16% to 20% of the annual budget has been allocated to support school meal production equipment. The percentage of school meal facility support was over 50% of the budget in 2007 and 2008, right after implementing mandatory self-operated foodservice systems, but has decreased since 2008.

Figure 3-3. Seoul: School Meal Program Budgets 2005~2016[26)]

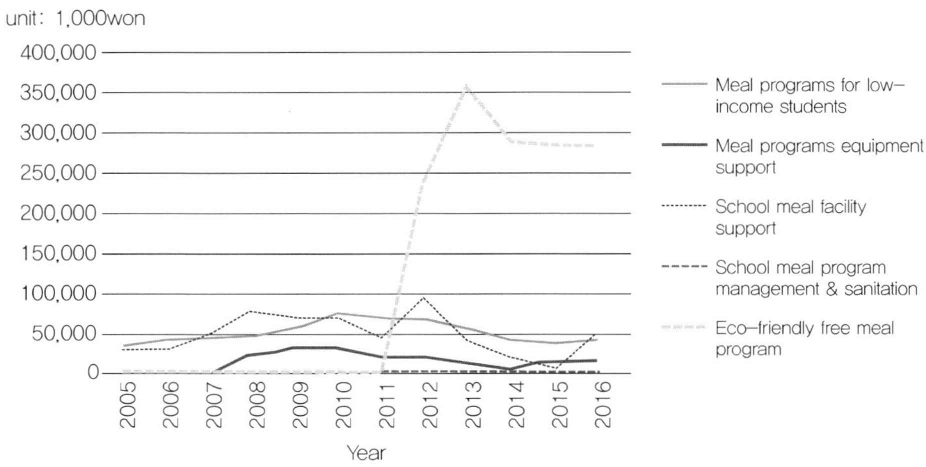

Table 3-15 provides information that may be useful to analyze the 2015 foodservice expenses in Seoul metropolitan area schools. Expense categories include facility and equipment support, maintenance costs, food costs, labor costs, and costs for fuel and other supplies.

The total costs for each category for the entire school year can be calculated and a comparison by foodservice operation types is possible (See Table 3-17). For instance, in terms of labor costs for high schools in Seoul, each school with a self-operated conventional foodservice system spent a total of 184.8 million won on average,[27)] while each school with a contracted conventional foodservice system spent a total of 202.3 million won on average. In terms of facility and equipment costs, each high school with a self-operated

26) Seoul Metropolitan Office of Education (2016). Internal Document.

27) For calculation, a sum of labor expenditures from four sources is divided by the number of schools. [(3,984,400+4,103+9,136,751+1,766)/71=184,877.6]

Table 3-15. Seoul Metropolitan Office of Education: School Meal Program Budgets 2005~2016[28)]

Year	School meal program for low-income students		School meal equipment support		School meal facility support		School meal program management		Eco-friendly free meal program		Total
	Won	%	Won	%	Won	%	Won	%	Won	%	Won
2005	34,516,170	53.33	-		30,197,795	46.65	12,600	0.02	-		64,726,565
2006	41,459,263	54.61	-		34,143,396	44.97	314,870	0.41	-		75,917,529
2007	43,199,054	46.80	-		48,657,801	52.71	450,593	0.49	-		92,307,448
2008	47,162,613	32.22	23,419,167	16.00	75,251,097	51.41	548,419	0.37	-		146,381,296
2009	57,690,871	35.57	32,738,756	20.19	70,694,200	43.59	1,068,633	0.66	-		162,192,460
2010	73,035,579	41.42	31,183,226	17.69	71,371,341	40.48	719,860	0.41	-		176,310,006
2011	68,435,098	51.82	17,736,086	13.43	45,101,141	34.15	792,364	0.60	-		132,064,689
2012	68,361,618	16.43	18,478,518	4.44	92,071,297	22.13	728,565	0.18	236,370,857	56.82	416,010,855
2013	55,446,580	11.97	11,786,923	2.54	41,762,966	9.02	719,915	0.16	353,519,218	76.32	463,235,602
2014	42,615,872	11.87	6,075,721	1.69	17,786,747	4.96	850,774	0.24	291,600,953	81.24	358,930,067
2015	38,152,977	11.03	12,694,992	3.67	7,911,287	2.29	721,052	0.21	286,551,405	82.8	346,031,713
2016	41,263,054	10.60	14,225,172	3.65	46,304,108	11.90	880,378	0.23	286,569,621	73.62	389,242,333

* Note: (unit: 1,000 won)

conventional foodservice system spent a total of 17.5 million won on average, while each high school with a contracted conventional foodservice system spent a total of 29.3 million won on average. In terms of facility and equipment costs, each school with a self-operated conventional foodservice system spent a total of 17.5 million won on average, while each high school with a contracted conventional foodservice system spent a total of 29.3 million won on average. In terms of food costs, each high school with a self-operated conventional foodservice system spent a total of 437.4 million won on average, while each high school with a contracted conventional foodservice system spent a total of 542.1 million won on average.

Combining all three operation types, Table 3-16 summarizes and compares the high school expenditures in Seoul by foodservice management types. Each school with a self-operated foodservice management system spent

28) Seoul Metropolitan Office of Education (2016). Internal Document.

783.2 million won on average, while each school with contracted foodservice management system spent 736.7 million won on average. For the categories of facility/equipment and food costs, the expenses per school of self-operated systems are higher than those of contracted systems.

Table 3-16. Seoul Metropolitan Office of Education: High School Expenditures by Foodservice Management Types (2015)[29)]

Foodservice Management Type	Schools (students) with meal program		Expenditure					
			Facility/ Equipment	Mainten-ance	Food	Labor	Fuel/ Supplies	Total
Self-operated	166 (148,610)	Total	5,788,571	1,024,722	83,809,549	32,489,456	6,908,678	130,020,976
		Per school	34,871	6,173	504,877	195,720	41,619	783,259
		Per students	39.0	6.9	564.0	218.6	46.5	874.9
		Percent	4.45%	0.79%	64.46%	24.99%	5.31%	100.00%
Contracted	152 (149,207)	Total	4,400,338	1,035,688	69,918,023	30,235,399	6,396,570	111,986,018
		Per school	28,950	6,814	459,987	198,917	42,083	736,750
		Per students	29.5	6.9	468.6	202.6	42.9	750.5
		Percent	3.93%	0.92%	62.43%	27.00%	5.71%	100.00%

* Note: (unit: 1,000 won)

29) Ibid.

Table 3-17. Seoul Metropolitan Office of Education: 2015 Expenditure of Education Budget by Expense Category[30)]

Category				Schools with meal program	Schools with cafeteria	Expenditure									
						Facility & Equipment			Maintenance			Food			
						Education Budget	Local funding	Misc.	Education Budget	Local funding	Misc.	Education Budget	Local funding	Parents payment	Misc.
Elementary	Self-operated	Conventional foodservice		592	299	10,790,514	2,014,272	13,751	3,373,780	107,579	24,325	117,403,804	114,450,224	12,178,431	6,275
		Commissary foodservice	central kitchen	1	0	40,182	0	0	6,717	0	0	108,733	113,990	0	0
			satellite service center	5	3	4,007	-	-	4,905	-	-	100,143	64,567	657,217	-
Middle	Self-operated	Conventional foodservice		306	217	4,551,592	940,439	7,344	1,646,430	48,638	1,033	56,774,025	57,695,728	308,510	3,469
		Commissary foodservice	central kitchen	2	2	78,515	-	-	1,133	-	-	284,965	305,223	47,091	-
			satellite service center	592	6	598,481	22,408	4,950	143,242	4,741	-	10,975,639	10,711,934	170,892	-
High	Self-operated	Conventional foodservice		71	69	971,185	260,172	16,728	312,552	-	11,861	5,459,449	632,259	24,960,017	4,650
		Commissary foodservice	central kitchen	80	79	4,010,934	184,514	320,111	541,529	27,921	64,340	6,180,012	1,270,383	38,429,085	12,308
			satellite service center	15	1	24,927	-	-	66,519	-	-	893,875	74,142	5,890,697	2,672
	Contracted	Conventional foodservice		138	131	3,253,322	609,252	183,237	799,213	24,489	22,484	9,797,516	1,855,791	63,141,086	22,936
		Commissary foodservice	central kitchen	7	6	37,224	81,585	21,773	103,961	-	-	455,928	148,363	2,880,249	-
			satellite service center	7	0	174,502	-	14,516	19,022	-	-	423,113	69,448	1,800,150	-

* Note: (unit: 1,000 won)

30) Ibid.

Table 3–17. Seoul Metropolitan Office of Education: 2015 Expenditure of Education Budget by Expense Category (continued)

Category				Schools with meal program	Schools with cafeteria	Expenditure							
						Labor costs				Fuel, supplies cost			
						Education Budget	Local funding	Parents payment	Misc.	Education Budget	Local funding	Parents payment	Misc.
Elementary schools	Self-operated	Conventional foodservice		592	299	90,534,419	10,512,129	3,744,653	-	13,004,005	2,517,174	563,328	-
		Commissary foodservice	central kitchen	1	0	115,099	7,380	0	0	24,260	4,834	0	0
			satellite service center	5	3	112,660	15,034	232,402	-	14,687	1,348	45,056	-
Middle Schools	Self-operated	Conventional foodservice		306	217	27,141,119	17,947,397	139,524	8,382	4,644,756	3,976,654	10,259	3,311
		Commissary foodservice	central kitchen	2	2	144,272	87,209	10,971	-	30,993	24,561	3,575	-
			satellite service center	592	6	5,061,754	3,270,589	43,877	-	802,128	775,434	16,167	-
High Schools	Self-operated	Conventional foodservice		71	69	3,984,400	4,103	9,136,751	1,766	582,759	646	1,514,174	16,997
		Commissary foodservice	central kitchen	80	79	4,093,839	93,943	12,204,961	246,333	596,821	21,709	3,598,813	1,376
			satellite service center	15	1	652,097	18,587	2,051,990	686	97,889	4,066	473,176	252
	Contracted	Conventional foodservice		138	131	5,881,979	44,650	21,950,240	45,317	1,127,137	812	4,780,142	6,805
		Commissary foodservice	central kitchen	7	6	418,509	-	929,072	-	43,601	-	228,208	-
			satellite service center	7	0	364,094	-	601,538	-	37,891	-	171,974	-

* Note: (unit: 1,000 won)

References

Cha, Y. S., Kwak, T. K., & Hong, W. S.(2004). The Analysis of Customers' Satisfaction with Foodservice Quality According to the Types of Foodservice. *Journal of the Korean Dietetic Association*, 10: 309–321.

Kim, S. H., Lee, K. A., Yu, C. H., Song, Y. S., Kim, W. K., Yoon, H. R., Kim, J. H., Lee, H. S., & Kim, M. K.(2003). Comparisons of Students Satisfaction with the School Foodservice Programs in Middle and High Schools by Food Service Management Types. *Korean Journal of Nutrition*, 36: 211–222.

Shin, S. Y.(1999). *Satisfaction of the Middle School Students for the School Lunch Program*. DM Chungbuk University.

For Further Reading

[Contracting Out]

Amirkhanyan, A. A.(2007). The Smart–Seller Challenge: Exploring the Determinants of Privatizing Public Nursing Homes. *Journal of Public Administration Research and Theory*, 17(3): 501–527.

Bertelli, A. M., & Smith, C. R.(2010). Relational Contracting and Network Management. *Journal of Public Administration Research and Theory*, 20 (suppl 1), i21–i40.

Boyne, G. A.(1998). Bureaucratic Theory Meets Reality: Public Choice and Service Contracting in U.S. Local Government, *Public Administration Review*, 58(6): 474–484.

Brown, T. L., & Potoski, M.(2003). Contract–Management Capacity in Municipal and County Governments. *Public Administration Review*, 63(2): 153–164.

Brown, T. L., Potoski, M., & Van Slyke, D. M.(2006). Managing Public Service Contracts: Aligning Values, Institutions, and Markets. *Public Administration Review*, 66(3): 323–331.

Hirsch, W. Z.(1995). Factors Important in Local Governments' Privatization Decisions. *Urban Affairs Review*, 31(2): 226–243.

Hodge, G. A.(1998). Contracting Public Sector Services: A Meta–Analytic Perspective of the International Evidence. *Australian Journal of Public Administration*, 57(4): 98–110.

Niskanen, W. A.(1968). The Peculiar Economics of Bureaucracy. *The American Economic Review*, 58(2): 293–305.

Savas, E. S.(1987). *Privatization: The Key to Better Government*. Chatham, N.J.: Chatham House.

______(2000). *Privatization and Public–Private Partnerships*. New York: Chatham House.

Van Slyke, D. M.(2003). The Mythology of Privatization in Contracting for Social Services. *Public Administration Review*, 63(3): 296–315.

[Contracting Back In]

Chen, C.(2009). Antecedents of Contracting−Back−In: A View Beyond the Economic Paradigm. *Administration & Society*, 41(1): 101−126.

Hefetz, A., & Warner, M.(2004). Privatization and Its Reverse: Explaining the Dynamics of the Government Contracting Process. *Journal of Public Administration Research and Theory*, 14(2): 171−190.

Warner, M., Ballard, M., & Hefetz, A.(2003). Contracting Back In: When Privatization Fails. *The Municipal Year Book*, 30−36.

[Contracting Performance]

Amirkhanyan, A. A., Kim, H. J., & Lambright, K. T.(2014). The Performance Puzzle: Understanding the Factors Influencing Alternative Dimensions and Views of Performance. *Journal of Public Administration Research and Theory*, 24(1): 1−34.

Bel, G., Fageda, X., & Mur, M.(2014). Does Cooperation Reduce Service Delivery Costs? Evidence from Residential Solid Waste Services. *Journal of Public Administration Research and Theory*, 24(1): 85−107.

Fernandez, S.(2009). Understanding Contracting Performance: An Empirical Analysis. *Administration & Society*, 41(1), 67−100.

[Resources Related to the Korean School Foodservice Management]

Food Safety Information Portal: http://www.foodsafetykorea.go.kr/portal/main.html

Ministry of Food and Drug Safety: www.mfds.go.kr/eng

School Meals Act: https://elaw.klri.re.kr/kor_service/lawView.do?lang=ENG&hseq=18889

Seoul Metropolitan Office of Education: https://www.sen.go.kr/

South Korean Ministry of Education: www.moe.go.kr/

Teaching Note

Contracting Out or Contracting Back In: School Foodservice Contracts in South Korea

Purpose of the Case:

This case demonstrates most clearly the challenges to sustaining contracting relationships. By examining the different steps of school foodservice management policies in South Korea, this case also highlights potential benefits of and challenges to contracting-related issues with an approach that involves a diverse set of stakeholders.

The primary purpose of this case is to give students practice at diagnosing the underlying service delivery problems that could occur in the process of privatization. A secondary purpose is to help students understand the advantages and limitations of both contracting out and contracting back-in strategies as management tools.

This is a longitudinal case of school foodservice programs in South Korea. Since the difficulties of the agency that was in charge of service delivery are readily identifiable, it is a fairly simple case to teach. This case provides students an opportunity to diagnose problems of privatization and understand various actors who have impacts on the policymaking process and implementation process. This case also introduces to students a series of changes in public service delivery methods and helps them to develop solutions targeted at the specific problems they identify.

Teaching Uses:

This case can be utilized in many different academic settings. Courses on public management, contracting, public–private partnership, organizational theory, leadership, collaboration, and policy process may find relevance in this case. In particular, this case illustrates the following themes and the inherent tensions they present:

- shifting back and forth from in–house production to contracting out to contracting back in;
- contracting performance (e.g., cost saving and quality improvement) arguments;
- stakeholder involvement in the policy process;
- linking theories (principal–agent theory and transaction theory) and practices;
- strategic management issues, environment scanning, stakeholder analysis.

This case can be used to achieve the learning objectives as follows:

- Learn critical concepts and ideas related to contract management
- Articulate how theory and practice are linked to contract management
- Engage in discussions and exercise to develop a sense of how to apply the contracting cases and ideas covered in the course
- Cultivate critical and strategic thinking skills relevant to managerial choices in a turbulent and complex organizational environment

Suggested Conceptual Background: Contracting Out or Contracting Back In

The Korean school foodservice case combines considerations of decisions to contract out and later contract back in with the need to respond to stakeholder perceptions of operational problems. This case illustrates changes in the school foodservice policies in South Korea, focusing on the decision of the Ministry of Education to contract back in foodservices for public schools in South Korea as a key tool to address the problem of contracted foodservice management. There are two caveats to this case guidance. First, it is acknowledged that across countries and initiatives, contracting out practices vary in terms of legal frameworks, levels of private sector involvement, and the nature of services to be contracted. Therefore, readers should understand specific contextual backgrounds to tailor various strategies of contracting arrangements. Second, in covering many topics related to contracting out, this entry contains limited information and insufficient details to evaluate and analyze the impact of contracting on the efficiency, equity, and quality of the program. Additional readings and resources are therefore provided in the case.

The decision to privatize public services is a critical policy decision. Government contracting has been promoted on the basis of theoretical foundations, mainly public choice theory, with the argument that market competition in the bidding process of contracting out can reduce costs and improve service quality (e.g., Savas, 1987, 2000). However, a growing body of research states that cost savings are minimal and problems with quality management, control, or accountability are more frequently observed when services are outsourced. When contracts fail, it is not unusual for these services to be brought in-house for direct public provision. Warner, Ballard, & Hefetz (2003: 32) call this "contracting back in" and define it as "bringing back in house any service that the local government previously contracted out."

This table compares the reasons why governments contract out and why they contract back in. As shown in this table and in the empirical evidence, the effects of contracting in terms of efficiency, performance, and quality of services have been subjects of controversy. Considering these theoretical and conceptual arguments on contracting, students will be able to illustrate the case overview and discuss it in terms of attaining the goals of achieving better service quality and cost reduction.

Why Governments Contract Out	Why Governments Contract Back In
• Increased accountability by providing services at an acceptable minimum level • Lower spending on services that are produced by an external agency • Productivity enhancement, efficiency, and cost saving ▪ Economies of scope ▪ Market competition ▪ Bulk purchases • Efforts to overcome fiscal pressure facing the government unit	• Lack of monitoring: contracting back in is a substitute for monitoring • Problems with contractor performance: Lack of cost savings, poor service quality–as identified by professional monitoring • Opposition from labor, department heads, elected officials, or citizens • Problems with contract specification • Insufficient private competition • Competitive bidding: In–house crews bid to get the work back

• Improved performance through a competitive market mechanism • Political benefits for reforming and shrinking government, thereby reducing taxpayer burden • Desire to reduce both fixed and variable costs, to allow a client organization to focus on its core business, to offer access to skills and technology, to expand an organization's operational capacity and flexibility, and to increase an organization's accountability by formalizing service delivery	• Internal process improvement: Labor management cooperation makes contracting out unnecessary • Flexibility in responding to citizen demands • Attempts to decrease costs • Desire for more public participation in the service delivery process

Source: Boyne (1998); Hirsch (1995); Niskanen (1968)

Source: Warner, Ballard, & Hefetz (2003: 36)

Suggested Summary of Comparisons of Pros and Cons by School Foodservice Operation Types[31)]

The Ministry of Education (2008) published the manual for local schools to help their transition from contracted to mandatory self-operated foodservices. This manual contains the analysis of the comparison between two foodservice operations types as below. After the case study, instructors may encourage students to develop this kind of summary table to compare the pros/cons of self-operated versus contract-managed operation systems.

	Self-operated	Contract-managed
System	[pros] • Everything including cooking controlled by schools • A part of education, e.g., eating behavior • Guidance in healthy eating habits, table manners, communalism, reducing food waste etc. [cons] • School personnel have additional work duties related to foodservice management	[pros] • A variety of management types under school foodservice law • Acceleration of schools' foodservice adoption and saving of educational funds through inducement of private investment • Reduction of work load related to foodservice management [cons] • Limits of educational purposes regarding guidance of healthy eating

31) Ministry of Education (2008). Manual for Transition from Contracted to Mandatory Self-Operated Foodservice.

		• Conflict between nutrition teachers and employees affiliated with foodservice contract companies
Budget	[pros] • Government support of food, labor, operation costs → Reduced burden of meal payments on parents [cons] • Financial burden of support for equipment, food, labor, operation costs on Offices of Education	[pros] • Reduced financial burden on Offices of Education through inducement of private investment [cons] • Increased burden of meal payments on parents
Labor	[pros] • Expected high responsibility and sense of duty of employees affiliated with schools • Prompt changes in management and transparency of work through an effective communication system [cons] • Difficulties securing full-time employees and additional workload of managing foodservice employees	[pros] • Reduced workload for foodservice labor management [cons] • Difficulties intervening in foodservice management • Difficulties with systematic management because of low responsibility and sense of duty of employees affiliated with foodservice contract companies
Menu	[pros] • Priority on health improvement → Provision of traditional and nutritionally-balanced diets • Noncommercial → nutritious meals with low costs • Reduced food waste by educating students about a well-balanced diet [cons] • Limits of securing various food ingredients due to difficulties of management	[pros] • Priority on students' preference • Varying menus by hiring professional chefs and multifunctional cooking equipment (large foodservice management companies) [cons] • Use of low-quality ingredients such as frozen, instant, or imported foods to increase profit • Low efforts to improve students' health by focusing mainly on preference
Sanitation, Safety and Others	[pros] • Systematic management through investigation/training twice a year by professional personnel affiliated with Offices of Education • Administrative/financial support to solve problems [cons] • Limited sanctions for foodborne illness outbreak	[pros] • Sanctions for foodborne illness outbreak, e.g., contract termination [cons] • Overall low quality of food and limits to management improvement because authority lies with the contract companies

Discussion Outlines and Question Sequence:

1. Intro to Use and Limitations of Contracting Out

2. Problems and Decisions Facing the Ministry of Education

- As indicated in the case narrative, the Korean government wholly amended the School Meals Act in 2006 right after massive foodborne illness outbreaks. What decisions did the Ministry of Education make after the 2006 foodborne outbreaks?
- Before making this decision, what should the Ministry of Education first consider?
- Do you think that a change in the operation mode of school meal services was the best option that the Ministry of Education might choose? If not, what other potential alternatives could be considered?
- How would be the impact of the 2006 amendment on each stakeholder group, such as parent groups, principals, superintendents, etc.?

3. Evaluate the Decision: Contracting back-in after the 2006 amendment

- What features of the agency or specific contexts do you think contributed to the quality of school meal programs?
- Where are the weaknesses and problems?
- How would you assess the success/failure of this service delivery method?
- What do you think of the influence of media when deciding about contracting back in?
- What about management practices when changing the program?

4. Evaluate the Current Self-operated School Meal Program

- How would you evaluate the performance of self-operated school meal services? What method(s) or approach(es) would you use to assess the performance of self-operated foodservice system? Would you use different method(s) or approach(es) for self-operated versus contracted delivery? Why or Why not?
- What kinds of performance criteria should be used when evaluating the program?
- What incentives and penalties can be used in evaluating the self-operated services to ensure desired performance?

5. What can be done to improve the Ministry of Education's performance, especially to enhance the quality of school foodservices?

- What are possible actions?
- What are the obstacles?
- What factions or groups within the agency may be impediments?

- What groups outside of the agency can affect agency action?
- What about the teachers union's role and interests?
- What about the parents and media's role and interests?

6. In view of the obstacles and opportunities you have identified, how would you assess the implementation effort so far?

7. Summary and Lessons
   - Compare the values of contracting out and contracting back–in
     - What are potential advantages/disadvantages of contracting out the school meal services? Do you think there is any difference between using private companies to provide school meal services versus having their own operation system?
     - What are the main reasons why governments contract out and why they contract back–in? How do the evidences shown in this case support the arguments on contracting out and contracting back–in?
   - Share lessons learned from this case
     - What are the implications for implementation and leadership to successfully manage contracting out?
     - What lessons do you find from this case, particularly in terms of contract decisions and management?

The following questions may be used to prompt a discussion of the current case and a consideration of its implications and applications for other contexts:

- What should the Office or Minister do to monitor the performance of contracting out/back in? What should their first step be? What kinds of performance criteria should be used?
- What are the benefits and costs to the Office sustaining the in–house production of school meal programs?
- What are the tensions school principals face?
- How do the students and parents benefit from the changes in school meal operations? What steps should the school and the Office of Education take to maximize those benefits?
- Can you anticipate a situation in which the Office might be held back from achieving what they want to because how they operate? What could you do to avoid a situation like that? How could those precautionary steps hurt the Office?
- What would 'success' look like? Think about the answer from the perspective of school principals, students and parents, the Ministry of Education, and

food–service contractors. You could divide the class up into each of these different role assignments (schools, kids, Ministry, contractors) and have each group identify what success would look like for their assigned role, and then identify conditions that would enable them to succeed.

Suggested Supplementary Readings:

Suggested supplementary readings were provided at the end of the case narrative. In addition to them, the instructor might wish to add more readings on privatization, policy actors, contracting, and new public management.

04
Chapter

Work-Life Balance for Working Mom and Dad in South Korea

Taehee Kim

Work-Life Balance Policies in Public Organizations in South Korea

Demographic and sociological changes in the workforce along with the increasing participation of non-traditional employees (e.g., women, the disabled, the elderly, dual-career couples, and contingent workers) have been a compelling argument for creating an organizational environment where this heterogeneous group of people can work together (Riccucci, 2002; Kim, 2007; Kim & Mullins, 2016). In particular, it has been widely noted that these non-traditional employees may have greater difficulties balancing their work roles with their personal or family roles. Working women, for example, often need to perform their roles as primary care givers for their dependents at home while performing their roles in the workplace. As men are sharing the household burdens to a greater extent, especially those with a working partner, they are experiencing greater workloads and resultant role conflict between work and home. However, this is not limited to those with caregiving responsibilities. Interconnectedness between work and family/life can be an important issue to whoever has a need for balancing work and life. It is with the understanding that there can be either positive or negative spill-over between work and domestic responsibilities and identities (Halford et al., 1997). The conflict between work and life that results from incompatible roles and consequent job–related stress negatively affect job outcomes by lowering employees' attendance rates, job commitment, job satisfaction, and performance. Therefore, it becomes necessary for organizations to find ways to eliminate or minimize possible role conflict between work and life and help balance these dual roles effectively (Riccucci, 2002; Lapierre et al., 2008). In some western countries such as the United States, the government mandates various work–life policies such as child care subsidies, alternative work schedules, elder care, and paid leave. These are considered a major component of human resource management practices.

South Korea is not an exception to this trend. Several work–life balance policies have been implemented, with expectations that those policies would bring positive organizational outcomes. However, even though there have been increases in the number of available work–life balance promoting policies, questions remain as to whether or not those policies have brought expected or targeted outcomes and, if not, what should be considered to materialize the proposed benefits of work–life policies. This case report aims to introduce students to an overview of work–life balance policies in South Korea. Specifically, this case directs students' attention to challenges the universal application of those work–life balance policies may face when implemented without consideration of organizational conditions or culture.

Addressing Interconnectedness between Work and Family/Life: Proposed Benefits of Work-Life Balance Policies

It is suggested that the synergy from positive spillover between work and family would support well–being in all aspects of life and contribute positively to organizational performance. On the other hand, negative spillover between work and family in which either work or family obligations interfere with each other would undermine the employee's and family's overall well–being and result in negative organizational outcomes such as burnout, turnover, and lowered organizational productivity (Grzyward, 2000; Riccucci, 2002). Thus, it is critical for organizations to address work–life interconnectedness and actively seek ways to maximize the positive spillover while minimizing the negative spillover. In this regard, an increasing number of organizations, especially governmental organizations as a model employer, have made great efforts to introduce and implement so-called work-life balance policies seeking for the positive impacts on organizational outcomes such as job satisfaction, increased productivity, reduced turnover rate, and stronger job commitments. The benefits of these have been documented (Saltzstein et al., 2001; Riccucci, 2002; Kim 2007; Lee & Hong 2011). Work-life balance policies are defined as "any organizational programs or officially sanctioned practices designed to assist employees with the integration of paid work with other important life roles such as family, education, or leisure" (Ryan & Kossek, 2008: 295). These policies have been suggested to deliver positive organizational outcomes in several ways: (1) helping recruit and reach out to qualified but historically disadvantaged groups, especially female employees; (2) retaining qualified employees by creating a work environment conducive to meeting employees' multiple roles in both work and family; (3) addressing past gender-related discrimination in HR practices; and (4) motivating them to perform better by increasing their job satisfaction and commitment while reducing their turnover intention (see Figure 4-1).

However, when it comes to the practice, the under-use pattern[1] has been often reported even though a variety of programs under the work-life balance policies are available to employees. One of the reasons employees do not utilize those programs is because they do not want to identify themselves with employees of the so-called 'mommy track.' 'Mommy track'[2] employees are usually viewed by their supervisors or colleagues as less competent and qualified in comparison to their male colleagues or those without child-rearing responsibilities. Another explanation is that given the lack of su-

---

1) Citing the results of the 2011 Federal Employee Viewpoint Survey (2011), Kim & Mullins (2016: 84) pointed out this underuse pattern of federal employees especially in child-care programs compared to other work-life balance programs and noted, "availability of work-life balance policies does not necessarily result in perceived accessibility or even actual use by employees." For example, the use of an alternative work schedule could also be a reason for possible backlash and negative career outcomes even though it targets all employees. It is assumed that the use of flexible work scheduling creates more work for other coworkers in the same work unit. The use of flexible work schedules might negatively affect career outcomes for those who work with a supervisor who prefers to manage subordinates face-to-face. Kim & Wiggin (2011) noted a gender difference in the level of satisfaction with work-life balance programs. In their study, different pay grades also differently affect employees' satisfaction with alternative work schedule.

2) "Mommy track" refers to women who may be modifying their career aspirations to look after their family.

Figure 4-1. Proposed Benefits of Work-Life Balance Practices

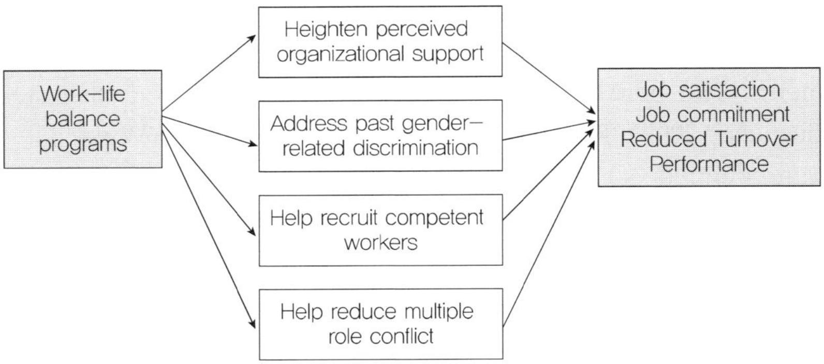

pervisory support or any supporting organizational culture, some employees are observed to feel hesitant to use family-friendly programs due to their fear over possible backlash and negative career outcomes. Moreover, recent studies note the tension those policies may cause between certain targeted demographic groups and non-targeted groups (e.g. between married couples with children and unmarried or childless employees).[3] The question of who has access to such policies becomes critical to shaping employees' perception

3) Working moms are categorized into two groups: the first group is a "career primary track" for women who prioritize work over their family and who are willing to spend long working hours if they are necessary and helpful for their career advancement, even when it means sacrificing time with their family. The second group is the "mommy track," or women who may be modifying their career aspirations to look after their family. The working mom in the mommy track is usually perceived as less competent and qualified compared to male colleagues. Bruce & Reed (1992: 120) noted, "What the track does is to affirm the traditional value of a 'mother's place' in a separate sphere, rather than offering a choice to either parent. … Truly family-friendly benefits will allow for a 'daddy track' and a 'parent track' as well as a mommy track. The key to providing family-friendly benefits is to provide choices, not paternalistic solutions." Increasing numbers of working men are assuming care giving responsibilities for children or elderly dependents, which means that family-friendly programs are not only for advancing women's interests. Nevertheless, colleagues who do not have any dependents may perceive that their colleagues with family responsibilities are treated with favoritism in their organization. Such policies targeting one specific group may create a so-called "family-friendly backlash," that is, resentment among employees who are single or childfree. That is, it is plausible to assume that employees may be reluctant to use those benefits for fear of facing negative judgments from others who may view them as less committed to their job (Allen, 2001), given the tension those policies may cause between certain targeted demographic groups and non-targeted groups (e.g., between married couple with children and unmarried or childless).

of fairness in adopting and implementing those policies as Kirby & Krone (2002: 51) note, "The fact that a policy exists on paper does not mean it is always accepted as legitimate or followed as written." These observations have fueled further inquiry into practical implications that work-life balance policies may have for different employees under different contexts.

Providing family friendly benefits is critical for setting up the context of managing a diversified workforce, but it is not enough to help employees coordinate their multiple work and life roles and bring positive returns to both their family and their employing organizations. The following description in the Korean context presented below and the hypothetical cases of an employee in South Korea may help understand what conditions should be met or needed to realize the benefits of work-life balance programs.

Context for Work-Life Balance Policies in South Korea

Due to the long-held Confucian ideology that imposes patriarchal values, South Korea has been a male-dominated society where women's role as a caregiver in the family is often taken for granted. In the past, it was women's primary responsibility to care for their elderly-in-law along with their own family members. Women, as the primary care giver, were expected to prioritize their family over their career whereas men were usually considered as their family's sole breadwinner. That is, even when women are highly educated enough to pursue a promising career, it was a social norm that women with family or children put their career aside and become housewives. Due to this gender role shaped by Confucian gender ideology, there have been limits in shared childcare responsibilities in marriage. Confucianism is not a dominating value in the current Korean society as it was in the past, but its influence still remains. In fact, South Korea's gender equality ranking is quite lower than that of other countries. According to the 2015 Global Gender Gap Report, South Korea was ranked 115st out of 145 countries in terms of gender equality. The range of jobs available to women has been restricted to medium-to low-status occupations such as secretaries, teachers, or clerical assistants (Kim, 2008). Women who have jobs often suffer from gender discrimination in the workplace such as sexual harassment or fewer opportunities for career advancement in the workplace. In order to address this issue, the

Korean government has taken many steps that include creating a work environment conducive to gender-equal employment; addressing the women's chronic career disruption; and helping women balance their work and life. For example, the Gender Equal Employment Act of 1987 was enacted to ensure equal opportunity and treatment in employment. The Infant Care Act (1991) was enacted to help poor families in their child-rearing responsibilities. The Women's Development Act was enacted in 1995 to protect women's rights and fight against workplace discrimination; it was later revised as the Framework Act on Gender Equality in 2014 to protect gender equality. A gender quota system in recruiting and preferential hiring for qualified women in government positions was introduced in 1997. Maternity Protection Laws took effect in 2001 to distribute the cost burden of pregnancy, childbirth, and parenting. Under the Kim Dae-jung administration, the Ministry of Gender Equality who is solely handling women's affairs was established to develop and implement women's polices and prevent gender discrimination in 2002. It was renamed the Ministry of Gender Equality & Family (MGEF) in 2005 to take responsibility for policies related to women, family and youth, and children. In 2014, a taskforce was created through a public-private partnership with the aim to develop plans and programs to promote gender equality. As a result, the status of women in South Korea has been greatly improved as shown in the Table 4-1 and Figure 4-2, though there is still room for improvement.

Women's Employment and Employment Type: Table 4-1 provides a snapshot of women's employment in South Korea. As the data show, while women's employment has increased over time since 2007, the ratio of non-regular workers, either temporary or part-time workers, is constantly around 40% of total employment.

When compared to men's employment, the ratio of non-regular employment of women is higher by about 10% (See Figure 4-1). As of 2016, 25% of male workers hold either temporary or part-time jobs, whereas 40% of women have those non-regular jobs. Women tend to be concentrated in non-regular employment compared to their counterparts. Regarding this trend, using a panel data analysis, the Korean Women's Development Institute (2015) provides further analysis showing that women's rate of taking non-

Table 4-1. Women's Employment Trend by Employment Type

	Total	full-time (regular)	temporary or part-time (non-regular)
2007	6,625	3,820	2,805
2008	6,756	3,962	2,795
2009	6,768	4,020	2,748
2010	7,075	4,132	2,943
2011	7,240	4,218	3,021
2012	7,499	4,379	3,119
2013	7,618	4,534	3,084
2014	7,968	4,791	3,177
2015	8,152	4,894	3,259
2016	8,423	5,028	3,395

Source: Statistics Korea.

Figure 4-2. Ratio of Temporary Workers

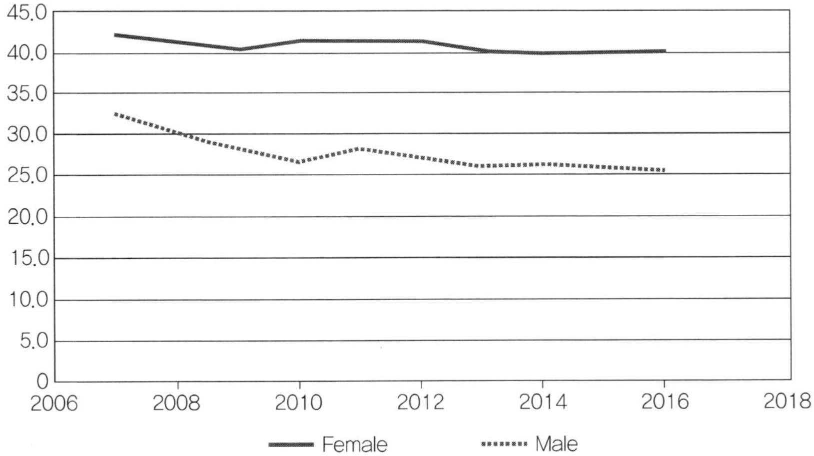

Source: Statistics Korea.

regular jobs increases in their 40's and 50's because after child-birth or due to childcare burdens, an increasing number of women abandon their full-time jobs or transfer to part-time or temporary status.

Women's Representation in Government: Table 4-2 provides a snapshot of women's employment in government jobs. It appears that representation of women in government jobs has been improved. The percentage of women holding government jobs has steadily increased to 33.7% of the civil service as of 2015.

Table 4–2. Women in the Korean Government

	2007	2008	2009	2010	2011	2012	2013	2014	2015
Total	275,484	275,231	278,303	279,636	281,035	284,355	287,299	289,914	296,273
Women	78,855	80,666	82,178	83,282	84,239	87,239	89,979	94,346	99,865
Ratio (%)	28.6	29.3	29.5	29.8	30	30.7	31.3	32.5	33.7

Source: Statistics Korea.

However, when it comes to upper–level managerial positions (Grade 4 and higher), women's representation is still quite low. While female employees constitute 32.5% of total government employment in 2014, only 9% held managerial positions in government. The ratio of women holding managerial positions in government has remained constant at about 8~9% (See Table 4–3).

Table 4–3. Ratio of Women Holding Managerial Positions in Government

	Grade 4 or higher	Ratio of Women (%)
2011	7,132	7.3
2012	7,326	8.2
2013	7,256	8.8
2014	7,444	9.7

Source: Statistics Korea.

Choi & Park (2014) noted a similar pattern when examining employment of women at all governmental levels including central and local governments. The percentage of female employees who hold upper–level jobs (Grade 4 and higher) is 6.5% when combining all career civil servants and contract civil servants at all governmental levels and only 4.4% in positions higher than Grade 4 in local government (See Table 4–4). These trends show that women continue to be concentrated in lower–level, non–managerial positions in government, indicating the existence of glass ceiling.

Table 4-4. Employment of Women in Korean Government (Executive Branch) by Grade

Classification	All governments		Central governments		Local governments	
	All empolyees	Female (%)	All empolyees	Female (%)	All empolyees	Female (%)
Total	964,158	42.0	622,737	47.2	341,421	32.4
Senior civil service	1,034	3.2	997	3.3	37	0.0
Grades 1-2	66	1.5			66	1.5
Grade 3	959	4.6	617	4.7	342	4.4
Grade 4	8,368	6.5	5,461	7.2	2,907	5.3
Grade 5	29,112	10.8	12,443	13.7	16,669	8.6
Grade 6	82,946	19.7	24,941	19.0	58,005	20.0
Grade 7	108,547	40.7	28,973	28.7	79,574	45.0
Grade 8	56,351	50.8	19,509	45.3	36,942	53.7
Grade 9	32,339	52.6	13,002	48.3	19,337	55.6

Source: Adapted from Choi & Park (2014, Table 2: 9).

Gender Pay Gap: When it comes to gender pay gap, it turns out that women continue to get paid less than their male counterparts. Even though the gap is becoming much narrower, the pay gap still exists. The latest figures show that female full-time workers earned about 68 percent of men's earning as of 2013.

Table 4-5. Gender Pay Gap

	2000	2005	2010	2011	2012	2013
Total	1,314	1,888	2,360	2,454	2,567	2,660
Female	954	1,396	1,772	1,862	1,958	2,033
Male	1,474	2,109	2,648	2,750	2,878	2,986
Ratio	64.7	66.2	66.9	67.7	68	68.1

Source: Ministry of Employment and Labor.

The occupational segregation between men and women is suggested as one of the major determinants of the gender pay gap. Men are tend to be employed in high-paying professions such as doctors, or professors, whereas women are more likely to be employed in low-paying professions such as clerks or secretaries. Park (2016) analyzed the occupational segregation status in South Korea by gender using the data from the International Labor Organization (ILO). Her study found that while more men hold professional or managerial occupations, more women were found in service, clerk or sales occupations, accounting for greater gender earnings gaps as shown in Figure 4-3. Childcare or dependent care responsibilities are suggested to greatly shape women's decision to choose a certain type of occupations, because being a good mother or good wife is a highly regarded value that women are expected to uphold in Korean society. Therefore, women are more likely to look for occupations where they can find flexibility with their working hours so that they can take time off for family related reasons when needed, even though they are lower-paying careers.

Figure 4–3. Occupation by male and female in South Korea

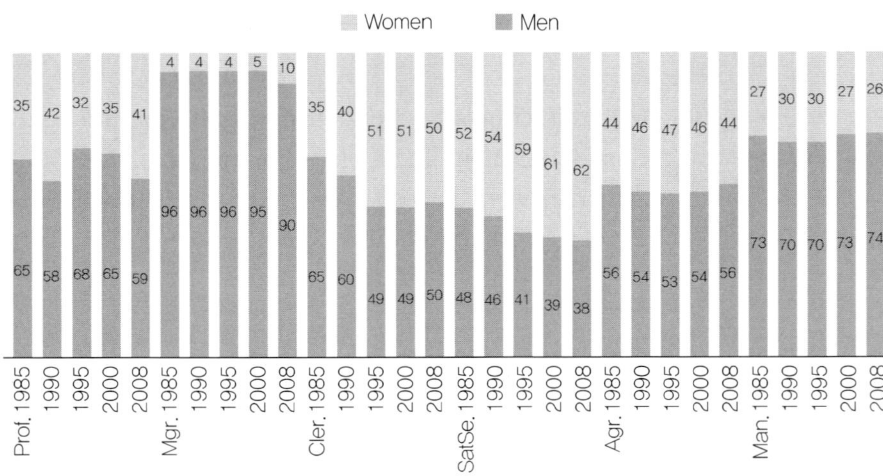

Source: Adapted from Park (2016: 27).

Childcare as Major Impediment to Women's Employment and career advancement: Work and family conflict, gender stereotypes and discrimination, and male-dominated workplace culture are suggested as major obstacles to women's employment and career advancement (Choi & Park, 2014). As for sharing household responsibilities, there have been changes in the perceptions of men with whom an increasing number perceive household responsibilities should be fairly shared. However, in reality, Korean working women still do more housework and childcare at home compared to their male partners. According to the 2014 social survey, 50 percent of those surveyed said that chores should be distributed fairly, while in reality 80 percent indicated that women performed the majority of chores at home when asked who regularly performs the majority of chores (see Table 4–6).

Table 4–6. Distribution of households

		Women primarily	Fair distribution	Men primarily
Opinion	2008	66.5	32.5	1.1
	2010	61.3	36.8	1.9
	2012	52	45.3	2.7
	2014	50.2	47.5	2.3
Reality	Husband	80.5	16.4	3.1
	Wife	81.5	16	2.5

Source: 2014 Social Survey.

Figure 4–4. Impediments to women's employment

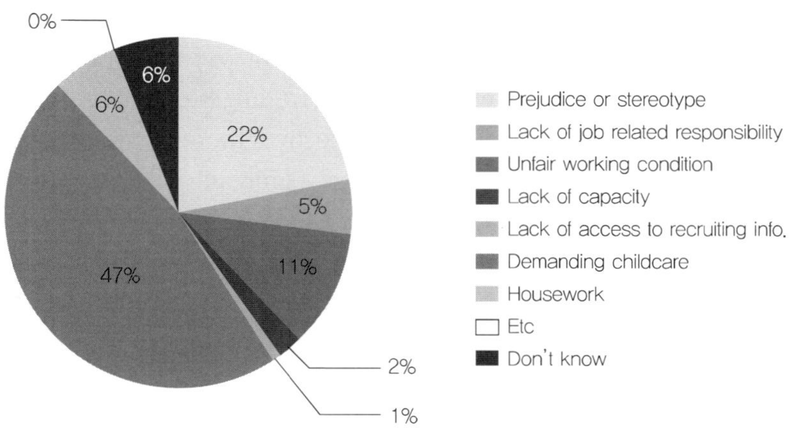

Source: 2015 Social Survey.

Figure 4–4 shows perceived impediments to women's employment according to a 2015 social survey. About 48% of respondents chose "heavy demands of childcare" as one of the main impediments to women's employment, while about 23% of respondents chose assumptions about women's job attitude or capacity or stereotypes.

Work-life Balance Promoting Policies: Given this context, the Korean government has implemented a variety of work–life policies for the purpose of helping female employees with their employment and career advancement. Examples of work–life balance programs include leave programs such as (1) ante–natal leave, which is one day of paid leave per month during pregnancy; (2) maternity leave, which offers 90 days of paid leave before and after the birth of a child (with the condition that after childbirth 45 days must be taken); (3) paternity leave offering three days of paid leave at the birth of a child; (4) parental leave of one year or up to three years of leave for each child; (5) leave for family reasons, such as one year of leave for caring for a sick family member; (6) health leave, which is one day of paid leave per month for women; and (7) breast–feeding leave, which is one hour of paid leave per day to care for a child.

Many of these types of leave specifically address women because female employees are more likely to have more needs for work/life balance due to their responsibilities as child bearers and their potentially inevitable need of a periodic leave for childbirth (Riccucci, 2002). For example, employed women can take maternity leave with three months of full payment. Working women or their husbands with a child under 8 years are eligible to take up to 3 years of childcare leave. From the employee's perspective, these leave programs enable working parents to balance their work and family life. From an employers' perspective, they help retain competent and qualified employees and foster their work motivation (Riccucci, 2002; Kim, 2008; Kim & Mullins, 2016).

Under the amended Gender Equal Employment Act of 1995 and the Infant Care Act, employers who have more than 300 women employees are required to have childcare facilities.

As a result, the number of organizations offering on–site childcare has slightly increased over time and as of 2014, 692 organizations offered on–site childcare (see Table 4–7). Choi (2007) found that about 32% of female respondents and about 17% of male respondents had used on–site childcare.

Table 4-7. Number of Available Childcare Centers

No. of available childcare centers	2012	2013	2014
National or Public childcare center	2,203	2,332	2,489
On-site childcare center	523	619	692

Source: Statistics Korea.

Flexible work schedules are available in some cases so that part-time work arrangement can be made, and some public organizations have tried to provide facilities for breastfeeding or pumping breast milk in the workplace or, depending on budgetary status, on-site childcare (Ministry of Government Administration and Home Affairs, 2005). As for the flexible work policies, the most common types of flexible work arrangements are flextime, adjusted work-hours and working from home. As of 2014, among 1,000 organizations examined, it turns out that about 13.8 percent of organizations adopted flextime; 3.4 percent adopted the option of working from home, and 4.7 percent adopted adjusted work-week schedule (4 days per week schedule). These accommodations are provided in the belief that the implementation of these policies and organizational support for facilitating employees' use are critical for recruiting and retaining talented and experienced workforces.[4)]

Table 4-8 and Figure 4-5 show the pattern of using maternity and paternity leave combined. The use of maternity and paternity leave increased over time. In particular, women's use of leave has constantly increased. On the other hand, while men are eligible to use this leave benefit, their use rate is slightly increasing but quite low when compared to women. As of 2014, only 4.5% of men used paternity leave. This may indicate that in South Korea, childcare is still regarded as women's duty or responsibility. Given that a working mother's relationship with her husband is traditional at home, it appears that husbands prioritize their careers while women take leaves in order to adjust to the needs of their families even when it means disrupting their career's advancement.

4) Moreover, to facilitate the adoption of family-friendly programs, the Ministry of Gender Equality & Family (MGEF) initiated a certification system that comes with financial incentives to public or private organizations who have successfully implemented family-friendly programs such as childbirth or childcare support or flextime. As of 2015, about 1,363 organizations had earned the certification.

Table 4-8. Maternity/Paternity leave Use Pattern

	2007	2008	2009	2010	2011	2012	2013	2014	2015
Total	21,185	29,145	35,400	41,733	58,137	64,069	69,616	76,833	87,339
Female	20,875	28,790	34,898	40,914	56,735	62,279	67,323	73,412	82,467
Male	310	355	502	819	1,402	1,790	2,293	3,421	4,872

Source: Statistics Korea.

Figure 4-5. Maternity/Paternity leave Use Trend Chart

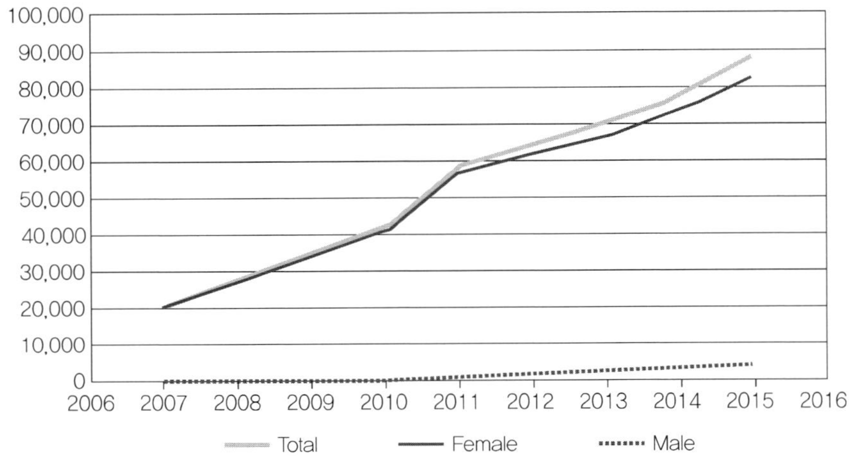

Source: Statistics Korea.

When asked about their employment status after taking maternity leave, about 60 percent indicated that as of 2013, they kept their job after they returned from maternity leave and its ratio is increasing over time. However, this statistics does not capture whether or not those employees returned to the position they were in before taking leaves.

In fact, according to the report released by Statistics South Korea in 2015, the unemployment rate of married women ages 15 to 54 is about 41 percent. About 22 percent of married women between the ages of 15 to 54 either quit their jobs or expressed intention to leave their jobs because of family reasons such as pregnancy, childbirth, childcare, and dependent care. As for the primary reasons for women's career disruption, marriage was listed highest (about 36.9 %), followed by infant-care (29.9%) and pregnancy and childbirth (24.4).

Table 4-9. Employment Status and Maternity leave

	2008	2009	2010	2011	2012	2013
Ratio	53.7	51.5	52.6	54.9	57.3	59.5
No.	15,642	18,243	21,936	31,942	36,712	41,418

Source: Ministry of Employment and Labor.

Note: The ratio indicates the percentage of employees who keep their job after taking maternity leave; No. indicates the number of employees who report staying in the same job after taking maternity leave.

Table 4-10. Working Mom's Career Disruption Rate

	2011	ratio	2012	ratio	2013	ratio	2014	ratio	2015	ratio
Total	1,900	100	1,978	100	1,955	100	2,139	100	2,053	100
Marriage	893	47	928	46.9	898	45.9	822	38.4	757	36.9
Pregnancy/Child birth	380	20	479	24.2	414	21.2	436	20.4	501	24.4
Infant-care	545	28.7	493	24.9	571	29.2	627	29.3	614	29.9
Child-care	81	4.3	79	4	72	3.7	93	4.3	80	3.9

Source: Statistics Korea.

Figure 4-6. Reasons for Women's Career Disruption Trend Chart

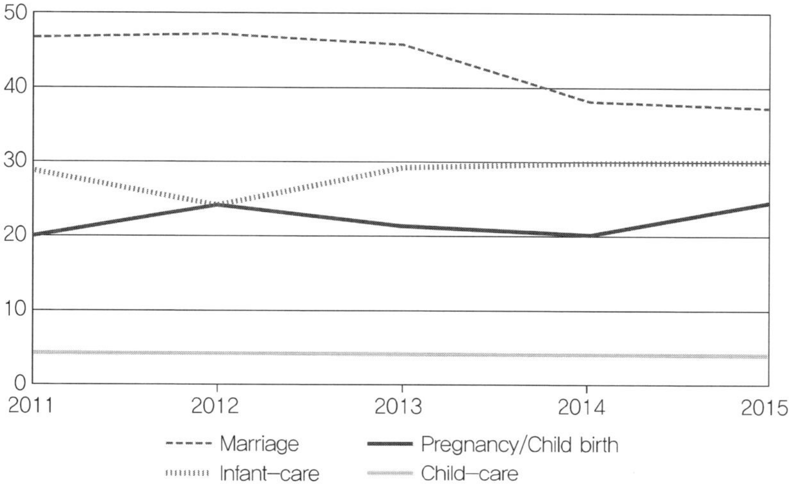

Source: Statistics Korea.

This may imply that many women still perceive their childbearing and childcare burden as a major obstacle to their career advancement. It may also be attributable to the lack of quality childcare facilities. As incidents of child abuse at daycare centers increase, an increasing number of working women have been asking their mothers-in-law to look after their kids even though this would cause travel problems. Citing the results of a 2007 survey of 1,000 participants conducted by the Ministry of the Interior, Yu & Kim (2009) reported that about 47% of respondents perceive the use of maternity or paternity leave negatively because they believe it negatively affects career advancement. As for their colleagues' use of leave, about 46% of respondents indicate that they understand the needs of their colleagues with childcare obligations but perceive that the absence of their colleagues may increase their workload. Choi (2007) also made a similar observation using a survey of 617 government employees conducted by the Korean Institute of Public Administration. While 56% of women indicate severe difficulties in balancing work and life, about 35% of men express difficulties. A majority of both men and women chose child-care as one of the major difficulties in balancing work and life. When asked about the reasons why they do not take maternity or paternity leave, a majority expressed concern about job security, career disruption, or negative impacts on promotion opportunities expected.

Moreover, there exist widespread concerns about career damage resulting from using extensive leave or alternative work scheduling for family purposes. In some cases, women who use leave for family purposes are likely to be viewed as "willing to trade some career growth and compensation for freedom from the constant pressure to work long hours and weekends" (Schwartz 1989: 70). Men are not an exception to this phenomenon because male employees seeking work-family balance by using those benefits may be confronted with career damage, especially when they have many colleagues who hold traditional views of gender roles and thus may not view a male employee's use of family-friendly programs positively. To measure working parents' attitudes toward family-friendly programs, Won & Pascall (2004: 281) conducted several interviews of working parents in South Korea. One of their interviewees noted, "In the current organizational culture, we are forced to choose between work and motherhood. … When I applied for leave, I made up my mind that it was OK for my career to go slow because of it." Another interesting observation was made by one of their male interviewees. He noted that when men take paternity leave, their colleagues and supervisor usually do not accept a "family-committed man," and this jeopardized their reputation in the workplace and eventually their career.

The issues addressed above suggest that making policy available cannot in and of itself help materialize the proposed benefits of work–life balance policies. The following two hypothetical cases illustrate experiences of a typical working mom in South Korea. They illustrate gap between government's work–life balance policy and working mom's reality in South Korea. Specifically, they provide examples that suggest consideration of cultural changes that are supportive of employee's balance between work, family, and personal life matters in overcoming challenges addressed above in relation to work–life balance policies.

Case 1. One Working Mom's Day

Jaehee is the mother of a 4–year–old girl, Yuna. Jaehee is currently working as a middle school teacher in a school located in the southern part of Seoul. Her typical day starts with waking up at 5 : 30 a.m. to prepare breakfast for her family and to get Yuna ready for school. The nearest and most affordable preschool is about 30 minutes away from her house and 7 : 00 a.m. is the earliest drop–off time with the latest time parents can pick up their children being 7 : 00 p.m. Since she needs to get to work by 8 : 00 a.m., she needs to make sure to send Yuna off to school by 7 : 00 a.m. so that she can have time to get ready to go to work. Yet somehow it always doesn't work as planned. She usually needs to squeeze a 30–minute commute into 20 minutes. She always needs to juggle among multiple household responsibilities between breakfast preparation and child–care including bathing, dressing, and feeding Yuna.

When her husband is available to share school drop–off duty, Jaehee can spend more time to take care of herself. However, in most cases, her husband is not available. Without a willing family member living nearby, she has little choice but to hire a nanny called an "attending school helper[5]" who would help drop off her daughter to school. This would cost her extra money, approximately $10 (10,000 won) per hour. Even though the latest hour is 7 : 00 p.m. at school, most kids are picked up by 4 : 00 p.m., and she may need to hire another nanny who would help pick up her daughter and spend some

5) It is called as Deung–gyo Doumi in Korean.

time with her until Jaehee or her husband comes home from work. Given the lack of any family members who live nearby, Jaehee must hire someone who can care for Yuna for 4 to 5 hours, costing her family an estimated $1,300.00 (1,400,000 won). This amount is equivalent to approximately one-third of Jaehee's monthly salary. Given this situation, the only available option is either for her to stop her career and stay at home until Yuna grows up while worrying about meeting the family expenses solely on her husband's income, or for her and her husband to remain as a dual-earning couple to continue working while paying for child care services and not being able to spend any quality time with her daughter.

While at work Jaehee always feels guilty for leaving her little daughter, especially when Yuna is sick. Since Jaehee works at a school where most of her colleagues are well into their late 30's or early 40's with small or school-aged children, there is a general understanding by her colleagues about her felt difficulties in balancing her work and family, and her needs to take off from her job on time to be back to home to cater for her daughter. However, the lack of latitude over her work schedule makes it difficult for Jaehee to concentrate on work and perform properly. Additionally, even though return-to-work is guaranteed for a school teacher like her, her use of about a year of maternity and childcare leave caused her to feel that her career is interrupted and makes her feel pressured to do more work to catch up on what's going on at school. Her husband cannot take a long leave either because his work at a private company means his return-to-work may not be guaranteed and he doesn't want to take unpaid paternity leave due to financial reasons.

Jaehee tries to get home immediately after classes are over, usually around 5 : 30 p.m. She then tries to serve dinner at about 6 : 00 p.m. because she values shared dinner gatherings with her family. However, meeting this after work schedule proves difficult as Jaehee must often stay at school later than expected, and her husband often does not return home from work until 10 : 00 or 11 : 00 p.m. After dinner, Jaehee helps Yuna with her homework, if any, and does the laundry. The domestic contribution by her husband is limited to rare occasions. It is only after her daughter is asleep that she can carve out some time to have a chat with her husband to catch up on each other's day or finish up the left over work. Due to her working schedule, Jaehee can never fully engage in Yuna's after–school activities, leaving her feeling guiltier about not being able to spend quality time with Yuna, and lamenting how good it would be for Yuna if she were a stay–at–home mommy. On one occasion, Yuna was going to have a ballet performance. Jaehee was excited to see her daughter perform, but on that same evening she was called to a mandatory assessment meeting on short notice and had no choice but to miss this precious event.

Case 2. High Workload and Work–Life Balance?

Jiyeon is a social worker working at a public senior welfare facility located in Seoul. She comes from a lower–middle–class family. Jiyeon chose her profession because she believed helping someone in need to be very rewarding.

She is required to work anywhere from an 11 to 12 hour shifts for three to four consecutive days with a day or two off after each set of consecutive days. Each floor of her four story workplace is fully packed with the elderly admitted to the facility, despite an insufficient number of staff needed to provide services at a satisfactory level. Making matters worse, working overtime is very common even though employees are not compensated for overtime work. Compared to other service industries the salary level of social workers is very low, and increasing workloads without any measures to address the staff shortage issue has resulted in a higher level of turnover. Even when she doesn't feel well, Jiyeon is always hesitant to take a day off because she doesn't want her colleagues to shoulder her work in her absence.

Besides the demanding work conditions, there have been several occasions where Jiyeon felt that her employer is not valuing or acknowledging her needs as a working mom. Last month, one of her colleagues Miso severely injured her back while helping elderly patient with moving his wheelchair, and needed to be hospitalized for two weeks. In Miso's absence, Jiyeon could overheard her other colleagues complain about their increased workload and even it was told by her supervisor that given a continuous absence, it may be difficult to keep her position. On another occasion, another colleague, Yunhee's young toddler came down with flu and needed to be taken to the doctor. In order to bring her child to the doctor for a two hour period and have a day off to take care of her sick baby, Yunhee skipped her lunch and persuaded her supervisor that she would make up those missed hours by working the night−shift. Even though employees are entitled to use their annual leave for these purposes, many do not feel their use of those types of leave is welcomed by either their supervisor or their colleagues.

In this context, Jiyeon feels increasing levels of anxiety and overwhelming stress while worrying about her future career and work−life balance. Jiyeon got married last year and now she is expecting a new baby. Although she has a right to take maternity leave, she is scared to take it given the past situations with her colleagues. Because of the intense workload, taking maternity leave would shift her share of work to her colleagues who already feel overwhelmed with their own workloads. In addition, her job may not be secured for her to return to. She also believe that unpredictable work schedules would be a big obstacle.

Jiyeon has seen many friends struggle to balance work and life and eventually drop their career because of family responsibilities. It would be, however, difficult for Jiyeon to quit her job because it would be very challenging to finance her life with a new baby with her husband's single income. Jiyeon keeps going to work even though her due date is quickly approaching.

Suggestions for Improvement

What are the dilemmas and challenges that two working moms, Jaehee and Jiyeon have faced? The preceding sections suggest that the overall status of women's employment has improved and the government has made a series of efforts to help address past discrimination in employment practices against women and help them balance their work and life. However, it turns out that there are still obstacles to women's employment, career advancement, and more importantly their utilization of the work−life balance policies that exist. As illustrated in those two cases, making policy available cannot in and of itself help materialize the proposed benefits of work−life balance policies. One of the major impediments might be the lack of supportive culture for successful implementation of work−life balance policies. Some prior studies address unique cultural norms that play a major role in shaping the attitude of managers and employees toward the use of work−life balance policies (Ryan & Kossek, 2008; Lee et al., 2011). Lee & his colleagues (2011) noted the cultural differences between South Korea and other Western countries such as the U.S.A. In South Korea as a collectivist society, rather than having work and life as a separate domain, work and family are interrelated and considered as an interdependent domain. Another distinctive cultural characteristic they suggest is Koreans' inclination to comply with in-group norms. For example, the culture of working long hours shapes in-group norms in which working long hours is viewed by colleagues and supervisors as a sign of loyalty to the employing organization and accountability for getting the job done even when the employee is aware that extended work hours would have negative impacts on work-life balance. The frequent use of flexible work schedule may conflict with this group norm, which would result in employees' hesitance to use it even when it is available. Another cultural characteristic is shaped by Confucian ideology that expects women to take exclusive responsibility for childcare and domestic work (Kim, 2007). As Kim (2007) noted, in this culture, working moms are usually not well-received as qualified workers and male workers who are willing to share domestic responsibilities with their partners are not well-received by their male colleagues. In order not to jeopardize their career advancement and secure their job or position, employees are encouraged to prioritize their work over their life or family needs. That is, in order to achieve the intended outcomes of work-life balance policies, there must be an inclusive culture in which different needs of individuals are recognized and respected and also a family-friendly culture in which the use of work-life balance policies is encouraged and its value is well-received. It is not an easy task to change a deep-rooted culture.

It can begin with top leadership's commitment to promoting and managing diversity matters (Riccucci, 2002). Government workers and managers also need to be educated about bias or stereotypes they have when judging someone's work-related competence and qualifications and about how to overcome bias and stereotypes (Riccucci, 2002; Choi & Park, 2014; Kim & Mullins, 2016). In implementing work-life balance policies, employees' perception of fairness and justice is critical to success. For this purpose, managers or supervisors need to be trained about how to fairly deliver this benefit to employees. They also need to communicate information on eligibility and available programs clearly. The use of programs should be encouraged when needed, and employers should ensure that there are no career disadvantages when using those programs. At the government level, rather than merely providing policies facilitating work–family balance by targeting working parents, it is recommended to develop and implement general work–life balance promoting programs that target anyone in the organization such as workplace health and wellness programs (e.g., nutrition services or health education).

References

Beauregard, T. A., & Henry, L. C.(2009). Making the Link Between Work–Life Balance Practices and Organizational Performance. *Human Resource Management Review*, 19 (1): 9–22.

Caillier, J. G.(2013). Satisfaction With Work–Life Benefits and Organizational Commitment/ Job Involvement Is There a Connection? *Review of Public Personnel Administration*, 33(4): 340–364.

Casper, W. J., & Buffardi, L. C.(2004). Work–Life Benefits and Job Pursuit Intentions: The Role of Anticipated Organizational Support. *Journal of Vocational Behavior*, 65(3): 391–410.

Choi, S. Y.(2007). Seeking for Measures to Improve Workplace Conditions of Women Public Employee, *Korean Institute of Public Administration (KIPA) Research Report*: 2007–23.

Choi, S., & Park, C. O.(2014). Glass Ceiling in Korean Civil Service Analyzing Barriers to Women's Career Advancement in the Korean Government. *Public Personnel Management*, 43(1): 118–139.

Choi, H. S., & Cho, J. H.(2010). Policy Suggestions to Effectively Utilize Female Employees in Science and Technology, *Industry and Economy Analysis*: 16–27.

Clark, S. C.(2000). Work/Family Border Theory: A New Theory of Work/Family Balance. *Human relations*, 53(6): 747–770.

Doherty, L.(2004). Work–Life Balance Initiatives: Implications for Women. *Employee Relations*, 26(4): 433–452.

Eisenberger, R., Armeli, S., Rexwinkel, B., Lynch, P. D., & Rhoades, L.(2001). Reciprocation of Perceived Organizational Support. *Journal of Applied Psychology*, 86(1): 42.

Foster Thompson, L., & Aspinwall, K. R.(2009). The Recruitment Value of Work/Life Benefits. *Personnel Review*, 38(2): 195–210.

Hoyman, M., & Duer, H.(2004). A Typology of Workplace Policies Worker Friendly vs. Family Friendly? *Review of Public Personnel Administration*, 24(2): 113–132.

Kang, H. R., & Rowley, C.(2005). Women in Management in South Korea: Advancement or Retrenchment? *Asia Pacific Business Review*, 11(2): 213–231.

Kim, S.(2008). Women and Family–Friendly Policies in the Korean Government. *International Review of Administrative Sciences*, 74(3): 463–476.

______(2007). A Comparative Study of Family–Friendly Policies and Benefits in Public Organizations: South Korea and the United States, *Korean Journal of Policy Studies*, 21(2): 1–22.

Kim, T., & Mullins, L. B.(2016). How Does Supervisor Support and Diversity Management Affect Employee Participation in Work/Family Policies?. *Review of Public Personnel Administration*, 36(1): 80–105.

Kirby, E., & Krone, K.(2002). "The Policy Exists but You Can't Really Use It": Communication and the Structuration of Work–Family Policies. *Journal of Applied Communication Research*, 30(1): 50–77.

Kim, J., & Wiggins, M. E.(2011). Family Friendly Human Resource Policy: Is It Still Working in the Public Sector?. *Public Administration Review*, 71(5): 728–739.

Kossek, E. E., Lewis, S., & Hammer, L. B.(2009). Work–Life Initiatives and Organizational Change: Overcoming Mixed Messages to Move from the Margin to the Mainstream. *Human Relations*, 63(1): 3–19.

Kossek, E. E., Pichler, S., Bodner, T., & Hammer, L. B.(2011). Workplace Social Support and Work–Family Conflict: A Meta–Analysis Clarifying the Influence of General and Work–Family–Specific Supervisor and Organizational Support. *Personnel Psychology*, 64(2): 289–313.

Lambert, S. J.(2000). Added Benefits: The Link Between Work–Life Benefits and Organizational Citizenship Behavior. *Academy of Management Journal*, 43(5): 801–815.

Lapierre, L. M., Spector, P. E., Allen, T. D., Poelmans, S., Cooper, C. L., O'Driscoll, M. P., & Kinnunen, U.(2008). Family–Supportive Organization Perceptions, Multiple Dimensions of Work–Family Conflict, and Employee Satisfaction: A Test of Model Across Five Samples. *Journal of Vocational Behavior*, 73(1): 92–106.

Lee, E. S., Chang, J. Y., & Kim, H.(2011). The Work–Family Interface in Korea: Can Family Life Enrich Work Life? *The International Journal of Human Resource Management*, 22(9): 2032–2053.

Moon, S. Y., & Roh, J.(2010). Balancing Work and Family in South Korea's Public Organizations: Focusing on Family–Friendly Policies in Elementary School Organizations. *Public Personnel Management*, 39(2): 117–131.

Park, Yoonhee(2016). "A Microdata Analysis of the Gender Pay Gap in South Korea: How Do Social Norms and Gender Role Attitudes Affect the Labor Force Participation of Korean Women?" Senior Projects Spring. Paper 329. http://digitalcommons.bard.edu/senproj_s2016/329

Parker, L., & Allen, T. D.(2001). Work/Family Benefits: Variables Related to Employees' Fairness Perceptions. *Journal of Vocational Behavior*, 58(3): 453–468.

Ryan, A. M., & Kossek, E. E.(2008). Work–Life Policy Implementation: Breaking Down or

Creating Barriers to Inclusiveness? *Human Resource Management*, 47(2): 295–310.

Sa, Y.(2013). Policy Implementation Framework and Family–Friendly Work Policy: Evidence from Flex–Working Programs in South Korea's Public Sectors. *Asian Social Science*, 9(15): 189.

Saltzstein, A. L., Ting, Y., & Saltzstein, G. H.(2001). Work–Family Balance and Job Satisfaction: The Impact of Family–Friendly Policies on Attitudes of Federal Government Employees. *Public Administration Review*, 61(4): 452–467.

Smithson, J., & Stokoe, E. H.(2005). Discourses of Work–Life Balance: Negotiating 'Gender Blind' Terms in Organizations. *Gender, Work & Organization*, 12(2): 147–168.

Swanberg, J. E., Pitt–Catsouphes, M., & Drescher–Burke, K.(2005). A Question of Justice Disparities in Employees' Access to Flexible Schedule Arrangements. *Journal of Family Issues*, 26(6): 866–895.

Schwartz, D. B.(1994). An Examination of the Impact of Family–Friendly Policies on the Glass Ceiling. New York: Families and Work Institute.

The Korean Women's Development Institute(2015). Korean Longitudinal Survey of Women & Families (KLoWF). *The Korean Women's Development Institute 20.*

Yu, H. L., & Kim, M. G.(2009). Developing Family–Friendly/Work–Friendly Services to Facilitate Work–Life Balance for Local Government Female Employees, *Korean Public Personnel Administration Review*, 8(3): 243–277.

Won, S. Y., & Lee, D. S.(2012). The Impacts of Work–Life Balance Policies on Gender Differences in Labor Participation: Using Cases of 16 OECD Countries. *Korean Journal of Policy Studies*, 21(3): 325–360.

Teaching Note

Work–Life Balance for Working Mom and Dad in South Korea

Teaching Note for Instructors

This case report is suitable for a general Public Management or specifically Human Resource Management course. The main objective of this case report goes beyond addressing the importance and benefits of work–life balance policies and programs. It aims to help students understand conditions necessary to create a family–friendly workplace and to effectively address a variety of needs that employees may have in their non–work domain. When teaching this subject, instructors may introduce the topic of work–life/work–family balance using suggests texts and readings below and explain about why it matters and what key conceptual or practical issues need to be addressed.

Most of the prior studies tend to use large scale cross–sectional surveys to provide evidence for the positive impacts of work–life balance policies and programs on organizational outcomes or gender equality. However, those studies are limited in explaining the policy context, for example, a culture at both organization and society levels or institutional characteristics which might be crucial to understanding why it works or not. It is because that the culture or institutional characteristics may shape employee's views or perspectives toward the use or non–use of work–life balance policies and in return, may affect the outcomes of work–life balance policies and programs.

As explained in the case report, in South Korea, with increasing participation of women in the workforce, governmental organizations must be prepared to provide programs that help those working women balance their possibly conflicting roles between work and family. Given the long history of gender discrimination, the government especially needs to provide programs that help recruit qualified women and eradicate past discriminatory practices against women in the workplace. More than ever, the low fertility rate is becoming a critical issue because it implies a labor shortage in the coming future. One of the major reported reasons for the low fertility rate is that women tend to regard being pregnant as a great impediment to their career advancement as well as their economic well-being. Therefore, for organizational success as well as for the general well-being of society, effective implementation of work-life balance programs becomes more critical than ever. In this regard, as introduced above, a variety of policies have been implemented. However those policies tend to target working parents or employees with family dependents, rather than targeting general employees who may be single or may not be married. Also, even when those policies are available, the evidence to support the actual or satisfactory use of those policies and programs remains limited.

The instructor can introduce work-life balance practices for government employees in South Korea using descriptive information and statistical evidence. The instructor needs to make students aware of available work-life programs in South Korea and its related laws. By using a hypothetical case given in the case report, the instructor may be able to initiate discussion about challenges faced by typical working parents when using those policies. The subsequent discussion can be made about the necessity of having a supporting culture. That is, in materializing the proposed benefit of work-life programs, the instructor needs to teach students about the importance of supportive culture which can be either shaped by diversity training or created by inclusive leadership.

In order to effectively organize and manage class discussion, instructors may consider using the followings as learning objectives.

Summary of Prior Studies on Proposed Work-Life Balance Policy Benefits

The availability of work-life balance policies is suggested to shape employees' perceived positive organizational understanding of their personal needs and make employees more likely to display positive work attitudes or behaviors. Perceived organizational support theory provides a support for this argument, in which a sense of obligation by employees can be incurred when there is a quality social exchange between employees and their employing organization. That is, the provision of work-life policies can be viewed by employees as the employer's support for their personal needs. This in turn contributes to developing the employee's perception of organizational support, which is the employee's belief that "the organization values their contributions and cares about their well-being" (Eisenberger et al., 1990: 51). The perception of organizational support would create felt obligations on the employee's side on the basis of the reciprocity norm to help achieve organizational goals by increasing commitment to the organization and improving job performance. In other words, the provision of work-life balance benefits would be viewed by employees as organizational-level active efforts to help address employees' work-life related multiple roles and therefore, their potential and career advancing objectives can be realized without being compromised by non-work related roles and responsibilities. Prior studies also noted that satisfaction with work-life programs is critical to helping employees balance their dual roles in work and family and increasing their commitment to the organization and satisfaction with their job (Ezra & Deckman, 1996; Saltzstein et al., 2001; Secret & Swanberg, 2008; Kim & Mullins, 2016). For example, Caillier (2012) analyzed data from the 2010 Federal Employee Viewpoint survey and found that employee's satisfaction with work-life balance programs significantly predicted their higher job commitment and involvement, both of which are suggested as major drivers for performance. Butts & his colleagues (2013) provided empirical support for the utility of providing work-family support policies using a meta-analysis. They found that either the availability or the use of work-family support policies would work as a signal to employees about the organization's concern for their well-being as well as an instrument for reducing the employee's work-life conflict. Given the relatively higher caregiving responsibilities on the women's side, the effect of work-family support policies on employee's job attitudes such as job satisfaction is greater for women than men.

In the Korean context, Moon & Yoon (2005) found a positive link between family-friendly programs and organizational outcomes in a study of employees from both public and private organizations. Won & Lee (2012) also found that government supports for child-care greatly help to address gender discrimination issues that may occur in the recruiting process. The provision of work-life balance programs is suggested to help recruit and retain qualified employees because workplaces with those benefits are regarded as ideal workplaces where employees can combine their work and private lives relatively easily. The attractiveness of organizations providing work-life balance policies to prospective applicants might be dependent on the degree to which they value or seek work-life balance. A few recent studies provide supporting evidence for the link between the availability of work-life balance programs and applicant's decision to seek employment. The findings suggest that the work-life benefits help increase job pursuit intentions. For example, Foster Thompson & Espinwall (2009) surveyed students enrolled in a large southeastern U.S. university and found that the availability of childcare benefits makes significant differences in the job choices of female applicants. Choi & Jo (2010) also point out the issue of career disruption of women in their 30's who have family obligations, especially for women in science and technology fields. They briefly introduced five relatively successful cases of corporate organizations with work-life balance policies (e.g., Samsung SDS) and suggest that the availability of work-life benefits would be very appealing to women in their early career and would positively affect their choice to work while raising children because those benefits give them flexibility.

Work-Life Balance Policy Category

Hoyman & Duer (2004) suggested that a much broader term is needed, like "worker-friendly" rather than "family friendly" because some policies like alternative work schedules target employees who are single or childless as well as employees with family responsibilities. In consideration of this, Hoyman & Duer (2004) classified worker-friendly policies into four types. Type 1 policies exist to help employees with family obligations and include pregnancy leaves, maternity or paternity leave, childcare, and so on. Type 2 aims to remove any possible impediments to employees' performing work. These policies target all employees and include telework, employee assistance programs, or flextime. Type 3 policies relate to training and educating employees such as programs for developing capacities or skills. These are distinguished from other policies in that they benefit employers as well as employees. Finally, Type 4 policies provide non-traditional incentives such as recognition awards, like an annual award dinner, that aim to boost employee's work motivation.

Learning Objectives

1) Discuss cost and benefits to organizations who adopt work-life balance practices
2) Discuss the development and management of gender equality policies in the Korean context
3) Discuss the impact of public human resource management reforms in relation to work-life balance have had on gender equality and organizational outcomes
4) Understand the importance of accommodating employees' needs for work-life balance

In order to solicit quality class discussion, instructors may use the following questions.

Discussion Questions

1) Who do you think has more access to family-friendly policies?
2) What outcomes (either positive or negative) do you expect from employees who use family friendly policies?
3) What impact does the use of family-friendly policies have upon career advancement?
4) If you were a manager, how would you address stigma that family friendly policy users may face from their colleagues and managers?
5) To what extent has the Korean government supported working mother's needs for work-life balance?
6) What laws apply to the issues surrounding Jaehee and Jiyeon's family including maternity and childcare leaves?
7) What lessons might be drawn from those cases?

As additional resources, the instructor may assign students to read or watch the following resources before class.

Additional Readings or Resources

- Case article: Mommy–Trach Backlash by Alden M. Hayashi, *Harvard Business Review* (2001, March)
  Available at https://hbr.org/2001/03/mommy–track–backlash
- Video clip: Nigel Marsh: How to make work–life balance work
  https://www.youtube.com/watch?v=jdpIKXLLYYM

Potential Assignments

1. Choose one or two work–life balance policies and programs of your choice in any countries. Find similarities and differences between the policy or program of your choice and ones of South Korea.
2. You've recently been hired as an assistant to HR manager in one local government agency with the task of redesigning work–life policies and programs. With consideration of cultural changes necessary to materialize the benefits of work–life balance policies and programs as well as employees' diversified needs in relation to balancing work and life, how would you examine the existing organizational culture in relation to implementing work–life balance policies and programs? How would you identify different needs of individual employees in relation to balancing their work and life and how would you accommodate them?

Chapter 05 Stakeholders in the Public Policy-Making Process: The Case of the Separation of Prescription and Dispensing in South Korea

Chul-Young Roh

Background

After the end of the Korean War in 1953, the Korean government made desperate efforts to recover infrastructure and to promote economic growth after the devastation from the War. Healthcare was mainly delivered by the private sector, such as physicians, pharmacists, and hospitals. In 1997, the government came onto the healthcare stage as key player when it established a national health insurance plan for government and industrial employees. The government also planned to implement universal health insurance to cover all citizens through a network of local as well as employer-based communities. The payment method was fee-for-service (FFS) by which the physicians were reimbursed for as much as they provided, but the physicians thought the fee schedule that the government set up was not enough. To supplement the insufficient reimbursement, physicians dispensed drugs in their clinics. The insurance policy provided the reimbursement for drugs that both physicians and pharmacists dispensed, and the reimbursement rates were higher than the prices that physicians paid for them. This price difference, called the "drug margin," made up almost half of the net income for physicians who had private clinics.

Meanwhile, South Korea experienced a shortage of physicians, especially in rural areas. In these places, pharmacists played the part of primary physicians by diagnosing patients and dispensing drugs. In other words, physicians and pharmacists were both able to prescribe and dispense drugs for outpatient care. This resulted to the over-prescription and erroneous prescription of prescribed drugs to maximize the economic profits of both physicians and pharmacists. Abuse of drugs, especially antibiotics, stimulated the call for healthcare reform in pharmacy practice.

Both physicians and pharmacists blamed each other for excessive misuse and abuse of drugs that caused an increase in the portion of the national debt attributable to the insurance reimbursement method (FFS). For example, the rate of antibiotic resistance in South Korea was the highest in the world before the pharmaceutical reform. The high drug spending in South Korea was a critical factor that promoted pharmaceutical reform. Drug costs occupied almost 30% of national healthcare spending before the reform.

These problems and the overlapping roles of both physicians and pharmacists came from confusion about the roles and function of the two groups. The public got more attention of the separation of the function and roles of two groups. But implementation of the reform was failed due to interests of stakeholders in pharmacy practice.

In response to the increased social negative externality and in order to provide the public with better quality of healthcare services and prevent the misuse and overuse of medicine by ensuring that the two major healthcare providers (i.e., physicians and pharmacists) operated within a framework of checks and balances, policy stakeholders, especially government, tried to reform the process of drug prescription and dispensing. The separation of prescription and dispensing has more critical policy implications than the separation of labor between physicians and pharmacists.

Policy Stakeholders in the Separation of Prescription and Dispensing in South Korea

Starting in the early 1980s, pharmaceutical reform (the separation of prescription and dispensing, or SPD) was attempted several times. Physicians, pharmacists, government and civic organizations participated as stakeholders in the policy-making process of pharmaceutical reform. However, each stakeholder had different degrees of political powers or influence in the policy-making process depending on the government regime in power.

Physicians

Physicians are the key players in health politics in South Korea, the Korean Medical Association (KMA) was always the most influential policy player in SPD reform. Physicians are recognized as the sole experts in the complex and scientific field of medicine. It is impossible to implement health policy without their cooperation. In the case of SPD reform, physicians wanted to maintain the status quo by opposing the reform. Even though the government set drug prices on the basis of the information that pharmacy companies and wholesalers released, physicians and hospitals purchased the drugs at lower prices than payers (insurance providers) reimbursed. To maximize their profits, physicians and hospitals wrote prescriptions and dispensed as much medication as they could. With their excellent political lobbying powers, they campaigned against SPD on the ground that it would be inconvenient and disadvantageous to patients. Physicians had critical influence on SPD through several nationwide campaigns and mass demonstrations that paralyzed the entire healthcare system in South Korea. These activities pushed the government and National Assembly to distort the elements of reform and address their interest, including increasing reimbursement rates to cover loss of physicians' income during the strikes and rallies. Physicians who were employed by hospitals and sole practitioners participated in strike and rallies.

Pharmacists

Pharmacists also opposed SPD reform at beginning. However, they later recognized that several serious conflicts existed between physicians and themselves. Physicians always got the upper hand over pharmacists in healthcare practice as well as in political power in the policy-making process. The professional power of physicians and was stronger than that of pharmacists, and the widespread demonstrations by physicians had the primary effect on policy decision-making in SPD reform. Even though pharmacists got a fee schedule with higher rates schedule in return for not striking, the SPD fundamentally changed the position and role of pharmacists who had played the role of primary care providers for a long time, especially in rural areas.

The professional and political power of pharmacists in the SPD reform rapidly ran out and they depended on physicians, though they still were influential in the SPD reform.

Government (Ministry of Health and Welfare)

Government (in this case, the Ministry of Health and Welfare) is crucial in the policy-making process. Government sets the reimbursement rates for healthcare services and decides the price of drugs in the universal healthcare system. While government allowed a narrow margin for inpatient and out-patient services, it permitted healthcare providers to get higher profits from prescribing and dispensing drugs. It still was skepticism about the feasibility of SPD reform, because there was an iron-triangle of the pharmaceutical industry, healthcare providers and government. The Ministry of Health and Welfare failed to be the major key player in SPD reform. Later the Ministry of Health and Welfare yielded to physician strikes by substantially increasing physician fees.

Civic Organizations

Healthcare was not a focus of civic organizations, which were more concerned about political and economic agendas than about social issues such as SPD. However, they played a critical role in breaking the "iron triangle" among the pharmaceutical industry, healthcare providers and government and in formulating healthcare policy such as SPD reform. Civic organizations were especially powerful in the Kim Dae-Jung government. They made SPD into a major social issue and forced the KMA and the KPA to come to the bargaining table to resolve the SPD reform.

Policy Context in South Korea

Democracy is unlike dictatorship or tyranny in that it provides opportunities for people to hold their leaders accountable and to oust them without the need for a revolution. It continues responsiveness of the government to the preference of its citizen. It achieves political and social equality and provides all citizens with means to formulate and signify their political and social preferences. Democratization is the process that changes an authoritarian political system to a responsive democratic system.

Democratization should promote a public policy-making process by a wide range of political and social spectrums to organize relationships and mobilize collective action. It also allows wider opportunities for social members to participate in public policy-making process. The result of democratization is to enlarge egalitarian rights and transparent decision-making structures. This case study focuses on how democratization influenced the result of public policy decision-making in South Korea in the specific case of SPD policy.

The Road to Separation of Prescription and Dispensing

During the period of rapid economic growth and progress in political democratization in the 1980s, the public became concerned about healthcare in South Korea. Before 2000, physicians were able to dispense medications directly to their patients in their office. Pharmacists were also allowed to dispense medication. Both physicians and pharmacists used this situation to maximize their profits, while patients were at a disadvantage. In the early 1960s, the Korean government had tried to separate the two functions of prescription and dispensing by enacting the Pharmaceutical Affairs Act, but the effort failed repeatedly due to government irresolution and opposition from both physicians and pharmacists.

Between 1982 and 1985, the Chun Doo-Hwan administration, which had taken power via coup d'état in 1980, ruled over South Korea. Chun's administration tried to implement the Separation of Prescription and Dispensing (SPD) program in the city of Mokpo, where physicians and pharmacists relatively practiced equally, and promoted it with an enforcement ordinance or by enforcing agreements between doctors and pharmacists, as a part of the pilot program of the 2nd Level Health Insurance Plan that expanded the National Health Insurance (NHI) to cover farmers and fishermen. The Korean Medical Association (KMA), which represents physicians, and the Korean Pharmaceutical Association (KPA), which represents pharmacists, were the major interest groups at this time. The KPA took the lead of a one-day shut-down to support compulsory implementation of SPD in May 1982, while the KMA did not support SPD and hinted at the possibility of boycott. None of the interest groups (KMA, KPA and government) would cooperate.

There was no official or unofficial committee or organization that each interest groups did take participate in the SPD reform. Government assumed all charge of implementation. The KMA and the MPA individually contacted policy stakeholders, such as politicians and senior government officials related with SPD to address their interests. The lobbying of the KMA was more successful than that of the KPA. The deputy secretary of the Ministry of Health and Social Affairs (MHSA), confirmed that the government would not enforce SPD and promised that compulsion would not be included in the policy. After a one-day strike by pharmacists in May 1982, the government organized a national-level committee that the KMA and the KPA participated in. Unfortunately, this committee did not contribute to the decision-making process, although it met three times in this period.

In 1984, the government implemented a SPD pilot program. MHSA worked directly with local KMA and KPA representatives in the city of Mokpo and forced them to make an annual contract that physicians have to issue prescriptions to pharmacists. The KMA did not support and refused to extend the annual contract in the following year. MHSA accepted KMA's opinion and terminated the SPD pilot program in 1985. In this period, the winner in this scenario was the KMA.

In 1987, with the transition to democracy in South Korea, Rho Tae-Woo, the presidential candidate from the authoritarian ruling party as well as the successor of authoritarian president Chun Doo-Whan, was elected by direct election. Although the Rho administration had an authoritarian image, his government worked to prevent popular unrest and allowed freedom to society. His government allowed citizens had the right to freedom of assembly and association. After 1987, many civic organizations were established and organized, but they did not participate in the policy-making process. Because these civic organizations were still new and not well organized in this period, and the most critical priority was democratic movements such as freedom of speech and augmentation of political and economic freedom, SPD policy did not draw as much of their attention as other democratic agenda items in this period. The civic organizations refused to participate in committees that the authoritarian government sponsored, and the Rho government also was reluctant to request that they join the committees. As a result, government, the KMA and the KPA were again the main stakeholders in SDP issues.

The Rho administration tried to enact universal National Health Insurance (NHI) that covered all the population to solidify the base of his regime. The MHSA comprised the committee for this goal. Again, SPD surfaced as a political agenda between physician and pharmacists. Political parties (National Assembly) were also involved in the policy–making process, but their influence was limited and meager in this period. Political parties just rubber–stamped bills based on the decisions of the committee.

The MHSA requested the committee to accept an incremental increase in compulsory SPD, but the new proposal reflected the KMA's intention that eliminated physicians' legal duty from the SPD. The KPA strongly opposed the new proposal and held a series of strikes and demonstrations. The government did not intend to break up a demonstration of pharmacists and was not willing to mediate in the conflict between physicians and pharmacists. Therefore, the government took a noncommittal attitude between physicians and pharmacists and suspended any decisions on the SPD. Instead, to reflect the interests of pharmacists, the MHSA offered the Pharmaceutical Insurance System (PIS) that reimbursed for certain medications dispensed without prescriptions.

In the Rho administration, the KMA increased its political power in policy–making. New public policy players, such as the People's Solidarity for Participatory Democracy, were not yet organized or did not intend to join the SPD reform committee. Although the KMA and the KPA were still key players in the policy–making process, the Rho administration favored the KMA and avoided any oppressive measures against the KMA. The KMA was able to become the most powerful player in the policy–making process.

After former opposition political leader Kim Dae–Jung won the presidential election in 1998, the government focused more on social and economic agendas than political ones. Kim's administration actively invited civic organizations into the policy–making process. These organizations were also friendly to the Kim administration, which had hired many members of these organizations to work for the administration and the ruling party. Through these social, economic and political environment changes, South Korea became more democratized in this period.

In May 1998, the Kim administration officially lunched SPD as a pharmaceutical market reform designed to promote the transparency of the market and the rights of consumers by disclosing the prescriptions to patients and pharmacists. The Ministry of Health and Welfare (MoHW – formerly the MHSA) organized committees, such as the SPD Steering Committee (SPDSC) and the SPD Executive Committee (SPDEC), in which the KMA, the KPA, MoHW and civic organizations joined. After South Korea became democratized, the civic organizations were no longer hostile to the government.

The MoHW organized those committees and prepared to pass bills for the revision of the Pharmaceutical Affairs Law (PAL). In this period, National Assembly played a critical role in getting stakeholders to accept and pass the bill that all policy stakeholders accepted for. The MoWH was not allowed to arbitrate on the SPD reform. The National Assembly endorsed the civic organization, The People's Solidarity for Participatory Democracy, that strongly supported SPD reform by authorizing it as an arbitrator between the KMA and the KPA. Ultimately, a bill that banned physicians and hospitals from dispensing drugs for outpatient services was passed based on agreement among all the policy stakeholders. Even though the KMA, which had an economic disadvantage from SPD, organized and led a series of anti-SPD rallies in 2000, they failed to stop the revised PAL. Public opinion did not support the KMA strikes, and government, ruling party and civic organizations were not willing to surrender to the KMA strikes. In spite of the KMA strikes, The KMA failed to hinder the implementation of the SPD. AS the civic organizations that support the SPD participated in the SPD reform committee, the KMA's influence relatively had waned. While the civic organizations had maintained friendly ties with Kim administration and were trusted by the national Assembly, the KMA did not expect government support in the manner that the KMA had once received it.

This case study focuses on how democratization influences the stakeholders in the public policy decision-making process. Specifically, democratization increased the opportunity of various stakeholders to participate in the public policy-making process.

References

Cho, H.(1999). Democratic Transition and Changes in Korea NGOs. In Proceedings of the Paper Presented at 1999 Seoul International Conference of NGOs' Hosted by CONGO, NGO/DPI of UN & GCS. Seoul, Korea. (in Korean)

Cho, B.(2000). Separation of Prescription and Dispensing, and Social Conflicts. In Preceding of the Paper Presented at the Fall Academic Conference of the Korean Society of Health Policy & Administration. (in Korean)

Immergut, E.(1992). Health Politics: Interests and Institutions in Western Europe, Cambridge, Cambridge University press.

Kim, Y.(2000). Health and Pharmaceutical Reform on the Separation of Prescribing and Dispensing. The Pharmaceutical Reform Symposium. Seoul, Korea. (in Korean)

Korea Ministry of Health & Welfare(2002). The Separation of Prescribing and Dispensing Roles. Seoul, Korea 2002. (in Korean)

Kwon, S.(2003). Pharmaceutical Reform and Physician Strikes in Korea: Separation of Drug Prescribing and Dispensing, *Social Science & Medicine*, 57: 529－538.

Teaching Note

Stakeholders in the Public Policy-Making Process: The Case of the Separation of Prescription and Dispensing in South Korea

This case study gives readers the opportunity to think about how policy stakeholders have behaved in the dynamics of policy change. It focuses on the healthcare policy of separating the prescription and dispensing of drugs in South Korea. This case study relies on the framework of public policy analysis by Kingdom (1995) to examine the context and process of this separation. The separation of prescribing and dispensing of drugs in South Korea has more critical public policy implications than a simple separation of labor among policy stakeholders. This case study emphasizes how public policy environment of democratization influences the behaviors of public policy stakeholders.

First, this case describes the environment of public policy in terms of the separation of prescription and dispensing of drugs in South Korea before 2000. At that time, a new authoritarian government that had taken political power via a coup d'état attempted to implement the separation of prescription and dispensing of drugs in order to provide the public with a better quality of healthcare services and to avoid misuse and overuse of drugs.

Second, this case study introduces the policy stakeholders in this matter. Tesbelis (2002) pointed out that the policy stakeholder is an individual and collective actor whose agreement is required for policy decision-making. Four major stakeholders were involved in pharmaceutical reform in South Korea: physicians, pharmacists, government and civic organizations. Traditionally, physicians enjoyed the status quo that they could prescribe and dispense drugs as much as they wanted to maximize their economic profits. With excellent political lobbying powers, they campaigned against the separation of prescription and dispensing (SPD) on the grounds that it would be inconvenient and disadvantageous to patients. The Korean Medical Association (KMA), the representative body of physicians, organized and led several nationwide rallies and strikes that shut down the entire healthcare system in South Korea.

Pharmacists also opposed SPD reform at the beginning. However, some time later, they recognized that several serious conflicts existed between physicians and themselves. Physicians always got the upper hand over pharmacists in healthcare practice as well as in political power in the policy decision-making process. Although pharmacists were still influential in SPD reform, their political power rapidly ran out and they were subordinated on physicians in practice.

Government (Ministry of Health & Welfare) occupies the critical position in the public policy-making process in South Korea. Government sets the fee schedule for healthcare services and determines the price of drugs in the universal healthcare system in South Korea. While government allowed a narrow margin for inpatient and outpatient services, it permitted healthcare providers to get higher profits from prescribing and dispensing drugs. There was an iron triangle among the pharmaceutical industry, healthcare providers and government in the SPD reform. Furthermore, government led and prepared SPD reform. An unusual aspect of this case is that political parties were not in critical positions in SPD reform.

Lastly, civic organizations such as the People's Solidarity for Participatory Democracy do not look at the SPD reform for the first time. After SPD reform changed from an economic agenda to a social agenda, civic organizations became actively involved. Civic organizations were especially powerful in the Kim Dae-Jung government, in which more freedom of speech and expression was allowed than in previous governments. The changed policy environment influenced the dynamics of the public policy decision-making process.

Democratization is the shift from an authoritarian regime to a democratic system. Dahl (1971: 1-2) defines democracy as 'the continuing responsiveness of the government to the preference of its citizen, considered as political equals' and political system should provide all citizens with means to formulate and signify their preference; there preferences should be weighted equally in the conduct of the government'. In this sense, democratization provides more chances for policy stakeholders to participate in the public policy-decision-making process. Changing the environment of public policy influences the stakeholders in the policy-making process.

During the first period (1980~1986), the authoritarian government (Chun Doo-Hwan Administration) ruled over the country. The key stakeholders in this period were the Korean Medical Association (KMA) and a government agency (Ministry of Health and Social Affairs) that promoted a pilot SPD program in the City of Mokpo between 1982 and 1985. The authoritarian government allowed to organize KMA only, and invited the KMA and the Korean Pharmaceutical Association (KPA) to participate in the healthcare policy-making process. The KMA enjoyed its autonomy under the authoritarian regime. The KMA is conservative and has excellent lobbying capacity compared with the KPA. Civic organizations were not allowed to be involved in the policy-making process.

During the second period (1987~1997; Rho Tae-Woo Administration), the policy window of opportunity began to open. Democratization was beginning to develop during this period. Although the Rho administration allowed more political autonomy and freedom compared with previous administrations, his administration still repressed some expression towards society. Newly organized civic organizations did not directly participate in SPD reform in this period and were not concerned about it. They focused on political agendas rather than social welfare (the SPD reform) in this period. The civic organizations recognized the Rho administration as the successor to the former authoritarian government and refused to participate in the policy-decision-making process even though the Rho administration the civic organizations asked to join in the SPD reform committee. The Rho administration was also reluctant to have civic organizations participating in the policy-making process. In this period, although the KMA and the KPA were the major interest groups in the SPD reform, the KMA was more powerful because of its greater political influence in the SPD reform.

During the third period (1998~2002), after Kim Dae-Jung was elected President, his administration actively invited civic organizations such as consumer protection organizations and the People's Solidarity for Participatory

Democracy into the policy decision-making process and recruited some members of the civic organizations into his administration and ruling party. His administration was on friendly terms with the civic organizations, which then began to turn their interests to more social agendas than political ones. In this period, the KMA failed to hinder the implementation of SPD. As the civic organizations had more voice in the policy decision-making process, the KMA became relatively less influential. This case study will examine the influence of the policy environment of democratization on the SPD reform in South Korea. Democratization allowed the freedom of participation of stakeholders and diversified the policy decision-making process. Most policy decision-making occasions conflicts among stakeholders. In this case study, although the KMA went on strike to maintain their interests, they could not overcome the changing policy environment resulting from democratization.

Chapter 06

Transforming Seoul: Rethinking Neighborhood

Hee Soun Jang & Jung Wook Kim

Seoul is a global megacity and a symbol of vibrant economic growth. With an estimated 10 million residents as of 2016, Seoul is the largest city in South Korea and the highest in density among OECD major cities. During the fast growth period of the 1970s through the 1990s, top-down policy approaches contributed pro-development projects that led to the construction of high-rise apartment blocks located in high-end areas and left low-end areas under-developed and marginalized.

Seoul's pro-development approach was criticized for promoting massive housing development at the expense of loss of community and social bonding. Over time, the problems of losing social value in neighborhoods have emerged as shown in the rise in crime that resulted in distrust of neighbors and left people feeling unsafe and lonely in their neighborhoods.[1] Growing problems caused by disputes among neighbors pushed the Seoul Metropolitan Government and local district governments develop solutions such as tougher building codes and regulations to mitigate neighborhood problems. However, those directive policy measures were not sufficient to effectively resolve community disorder related to

1) Kang, Hyun-kyung (2013, February 17). "Apartment Noise Hard to Handle." *The Korea Times*. Retrieved from http://www.koreatimes.co.kr/www/news/nation/2013/02/113_130616.html

crime, danger, segregation and other issues that are deeply rooted in fear and distrust. Government controls showed little impact on root causes of the growing neighbor conflicts caused by lack of social connections in the neighborhood. Disputes among neighbors may reflect a lack of communication with neighbors and the serious malfunction of the rushed housing development that has ruined the city's social and human values.

Seoul has experienced a decline of social structures that would make it possible for civil society to exist. The core elements of social structures are ideas, beliefs, and formal and informal institutions that foster the norms of tolerance, belonging, and altruism that govern the behaviors of members of the community to make our society a better place. Sharon Hong (2012) lamented Seoul's aggressive physical infrastructure development and argued that the city must be decoupled from construction-based development: "In Seoul, Korea, rapid urbanization in the twentieth century nearly destroyed 600 years of history."[2] Loss of social and human values from rapid development seems to make the city a victim of its own success. Experts on urban neighborhoods also have noted there is an intangible but equally important dimension of neighborhood that provides social goods such as understanding, fellowship, belonging, tolerance and mutual respect. While failing to generate social norms for individuals and communities to connect with each other, traditional voluntary clubs, gatherings, civic groups, and service activities have disappeared from the life of Seoul residents.

Skepticism about Seoul's new-town development played a role in the election of progressive leader Park Won-soon as mayor of Seoul in 2011. Encouraged by the frontier success of Sungmisan maeul (*maeul* translates to neighborhood), Mayor Park promoted qualitative participatory democracy via community building in an effort to provide opportunities to citizens to develop their own solutions to their service needs. The social activist Mayor was positive to turn Seoul a new city that is community based and produce desired outcome from CBP programs. Park argued, "Restoring sense of community is essential in creating a more humane society."[3] The core of Mayor Park's

2) Hong, Sharon (2013). Seoul: A Korean Capital. In Nihal Perera & Wing-Shing Tang (Eds.), *Transforming Asian Cities*. London; New York: Routledge. p.20.

3) Park, Won-soon (2014). In Seoul, the Citizens are the Mayor. *Public Administration Review*, 74 (4): 442-443.

Community Building Policy (CBP) is the belief that community organizations and activities of local neighborhoods will shape the social and human values of citizen life in Seoul in vital ways.

This idea of community building was well accepted and welcomed, especially by social progressives. Fouser (2011), a professor at Seoul National University, touted Mayor Park's Community Building Policy by saying, "As economic growth slows and democratic challenges mount, community building may be the only way to keep communities vibrant. It will be critical in attracting residents and businesses. Communities that pool their resources and work toward a common goal will prosper."[4)]

The political goals of a newly elected activist mayor who emphasized local initiatives and self-help (or self-governance) seem opportune and timely, but the notion of community building is less likely to be visible in short-term policy investment for a global city of 10 million people that is economically segregated and whose communities have been disintegrating over the past few decades. Community building had never been a high policy priority of any of mayors of Seoul until Mayor Park administration. Thus it has been a major policy effort to create new institutions and administrative systems that would integrate the new value of community and idea of citizen engagement into the bounds of history long "development" based administrative system of Seoul government.

Community Building Policy in Seoul Metropolitan Government

The Seoul Metropolitan Government launched a progressive community building effort called Community Building Policy (CBP), which provided administrative assistance and financial support for citizen-led civil society building plans. It was Mayor Park's expectation to transform conventional policy paradigms from controlling regulations to government support that would nurture citizens' potential to realize the true meaning of deliberative democracy and civil society. The policy was designed in expectation of the engaged citizens will seek solutions through sustained process of face-to-face interactions and then arrive at a legitimate consensus by embracing com-

4) Fouser, Robert J. (2011, December 5). Community Building in Korea. *The Korea Times*. Retrieved from http://www.koreatimes.co.kr/www/news/opinon/2011/12/314_100169.html

munity voices and encouraging grassroots participation in local initiatives.

As an initial effort, the city of Seoul had created and revised city ordinances and budget proposals multiple times and launched a citizen board that is to be main policy advisory mechanism for the implementation of CBP. Driven by the spirit of citizen engagement, CBP advisory board (named "Seoul Neighborhood Community Committee") is comprised of civic minded citizen leaders, professional activists and city council members, and city administrators. Since its creation in April 2012, the committee has been holding monthly meetings and acted as an advisory board for policy directions and corrections.[5)]

Under the system of CBP, the role of government changed significantly from a directive authority to a partner in co-creating legitimate and contextual solutions for the distinctive needs of each community. In his effort to create public-private partnership, Mayor Park made an appointment of non-career professional to be a head of community building policy initiatives. Seo Jin A, director of Local Community Division in Seoul is a longtime community building activist who has been expected to reinvent values and systems of city administration. Director Seo said from her *Herald newspaper* interview "Developing social connection among individuals in our neighborhood should be the first key step in community building in Seoul." Her strong focus on social connection was expressed in an application condition for the city's financial assistance program. The program manual specifies that more than three local residents have to be leading applicants of project application and this condition expects to make those citizen applicants more accountable and responsible of carrying out the entire process of community project. She mentioned in the interview that the local residents' engagement is a key check point for the financial support decision for community building project applications. This condition of grant application may not be a conventional approach in majority of social service programs that had been delivered mostly by the established nonprofit organizations.[6)]

The foundational principle of CBP is *citizen leads* and *government supports.*

5) Seoul Metropolitan Government (2013). *Seoul, Life, and People.* Seoul, Korea: Seoul Metropolitan Government.

6) Choi, Won-hyuk (2015, September 9). "Interview with the Director of the Local Community Division in the City of Seoul." *Herald,* Retrieved from http://biz.heraldcorp.com/view.php?ud=20150909000157

CBP strongly encourages ordinary citizens to take the initiative to build their own community programs and adopt grassroots approaches to realize public and private sector partnership. A socially connected community will be eventually developed if citizens have a social space to be together and resources to sustain the initial community building efforts. There are two assumptions in CBP. First, collective benefit will be generated if more people engage in civic activities and organizations. Second, those organizations and groups will encounter challenges to address the problems and need of government support due to their lack of physical and social resources.[7] The program aims to develop community capacity and allows citizens to identify their own problems and needs, handle the problems, and address common needs of the neighborhood by building connections and trust. As such, the city of Seoul initiated CBP to administratively and financially support communities and citizens in neighborhoods to respond to their unique problems and needs. CBP is considered a unique urban welfare approach that is based on culture and human values to ultimately strengthen the social capital of a neighborhood and help the community achieve civil society. Mayor Park administration was positive and ambitious about policy impact that CBP will be an alternative response to the welfare service demands for child care, education, services for youth, care for the elderly, safety, and so on and build a concrete mechanism that connects people through desirable social norms.

Seoul Community Support Center (SCSC): A Nonprofit Mediator

To implement administrative steps of CBP, the Seoul city government created a nonprofit organization to take charge of linking citizens to the government. In August 2012, the Seoul Community Support Center (SCSC) was established to connect community activities and community initiatives to the appropriate government agencies and mediate among diverse stakeholders including citizens, nonprofit organizations, local governments, and private businesses. As a key actor, SCSC is responsible for developing a collaborative governance that will benefit all participants in every stage of community building.[8] The

7) Seoul Metropolitan Government (2012). *Master Plan for Community Building in Seoul.* Seoul, Korea: Seoul Metropolitan Government.

8) Seoul Community Support Center (n.d.). *Hello? Seoul Community Support Center.* Retrieved on

three main activities of SCSC are:

- SCSC provides training, consulting, and counseling programs for citizens and communities that need government and private supports to facilitate community activities and community initiative.
- SCSC plays an intermediary role between citizens and government to match citizens' and communities' specific needs with customized governmental supports.
- SCSC promotes collaborative governance with administrative supports by mediating between the city of Seoul, local district governments in Seoul, private organizations, community groups, and individual citizens.

Currently, these functions of SCSC are integrated into two programs. The *Citizen Initiative Program* encourages citizens and community leaders to actively seek out alternative solutions to the specific service needs of their neighborhoods and assists in idea development by engaging in constant conversations with citizens. The program is implemented in such a way as to provide financial and administrative supports to citizens and community initiative groups to ultimately produce sustainable community organizations and their activities. SCSC proposes potential activities that can be organized by citizen groups such as community childcare services, promotion of environmentally friendly neighborhoods, crime and disaster prevention, diversity programs supporting multi-cultural families, parenting community, art galleries, and so on.[9] The *Community Capacity Building Program* supports community building efforts by passing on to applicants of community programs key know-how for nonprofit management and best practices of project development. This program offers tailored administrative support to cultivate community building and network development in a neighborhood. For example, education programs are offered to educate interested citizens about what community building is, why it is important, and how community capacity is built and to provide customized consulting services that fit to a unique neighborhood condition. Leadership training is provided as well to assist citizens to build supportive ties with other community groups to cope with everyday

---

August 23, 2016 from http://www.seoulmaeul.org/programs/user/eng/index.html

9) Seoul Community Support Center (2015). *Performance Report of Community Building Policy in Seoul*, Seoul Community Support Center.

challenges by providing opportunities for frequent gatherings to freely exchange ideas and resources with other interested parties.

In 2013, SCSC awarded 212 parent groups for their communal child care projects and each group was supported by the city of Seoul with up to 2 million won (about $1,700).[10] Parent community has been a major activity of CBP, and SCSC supports initial development stage groups to grow to be a focal point for building social connections. *Mom–moa* based in Nowon–gu is a community of local mothers cook for families with special needs children. The members of Mom–moa community group actively engage in local events and share their common interests and needs in issues of child care and education activities.[11]

Community Building Policy Creates Collaborative Governance

Community Building Policy designs the process of policy implementation through collaborative governance. As illustrated in the figure below, collaborative governance strongly emphasizes sustainable partnerships between citizens and government agencies that will ultimately create communities' unique solutions in the social context of neighborhoods. Community projects are supported in three stages of development, including the idea developing stage, the planning stage, and the action stage of the full–blown project that is expected to operate and generate positive outcome. Through collaborative governance in the three stages, SCSC as the nonprofit mediator plays a crucial role in managing community project applications and assisting citizens.

The figure shows the implementation process of the CBP. First, a citizen group applies for community project and receives consulting services from its local district government (*Gu*) including an investigation of existing conditions and assets of the neighborhood. After the process of consultation, this citizen group will propose their plan to SCSC. SCSC reviews the proposal and decides whether the project has potential to grow. After this initial review process by SCSC, the proposal is sent to the city of Seoul for final approval.

10) Seoul Metropolitan Government (2013). *Seoul, Life, and People*. Seoul, Korea: Seoul Metropolitan Government.

11) Seoul Metropolitan Government (2013). *Seoul, Life, and People*. Seoul, Korea: Seoul Metropolitan Government.

Then the city of Seoul decides on the proposed plan by assessing its feasibility and necessity of the activities. Accepted proposals receive seed funding and administrative assistance from Seoul.

In the process of implementation, SCSC provides tailored assistance for the various development stages of community projects. For a community or groups of citizens in the idea stage, SCSC helps them create networks or become involved in existing social networks in the neighborhood and educates them about meaning of civil society and practical steps of community building. Community project groups in the planning stage receive counseling services to design action plans for community organizations and projects. For the community project that is in the action stage, SCSC helps sustain community activities and projects and assesses potential assets, needs, and resources in the neighborhood to extend the scope and depth of community activities and projects. Urban farming project in Chungryangri, Dongdaemoon-gu has grown to be in the action stage project in rental apartment community.[12] From

Figure 6-1. Community Building Policy Governance

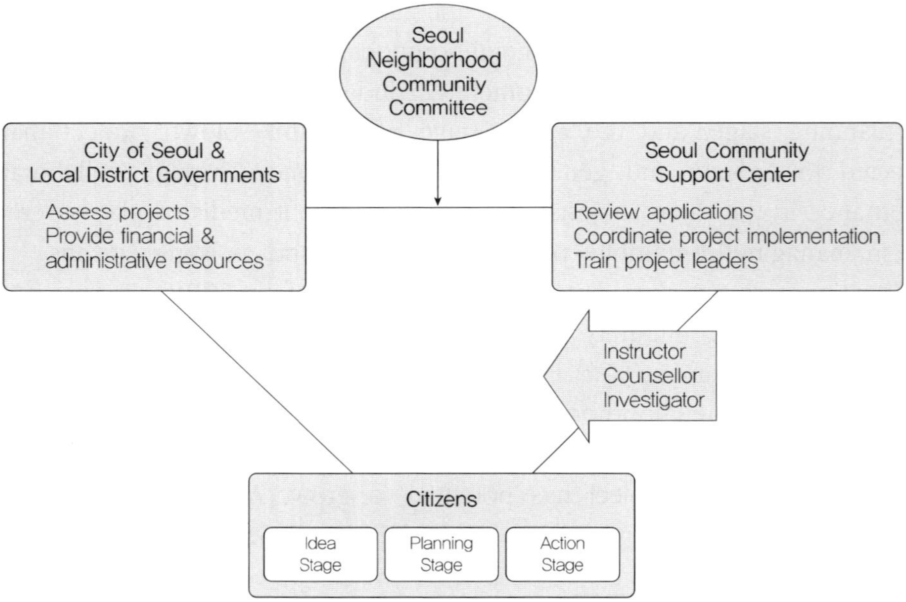

Resource: Modified from *Performance Report of Community Building Policy in Seoul* (2013).

12) Seoul Metropolitan Government (2013). *Seoul, Life, and People*. Seoul, Korea: Seoul Metropolitan Government.

the inception of idea, SCSC has provided instructional and administrative administrative assistance. In 2014 in developing stage of the project, the partnership of local leaders and SCSC developed educational opportunities for residents about community building and introduced diverse models of community based social clubs. There have been many workshop programs for better understanding of urban farming techniques.

SPOTLIGHT ON COMMUNITY BUILDING STORIES

Dobong-gu neighborhood association[13)]

Dobong-gu neighborhood association started community gathering in 2013 with the support of financial aid and civic leadership education from the Dobong-gu government. Social interactions among citizens created by community activities such as sport leagues, craft classes, etc., encourage them to concern more about community issues. A citizen leader who initiated community gatherings said, "Participation in those programs, I feel, helps us to create a sense of community and fellowship beyond our apartment complex because we are able to meet and communicate with neighbors who are not residents in our complex at the local sports league or craft classes." Mr. Kim, a member of an apartment complex neighborhood association, says, "Parents and teenagers have shown concern about community issues like care for the homebound seniors and green environment projects at the community gatherings." The interaction from community gatherings contributes to building social cohesion beyond mere interest-seeking. A member of a social club said "We have strong sense of social belonging that has been built from long residency in this community. Many residents show concern about issues and problems related to our community because people believe this is our community to live in and conserve." She placed an emphasis on stable residency as a key of success: "I believe we were able to carry out several community programs because lots of residents in our community have lived here for more than 20 years. I mean our people have a strong sense of belonging and their attachment to the neighborhood moves us forward to be dedicated to community building activities."

13) Interviews used for the case of Dobong-gu neighborhood association were conducted in May 2015.

Seoul is one of the busiest cities in the world. Citizens living in Seoul are too busy to have interest in and participate in community issues. "Nobody wants to be a board member of a neighborhood association because being a board member require lots of time and dedication, but people living in this city are so busy, and they are very tired of their own life matters," said a board member of a neighborhood association. A community leader said, "Our neighborhood is active in community gathering and events. But, younger families do not participate in community activities very well. I think they live very busy life. And there isn't much of immediate benefit to offer from community activities to them." An official in local government stated, "People do not want to participate in community building activities because they think that engagement in community issues is bothersome in their busy life."

Hanyang apartment complex[14)]

The Hanyang apartment complex had a difficult history of community conflicts caused by common area maintenance issues, and local government agencies received constant citizen complaints that blamed each other. The local government proposed the community to hold community-wide gatherings to listen to each other and learn their immediate and long-term demands. A team of government administrators and community leaders conveyed understanding of the situation and suggested a community social project that may foster open communication and mutual understanding among residents. With government support, residents initiated a recreation center building project to promote face-to-face interactions among residents. The citizen leader who led the project said, "Neighbors met a couple of times in a week to play table tennis. Because we met very often in the recreation center, we could become friends and the social bonding and sense of tolerance developed. I think the conflicts in our community have been reduced since we launched the social sports project at the community recreation center."

A chairperson in a sport club said, "Our community had suffered from chronic divisions of groups and constant conflicts that made the neighborhood unpleasant and unsafe. But, I saw that this community center supported by CBP funds played a vital role in conflict resolution of our community because neighbors who did not know each other before frequently met in the com-

14) Interviews used for the case of Hanyang apartment complex were conducted in May 2015.

munity center to play table tennis and other social sports. Their involvement in activities in this center provided opportunities for people to engage in conversations about life matters and community issues, then we became friends, and finally fostered constructive dialog for solving misunderstanding among neighbors. Now, our community has started community meetings to discuss community issues."

CBP have made various revisions and correction of application process to make it as simple as possible and easy to develop one for ordinary people. Seoul Community Support Center (SCSC) is also a nonprofit support organization for citizen to approach and interact for them to engage community building programs. However, ordinary citizens lack of professional skills and knowledge in community engagement and initiative for community building. A local district official said, "Community building and self-governing activities in apartment complexes are very difficult. It requires complex knowledge and skills to manage community common area and difficult issues." A citizen leader in Hanyang apartment complex said, "At first, I did not have any ideas what and how to do community gathering and activities. I wanted to secure a space for community activities but I did not know how to write a proposal that explains needs of such a space for receiving government grant. I should say consulting from local government was very helpful when I prepare applications."

Seongbuk-gu, Doosan apartment complex[15]

Local district governments in Seoul provide education programs, consulting services and grant-in-aid for citizens who are interested in community activities. As one of programs supported by CBP, local district governments in Seoul implemented green energy programs to reduce utility service charges and save energy for common area management for apartment complexes. By participating in this program, some of communities could reduce energy

15) The case of Seongbuk-gu Doosan apartment complex referred the resources: Sim, Jae-chul. (2014, December 30). Together with Security in Apartment. In The 15 Minutes that Change the World. Seoul, South Korea: CBS; Kim, Dong-hong (2013, December 23). "Seongbuk-gu, Community Building and Energy Saving." *Money Today*. Retrieved from http://www.mt.co.kr/view/mtview.php?type=1&no=2013122311112571090&outlink=1; Park, Sung-joon (2015, January 15). "Seongbuk-gu, Togetherness Movement in Apartment." *Ajunews*. Retrieved from www. ajunews. com/view/20150115095337539

expense and create a community fund from common area maintenance fee savings. For example, the neighborhood association of Doosan apartment in Seongbuk-gu was able to save costs for their common area lightening with educational and financial support provided by the CBP energy conservation program. The savings allowed the association create a community fund and strengthen job security for community maintenance employees (*Kyungbiwon*) from temporary part-time to full-time employment with benefits. A member of the association said, "We could make it possible because lots of residents engaged in this energy saving program and from those activities we could build trust among residents." The program also allowed citizens to be interested in energy conservation issues that affect everyone. A resident in the apartment complex said, "Through the energy program, we could understand how serious energy shortage is, and became more interested in various techniques in energy conservation as well as utility cost saving in common area of our neighborhood."

Doosan apartment residents have been engaged those programs and expressed their excitement about planned future activities. A local district official also noted that each of communities knows better than anyone else about their specific needs, culture, and assets as well as root causes of their unique problems. A public official in the city of Seoul said, "In implementation of CBP, we have to keep up accountability in evaluation of program results for each of community projects. Since each of community projects is unique to their specific needs there is no way to create universal indicators that would apply across the board at every local context. By knowing how hard to bring any visible outcome in one or two year (s), still we have to review and report the progress of policy goals." Although the Seoul government and 25 local district governments have agreed upon main principles and goals of CBP, each of stakeholders may have different viewpoints on policy priorities or performance criteria for the evaluation of policy impact.

Seongdong-gu, local community manager system[16)]

Seongdong-gu government operates a community manager system as a sub-program of CBP. The role of this community manager is to listen to

16) Interviews used for the case of Seongdong-gu local community manager system were conducted in May 2015 and January 2017.

residents' voices and foster community interactions and support collaboration among the diverse community groups to help them develop activities and programs that would benefit the community the most. In this process, CBP contributes seed funding along with expert advice on how to initiate and accomplish the planned projects. The director of the Seongdong-gu community manager system describes her main roles in CBP: "I make visits in local communities, listen to citizens' concerns and demands, and then inform city of Seoul and CBP agencies specific financial and administrative needs that may support citizens' initiatives and community activities."

Technical support and seed funding help communities to interact and may build their own capacity to solve their own problems. The chair of a neighborhood association in Seongdong-gu mentioned the essential role of government support in the process of program development: "The community manager of the local government made frequent visits to our community to meet us in person and listen to community issues and demands from local citizens. And she introduced us good opportunities to receive community leadership training and financial aid to start off some of the community projects that were needed most. From these training programs, we learned skills and tools to develop programs and how to write a grant proposal to receive grant-in-aid. And the seed funding was used to carry out several community programs such as a music class, eco-village project, and conflict resolution committee."

Seongdong-gu also provides programs for community leaders, community program development, and grant writing classes and constantly send information on grant opportunities and community resources for interested citizens. A member of a social club said, "We did not know what it was for community programs at first. We did not know how to write a proposal for the government funding program either." To address those difficulties, local governments provide leadership training programs and consulting services. A government official said, "Citizens learn about the important role of civic leadership in local problem solving and understand the need of dedicated individuals who could be a head of mothers' gathering or volunteer seniors for vegetable garden. When they have received training, local residents are motivated to take the leadership role in their community."

Seongbuk-gu neighborhood association[17)]

Citizens experience democratic practices in community gathering and programs. A team leader of local community in Seoul said, "Citizens who participate in community programs learn how to identify community issues and sources of conflicts through frequent communications with other neighbors in the programs." From the social gatherings and town hall meetings, citizens are able to learn how to discuss with others and make decisions. This process may not bring a perfect consensus but it increases understanding about diverse views, preferences and interests. The discussion in neighborhood meetings allows citizens to learn the meaning of democratic decision making to reach to a better resolution of their problem. For example, a neighborhood association of Seongbuk-gu changed its discussion style to more deliberative one to give opportunities for every resident chance to participate and express her/his own views and interests and examine each of the issues carefully.[18)] The board meetings often take more than three hours for examining various aspects of issues and weighing measures of alternatives. A chair of the neighborhood association said, "It takes usually three hours for each board meeting to discuss community programs and activities, and then board members may reach a consensus on any given topic. Throughout the process of lengthy conversation and discussions, we realize that consensus is difficult but possible."

The chair of board members in the association said, "I learned that we could reach to agreeable decisions on neighborhood issues through deliberative discussions. Deliberative discussions help us reduce misunderstanding by sharing information and listening to others opinions, and enhance understanding on our common issues like community recycling, use of parking space, noise complaints etc." And he said, "The role of community leader is important in the process because community leaders devote their time and effort to involve more residents in the deliberative process to reach to better decisions."

But the governments sometimes have to intervene in the internal matters of the neighborhood associations to promote transparency in their management

---

17) The interviews used for the case of Seongbuk-gu neighborhood association were conducted in May 2015 and January 2017.

18) Kim, Si-yeon (2015, July 04). "What Happened in An Apartment Complex?" *Oh My News*. Retrieved from http://www.ohmynews.com/NWS_Web/View/at_pg.aspx?CNTN_CD=A0002123906

and improve grant accountability. Government official in local district office said, "Our roles for community building are complicated and often confusing. We would like to respect local autonomy of neighborhood associations but at the same time it is our responsibility to examine and regulate neighborhood associations' finance to avoid mismanagement of community funding and mitigate potential conflicts for more transparent management of organizations."

Dobong-gu, social club[19)]

Officials of the city of Seoul and local governments indicate that the lack of trust in the community is a key obstacle impeding community initiatives and the effective operation of community building programs in their neighborhoods. A government official said, "Community Building Policy (CBP) has been challenging because many communities have suffered from distrust between residents and board members of neighborhood associations. Lack of trust makes it difficult to mobilize human, physical, and financial resources to initiate community gathering and programs." He also added, "In a community with broken trust to their formal or informal leadership, people are likely to be suspicious about the other groups and easily engage in a power game." Thus it is essential that all aspect of community building processes should be open and transparent. A chair of a social club in Dobong-gu, said, "Previously, we had some conflicts in our community. Residents did not believe neighborhood associations because the managers of our neighborhood association had operated financial secrecy and did not open financial information to the residents properly. But, several years ago, new members were elected as board leaders and they opened financial information and minutes of board meetings to community members on a website." She also stated, "After opening the information to the residents, they started to participate in discussion of community issues and community programs. We realized that we had common demand for community daycare programs through open discussions among residents. The whole process of daycare project made us very proud to work together to achieve common goals." She mentioned that transparent management of community organizations helped the community overcome distrust and rebuild a positive culture for community engagement.

19) Interviews for the case of Social club Dobong-gu were conducted in May 2015 and 2017.

Although many community projects have done by residents themselves, government officials still concern about whether local recipients of government grant have proper representation of the people in the neighborhood. It is difficult for administrators to identify which project representing better and closer of the demands and needs of people in the neighborhood. An official in Local Community Division of Seoul said, "When we are screening for government funding for CBP applications, it is very difficult to say whether these CBP grant applicants truly represent needs and interests of their neighborhood. Skeptics worry about tax money will be used only for those professional activists who have knowledge and experience to receive government grant. I admit this skepticism reflects some parts of reality whenever I see familiar names from applications over and over again."

What is Next? Priorities for Effective Community Building

One and a half years after the establishment of the Seoul Community Support Center (SCSC), almost two thousand community projects had been applied for, and 776 applications received funding and administrative assistance from Seoul city government.[20] In neighborhoods in Seoul, community organizations and groups of citizens have been providing social services to mitigate service needs and respond to their distinctive local problems. Their stories offer best practices that might be implemented elsewhere. The evidence is clear that community-based initiatives are spreading and increasing in Seoul. Transformation of our neighborhoods remains slow, but change is occurring. In furthering community building today, a high priority should be given to addressing immediate obstacles in an effort to recognize effective community building practices. While the Community Building Policy (CBP) of the Seoul city government may create social platforms for civil society in the urban communities of Seoul, it is important to note that the role of government has to be limited in facilitating and assisting if CBP intends to develop citizen-led initiatives.

20) Seoul Metropolitan Government (2013). *Seoul, Life, and People*. Seoul, Korea: Seoul Metropolitan Government.

References

Choi, Won-hyuk(2015, September 9). "Interview with the Director of the Local Community Division in the City of Seoul." *Herald*, Retrieved from http://biz.heraldcorp.com/view.php?ud=20150909000157

Fouser, Robert J.(2011, December 5). Community Building in Korea. *The Korea Times*. Retrieved from http://www.koreatimes.co.kr/www/news/opinon/2011/12/314_100169.html

Hong, Sharon(2012). Seoul: A Korean Capital. In Nihal Perera & Wing-Shing Tang (Eds.), *Transforming Asian Cities*. London; New York: Routledge.

Kang, Hyun-kyung(2013, February 17). "Apartment Noise Hard to Handle." *The Korea Times*. Retrieved from http://www.koreatimes.co.kr/www/news/nation/2013/02/113_130616.html

Kim, Dong-hong(2013, December 23). "Seongbuk-gu, Community Building and Energy Saving." Money Today. Retrieved from http://www.mt.co.kr/view/mtview.php?type=1&no=2013122311112571090&outlink=1

Kim, Si-yeon(2015, July 04). "What Happened in An Apartment Complex?." Oh My News. Retrieved from http://www.ohmynews.com/NWS_Web/View/at_pg.aspx?CNTN_CD=A0002123906

Park, Sung-joon(2015, January 15). "Seongbuk-gu, Togetherness Movement in Apartment." Ajunews. Retrieved from www.ajunews.com/view/20150115095337539

Park, Won-soon(2014). In Seoul, the Citizens are the Mayor. *Public Administration Review*, 74(4): 442-443.

Seoul Community Support Center(2016)(n.d.). *Hello? Seoul Community Support Center*. Retrieved on August 23, 2016 from http://www.seoulmaeul.org/programs/user/eng/index.html

______(2013). *Performance Report of Community Building Policy in Seoul*, Seoul Community Support Center.

______(2015). *Performance Report of Community Building Policy in Seoul*, Seoul Community Support Center.

Seoul Metropolitan Government(2012). *Master Plan for Community Building in Seoul*. Seoul, Korea: Seoul Metropolitan Government.

______(2013). *Seoul, Life, and People*. Seoul, Korea: Seoul Metropolitan Government.

The 15 minutes that Change the World(2014, December 30). *Sim, Jae-chul: Together with Security in Apartment*. Retrieved from https://www.youtube.com/watch?v=u7FrntqFKPA\

Teaching Note

Transforming Seoul: Rethinking Neighborhood

Background

Korean society has suffered from pervasive social disorder, including a high suicide rate, troubled schools, murder and other crime, deepening unemployment and poverty. Some believe this results from a loss of human values and social goods in our communities. As a policy response to these serious social ills, Seoul's Mayor Park Won–soon offered community building as a solution to the problems. The Seoul Metropolitan Government has made ambitious Community Building Policy choices that are expected to create social spaces where people come together, social interactions occur, and social capital emerges. Moving away from government–directed uniform solutions, Community Building Policies foster citizen–led approaches in seeking solutions to neighborhood problems and eventually enable citizens to become civic–minded leaders who are promoting their own activities and services. The ultimate goal of Community Building Policy efforts is to give communities ownership of their own programs and build shared understanding and trusting relationships among various stakeholders.

Purpose of the Case

This case explores the city of Seoul's Community Building Policy (CBP) and spotlights some projects and activities in urban neighborhoods of Seoul.

The case provides opportunities for students to learn about the meaning of community and the importance of social capital as a key component to neighborhood as well as how government policies may support community building processes and what benefit government can offer for more effective community building initiatives. The collaborative governance model proposed by CBP provides a useful guide for understanding relationships between government agencies, nonprofit mediators and citizens and the way the Seoul Community Support Center (SCSC) links government and citizens and supports the growth of citizen initiatives. In addition, this case suggests specific factors that are critical for the success of community building initiatives and challenges to community building. The review of Seoul's CBP fills a unique niche that offers theory-driven public policy practices and analyses of real applications of policy intentions in a diverse urban context. This case is ideal for undergraduate and graduate instruction in areas such as public administration, nonprofit studies, public policy, urban planning and political science. Instructors can focus on their particular disciplines and use the dimensions of this case that are fitting to their needs to supplement their main class materials.

Summary of Community Building Policy (CBP)

Urban communities in the city of Seoul are suffering from severe conflicts and social exclusion caused by rapid urbanization and pro-development focused urban planning practice. Responding to these problems, the city of Seoul has initiated Community Building Policy (CBP) to cultivate civic health, self-governing capacity, and livable communities. The basic approach of CBP is a citizen-led and government-supported model of government-citizen partnership. The Seoul city government and local governments have helped groups of citizens to promote citizen initiatives for community building projects with financial and administrative supports such as leadership training, counseling, and coordinating to match community needs and government aid through the Seoul Community Support Center (SCSC) established to develop and support CBP programs.

Some communities have experienced positive changes in their neighborhoods that have made a real impact on social capital building. The SPOT-

LIGHT stories in the case demonstrate that CBP contributes to:

- Civic culture nurtured (refer to Dobong-gu neighborhood association)
- Sense of mutual understanding and tolerance promoted (refer to Hanyang apartment complex)
- Community capacity built (refer to Seongbuk-gu, Doosan apartment complex)
- Community leadership trained and developed (refer to Seongdong-gu, local community manager system)
- Democratic practices developed (refer to Seongbuk-gu neighborhood association)
- Trust rebuilt (refer to Dobong-gu, social club)

Key Conditions to Achieving Effective Community Building

As the SPOTLIGHT stories above demonstrate, CBP in Seoul has engaged communities, fostered their capacity to solve their own problems, and created social norms for civic culture in many communities. The CBP of Seoul and local governments demonstrate the importance of grassroots approaches to community building as an effective model for resolving conflicts and instilling social capital in urban neighborhoods. The process varies depending upon the local context, but there are key conditions for success in the cases of CBP in Seoul.

First, **community leaders' commitment** is the most important condition for successful community building. A community leader may be a person who is well connected to the local community and is passionate about the cause of community building. Several successful cases show community leaders of projects or activities have to invest considerable time in listening to diverse voices from neighborhood groups and encouraging local residents to engage in activities and programs. They must always be answerable to the community, helping people to leave behind any resentment from past history and instead work together to improve situations. Whether through a contribution of labor, expertise, or (and) social network, a committed leader pools community resources and implements action plans with deep dedication. Board members of neighborhood associations spend considerable time in program planning, neighborhood meetings, designing proposals, and making contacts to the local residents and government officials and all of these efforts help accomplish a community driven self-governance in a long run (refer to Dobong-gu neighborhood association, and Seongdong-gu, local community manager system).

Second, **facilitative leadership of the government agency** is also a critical condition for the success of community building efforts. The role of government especially in the early stage of community project development is important to break down barriers in the growth of civic culture. Government officials have to demonstrate to citizens the benefits of community-led projects and raise awareness of positive community potential that will lead to collective efforts toward winning results for all stakeholders (refer to Seongdong-gu, local community manager system).

Third, **a physical community space** that can be considered as basic and minimum infrastructure for sustainable community activities is a factor in successful community building programs. Existence of a physical space that attracts social interactions and gatherings is important for continued face-to-face interactions among people that generate social capital that will alleviate conflicts and distrust in a community (refer to Hanyang apartment complex).

Fourth, **a sense of social belonging** that mainly comes from long and stable residency helps community building efforts to be effectively implemented. This is because citizens who have a sense of belonging in their community are more concerned about their community issues and have better understanding about community needs (refer to Dobong-gu neighborhood association).

Challenges in implementing Community Building Policy

Accountability Social value is not created in a short period of time but tax paid programs have to report visible outcome in every budget cycle. Although the Seoul Metropolitan Government and 25 local district governments have agreed upon main principles and goals of CBP, each of stakeholders may have different viewpoints on policy process or performance criteria for the evaluation of policy impact (refer to Seongbuk-gu, Doosan apartment complex).

Blurred Role of Administrators Key principle of CBP is that local residents lead community building activities and government supports and assists them to succeed. But the governments sometimes have to intervene in the internal matters of the neighborhood associations to promote transparency in their management and accountable management of government grant (refer to Seongbuk-gu neighborhood association).

Representation Questioned Administrators concern about whether local recipients of government support have representations of people in the neighborhood. But, it is difficult for them to identify who is a representative for people in a neighborhood (refer to Dobong-gu, Social club).

Lack of Professionalism and knowledge CBP have made various revisions and correction of application process to make it as simple as possible and easy to develop one for ordinary people. SCSC is also a nonprofit support organization for citizen to approach and interact for them to engage government supporting programs. However, ordinary citizens lack of professional skills and knowledge in community engagement and initiative for community building (refer to Hanyang apartment complex and Seongdong-gu, local community manager system).

Learning Objectives: What do Students Learn from the Case?

- Importance of social capital and civic culture for the generation of social goods: tolerance, altruism, and behaviors to support collective benefits
- Changes in the public policy approach for urban development from pro-development to community building
- Changes in the role of government in addressing social conflicts in Seoul from directive control to assisting partner
- Government-driven civil society: how government designs policy for civil society building and assists to build a civil society
- Community capacity formed from community building to address social problems
- Democratic practices fostered by self-governing practices and community gatherings in neighborhoods
- Tension between private sphere and public sphere in government-driven civil society building

- Challenges of policy implementation from administrator's perspectives
- Key concepts and terms associated with Community Building Policy processes

Policy maker's dilemma

Seoul Mayor Park Won–soon made a paradigmatic turn from a pro–development approach to a community building approach in the urban communities of Seoul. This shift garnered harsh criticism from groups that had enjoyed the benefits of previous policy direction. Critics of Park administration attack CBP an expensive policy for no return. CBP has an inherent dilemma for Mayor Park in relation to how to show the positive outcome in the short run of policy operations. The nature of CBP that aims at social transformation of neighborhoods makes it very difficult to expect a positive return on investment as visible proof of effectiveness of the policy in a short period of time. Furthermore, policy maker might face with dilemma when expectations from CBP between policy maker and citizens are different.

Administrators' dilemma

It is a key policy assumption that citizens are able to lead and grow by themselves if they are trained and supported with seed funding. However, the role of administrators in developing programs for community building is blurred between directing or controlling and assisting or supporting community building. While the Community Building Policy (CBP) of the Seoul city government may create social platforms for civil society in the urban communities of Seoul, it is important to note that the role of government has to be limited in facilitating and assisting if CBP intends to develop citizen–led initiatives.

Another dilemma for administrators is assessing the potential of community project applications and making decisions about to whom local governments should provide administrative supports and resources for better promotion of community building. For example, some applicants submit their proposal for their group members' exclusive benefit rather than represent their neighborhood's welfare as whole. In some neighborhoods, several groups of people have a severe turf war on neighborhood initiative, thus, government could not offer resources and support to a particular group of people.

Citizens' dilemma

Citizens have inherent limitations if they are engaging in community building projects as part of CBP because citizens are limited in time, knowledge, interest and proper authority (and accountability) to take on actions to serve the needs of the community. In particular, the responsibility for serving the needy and poor requires citizens' dedication and selfless passion to pursue sustainable service mechanisms at the community level. Basically, private citizens do not have the responsibility to address community issues and problems. Their busy private lives are also a challenge to their interest in and engagement with community issues. Even for citizens who are interested in community engagement, their lack of knowledge might restrict their ability to develop projects and carry them out.

Discussion Questions

- What is the basic rationale of CBP for positive change of urban communities?
- What are some reasons why Mayor Park might have proposed CBP?
- Describe the community building process designed by CBP and identify key features of the CBP framework that governs policy development and growth of community projects.
- What are the defining characteristics of CBP that are different from previous urban development policies in Seoul?
- What are the main benefits for citizens and communities from building communities?
- Is CBP replicable in other communities? What are the conditions that are required to be successful in community building?
- Why is it difficult for some communities to carry out effective community building projects?
- How does government help communities to be successful?
- Is community building policy successful? What is your advice for administrators for measuring outputs and outcomes community building?
- Identify a community organization that is effective at responding to the community's needs and analyze the conditions that make them successful. Use news articles or information from credible websites.

- Given the role that Mayor Park's administration has played in the CBP initiative, how would you advise other city governments to go about building community in their own cities?
- What challenges do citizens have when they are involved in community building? How does government encourage citizens to be interested in and actively engage in community building? How does government provide support for communities which lack knowledge and trust?
- What advice would you give to policy makers and administrators about community building?

Key Terms

- **Civil society** is defined in several ways. Newton (2001: 208) defines civil society as "a social context in which there is a broad range, great diversity, and high density of social networks and formal and informal social organizations." Anheier (2005) states that civil society is voluntarily organized by individuals and associations to pursue common interests between family, market, and the state. Edwards (2009: 403) refers to civil society as "all associations and networks between family and the state," including "registered NGOs of many different kinds, labor union, political parties, churches and other religious groups, professional and business associations, community and self-help groups, social movements, and the independent media."
- **Social capital** refers to capital embedded in social relationships. The concept of social capital is differently addressed in various studies. Putnam (2000: 239) refers to social capital as "connections among individuals—social networks and the norms of reciprocity and trustworthiness that arise from them" and argues that social capital embedded in connections facilitates cooperation and coordination to achieve a common goal. Coleman (1988) approaches it as a structural aspect which encourages people's actions. Fukuyama (2001: 7) defines it as "an instantiated informal norm that promotes co-operation between two or more individuals," focusing on social trust among features of social capital to promote economic development.
- **Community building** is an effort to build networks among people and

associations in a geographical area to achieve common goals. Weil (1996: 482) defines community building as "activities, practices, and policies that support and foster positive connections among individuals, groups, organizations, neighborhoods, and geographic and functional communities." Chaskin & Abunimah (1999) refer to it as connections among individuals, organizations, and resources to seek common benefits in their community.

- **Social norms** are shared guidelines that influence the behavior, attitude, and thought of people in a society. Ostrom (1999: 15) defines social norms as "shared understanding about actions that are obligatory, permitted, or forbidden." In cognitive science, social norms are defined as "standards of behavior that are based on widely shared beliefs about how individual group members ought to behave in a given situation" (Fehr & Fischbacher, 2004: 185).
- **Self-governance** is in general defined as a governing system by which a group of people or social organizations govern their affairs by means of regulations the members of the organizations establish. Kooper, Maes, & Lindgreen (2011: 199) define self-governance as "the capacity of social entities to govern themselves autonomously." Telemo (2015: 17) refers to self-governance to "a system in between private and state ownership where the appropriators themselves manage the resource."

Suggested Reading List

Bryer, T. A.(2009). Explaining Responsiveness in Collaboration: Administrator and Citizen Role Perceptions. *Public Administration Review*, 69(2): 271-283.

Chaskin, R. J.(2001). Building Community Capacity a Definitional Framework and Case Studies from a Comprehensive Community Initiative. *Urban Affairs Review*, 36(3): 291-323.

Chaskin, R. J., & Greenberg, D. M.(2013). Between Public and Private Action: Neighborhood Organizations and Local Governance. *Nonprofit and Voluntary Sector Quarterly*, 44(2): 248-267.

Fontan, J. M., Hamel, P., Morin, R., & Shragge, E.(2009). Community Organizations and Local Governance in a Metropolitan Region. *Urban Affairs Review*, 44(6): 832-857.

Glaser, M. A., & Denhardt, J.(2009). Community Policing and Community Building: A Case Study of Officer Perceptions. *The American Review of Public Administration*, 40(3): 309-325.

Graddy, E., & Wang, L.(2009). Community Foundation Development and Social Capital. *Nonprofit and Voluntary Sector Quarterly*, 38(3): 392–412.

Jung, K., Jang, H. S., & Seo, I.(2016). "The Government–Driven Social Enterprises in South Korea: Lessons from the Social Enterprise Promotion Program in the Seoul Metropolitan City." *International Review of Administrative Sciences*, 82(3): 598–616.

Jun, K. N.(2013). Escaping the Local Trap? The Role of Community–Representing Organizations in Urban Governance. *Journal of Urban Affairs*, 35(3): 343–363.

Kim, J. W., & Jang, H. S.(Forthcoming). Why do Residents Participate in Neighborhood Associations? The Case of Apartment Neighborhood Associations in Seoul, Korea. *Journal of Urban Affairs*.

Lelieveldt, H., Dekker, K., Volker, B., & Torenvlied, R.(2009). Civic Organizations as Political Actors: Mapping and Predicting the Involvement of Civic Organizations in Neighborhood Problem–Solving and Coproduction. *Urban Affairs Review*, 45(1): 3–24.

LeRoux, K.(2008). The Effects of Descriptive Representation on Nonprofits' Civic Intermediary Roles: A Test of the "Racial Mismatch" Hypothesis in the Social Services Sector. *Nonprofit and Voluntary Sector Quarterly*, 38(5): 741–760.

Marwell, N. P.(2009). *Bargaining for Brooklyn: Community Organizations in the Entrepreneurial City*. University of Chicago Press.

Musso, J., Weare, C., Bryer, T., & Cooper, T. L.(2011). Toward "Strong Democracy" in Global Cities? Social Capital Building, Theory–Driven Reform, and the Los Angeles Neighborhood Council Experience. *Public Administration Review*, 71(1): 102–111.

Nelson, R. H.(2005). *Private Neighborhoods and the Transformation of Local Government*. The Urban Insitute.

Power, E. R.(2014). Placing Community Self–Governance: Building Materialities, Nuisance Noise and Neighbouring in Self–Governing Communities. *Urban Studies*, 52(2): 245–260.

Putnam, R. D.(2001). *Bowling Alone: The Collapse and Revival of American Community*. Simon and Schuster.

Read, B. L., & Pekkanen, R. (Eds.)(2009). *Local Organizations and Urban Governance in East and Southeast Asia: Straddling State and Society*. Routledge.

Schneider, J. A.(2007). Connections and Disconnections Between Civic Engagement and Social Capital in Community–Based Nonprofits. *Nonprofit and Voluntary Sector Quarterly*, 36(4): 572–597.

Shrestha, M. K.(2013). Internal Versus External Social Capital and the Success of Community Initiatives: A Case of Self–Organizing Collaborative Governance in Nepal. *Public Administration Review*, 73(1): 154–164.

Stanley, J., Stanley, J., & Hensher, D.(2012). Mobility, Social Capital and Sense of Community: What Value? *Urban Studies*, 49(16): 3595–3609.

van Houwelingen, P.(2012). Neighborhood Associations and Social Capital in Japan. *Urban Affairs Review*, 48(4): 467–497.

Wissink, B., & Hazelzet, A.(2012). Social Networks in 'Neighborhood Tokyo.' *Urban Studies*, 49(7): 1527–1548.

Suggested Web Resources

- City of Los Angeles Neighborhood Council http://empowerla.org/
- City of Portland Neighborhood Involvement https://www.portlandoregon.gov/oni/
- Democracy Collaborative http://democracycollaborative.org/
- Community Wealth http://community-wealth.org/
- United Nations Development Program http://www.undp.org/content/undp/en/home/ourwork/democraticgovernance/overview.html
- Ted Talk Eric Liu: Why ordinary people need to understand power https://www.ted.com/talks/eric_liu_why_ordinary_people_need_to_understand_power/transcript?language=en

07
Chapter

Critical Assessment of the 2012 Gumi Chemical Spill: An Adaptive Governance Approach

Kyujin Jung

Introduction

An industrial accident in a plant operated by the Hube Global Chemical Corporation in Gumi, South Korea, released 8 tons of hydrofluoric acid into the surrounding area on September 27, 2012. The leak killed 5 workers and injured 18, affected 12,243 residents, and damaged 212 hectares of agricultural land and killed or injured 3,944 animals. About 300 residents were evacuated to nearby temporary shelters.

Although rare, such an industrial disaster demonstrates the importance of a crisis management system which can identify, assess, and handle a crisis at high-hazard sites. The challenges facing public agencies reflect the complexity and ambiguity of the administrative authority of those charged to deal with the crisis.

This case study examines how the local, regional, and national governments dealt with an unanticipated crisis by examining the information available and the announcements that were reported by various public agencies during the crisis. Particularly, this case study focuses on the management of complicated issues derived from new or unanticipated situations by using an adaptive governance approach. Thus, the guiding questions for this case study are:

- How was the 2012 Gumi chemical spill crisis managed in practice?
- What decisions made in crisis management impacted collaborations and the effectiveness of the overall response, and what changes should be made in reference to what we learned from the crisis response?

This case study adopted an adoptive approach which aims to critically evaluate the crisis response to the Gumi chemical spill incident in South Korea. A main focus is on the public sector coping with challenges to emergency management agencies under a crisis situation. The analytical methods used to gain insight into the subject matter was a combination of the mass media, government reports, and press releases from national, provincial, and local government. To reinforce validity of the data derived from diverse sources, the method was to compare the reports and releases in a chronological order. The following subsections present the background on emergency management in South Korea and a brief outline of the 2012 chemical spill incident in Gumi.

Background of the 2012 Chemical Spill in Gumi, South Korea

On September 27, 2012, a toxic chemical leak released hydrofluoric acid at Gumi's National Industrial Complex, located 124 miles southeast of Seoul. The accident occurred when two Hube Global Chemical Corporation workers working on a tanker attempted to unload hydrofluoric acid into a storage tank. About 8 tons of hydrofluoric acid escaped into the atmosphere, spreading across a 4 km radius, killing 5 workers, affecting 12,243 residents, and damaging 212 hectares of agricultural land and 3,944 killed or injured animals. As of 22 October 2012, it was reported that about 11,083 people had received treatment for nausea, chest pain, rashes, or sore eyes after inhaling fumes from the chemical leak. More than 300 residents including elderly persons were evacuated to public-run facilities in Bongsan-ri, Incheon-ri, and Baekhyeon-ri. Residents living within 1.5 km of the chemical spill site were advised to go for a medical check-up. Figure 7-1 shows an illustration of the affected area.

Figure 7-1. The Spatial domain of the Gumi chemical spill

Source: Naver Maps (2012, November 22) and YNA (2012, October 16).
Note: One centimeter to respectively one thousand and hundred meters i.e., 1:100,000 and 1:10,000.

As summarized in Table 7-1, Jung & Park (2016) illustrate that "about 12,243 residents including industrial workers, and public servants had received treatment for nausea, chest pain, rashers, or sore eyes as a result of exposure or inhalation of fumes from the chemical leak." The City government of Gumi continued advising residents living within 1.5 km of the chemical spill site to go for a medical check-up at the three temporary *ad hoc* healthcare centers as part of the first response. Despite that all risk in polluted areas was associated with the chemical leak, the national government has delayed in identifying its damages; local government also ignored the seriousness of the toxic gas and was not quick in evacuating its residents (Jung & Park 2016). All emergency response activities are summarized in chronological orders of Table 7-1.

As the initial function of emergency response, emergency assessment was caused by late emergency recognition of Ministry of Environment (MOE), indicating that the main elements of this functions also was not accomplished in the first response. According to NEMA (2011: 29), the lead agency for responding to crises related to the toxic chemical substance is the Ministry of Environment, and the ministry is obligated to establish the national safety management basic plan, respond to the chemical spill, and recover its damages. Despite that, the DREA under the ministry of environment unsuccessfully responded to the leak, and even issued a serious emergency warning over

Table 7-1. Chronological orders of the Gumi chemical spill

Date	Time	Agency	Events
September 27, 2012	15:43	N/A	The Gumi chemical spill occurred
	15:47	LFS/NEMA	Starting agency notification and mobilization
	16:00	LFS	Starting hazard Operations
			Initial Emergency medical care
	16:10	LPS	Impact zone access control and security
	16:30	LESOH	Operating local EOC
	17:00	MOE	Accepting the chemical spill
	17:50	LFS	Chemical response equipment mobilization
	17:45	MOE	Providing Crisis response information
	19:00	DREA/MOE	Threat detection and emergency classification
	19:10	LESOH	Population warning
			Starting Population monitoring and assessment
	23:30	LESOH	1st hazard exposure control
September 28, 2012	00:00	NIER	Chemical assessment equipment mobilization
			Damage assessment
	01:00	DREA	Hazard & environmental monitoring
	01:30	LESOH	2nd hazard exposure control
	03:30	MOE	Terminating the crisis response phase
	08:30	LESOH	Declaring emergency termination
	11:00	LESOH	returning residents home
	13:25	LESOH	3rd hazard exposure control
	14:40	DREA	Hazard & environmental monitoring termination
October 6, 2012	Prime Minister's Office		Sending a 26-member team to conduct a three-day assessment of the severity of the crisis
October 24, 2012	Korean Food and Drug Administration		Authorizing to dispose of crops and livestock; Rural Development Administration conducted clean-up operations using lime powder to detoxify agricultural soil

Source: Adopted to Jung & Park (2016).

Note: NEMA (National Emergency Management Agency); MOE (Ministry of Environment); NIER (National Institute of Environment Research); DREA (Daegu Regional Environment Agency); LESOH (Local Emergency Safety Operations Headquarter); LFS (Local Fire Station); LPS (Local Police Station).

6 hours 47 minutes. Because the Daegu Regional Environment Agency (DREA) broke the crisis response manual for mitigating the secondary damages without any other consideration, the residents were not evacuated over about 4 hours from the accident and gravely affected by HF (YNA 2012, October 16).

Despite the National Institute of Environmental Research (NIER) is a professional agency obligated to analyze the toxic chemical substances and to suggest effective operations on the crisis, moreover, the agency delayed to dispatch a special chemical analysis vehicle to the scene because the vehicle was not prepared for the potential crisis such as the chemical spill (Chosun 2012, October 23). The crisis response manual on toxic chemical substances (2012: XX) states that the cancellation of the serious emergency warning depends on the decision of the crisis evaluation committee in the ministry of environment. The DREA, however, "canceled the warning after 5 hours after the spill" (YNA 2012, October 16). The city government of Gumi also disputed that since the NIER offered the toxic chemical analysis results that the degree of the HF pollution within .31 mile from the accident was about 1 ppm under 30 ppm as the significant level, we allowed local residents to return to their home even though it was uncertain whether the area was safe from contamination (LESOH 2012, October 4).

On top of that, although rapid hazard operations were performed by local fire fighters as the first responder, they did not effectively mitigate hazard during the initial response. The reason is that MOE and DREA did not provide accurate emergency assessment to local agencies despite rapid hazard operations need the accurate emergency assessment (YNA 2012, October 16). In terms of the hazard operations, NEMA released an announcement about the reason why local fire fighters responded to the chemical leak by using water, noting that the key information guide for the chemical substance provided by the ministry of environment illustrates that the spilled HF gas should be diluted and dispersed by using abundant amounts of water (NEMA 2012, October 10). It implies that the information flow during the crisis caused inappropriate responses resulting in secondary damages to local communities.

As the crisis unfolded, secondary damages cost the local economy and residents' livelihood. Between 77 and 80 companies in the industrial zone were forced to shut down temporarily, reporting about U.S. $15.9 million in production lost and U.S. $1.7 million estimated costs in property damages (Chung, 2013). As of 6 October 2012, the media reported that crops on more than 90 hectares of agricultural lands were were being grown 200 meters from a chemical plant and animals affected by the chemical leak were exhibiting symptoms of chemical poisoning. The amounts of air pollution and water contamination caused by the chemical leak are unknown, but the government assured the public that only one to five parts per million (ppm) of hydro-fluoric acid were found in the air.

According to the National Institute of Environmental Research ([NIER] 2012: 4), hydrofluoric fluoride (HF) is "a highly caustic liquid, and should be managed with extreme care." The symptoms of exposure to hydrofluoric acid may not be immediate. If untreated, however, it can interfere with nerve function as well as result in serious injuries (Korea Medical Association 2012, October 10). The U.S. National Institute for Occupational Safety and Health (NIOSH), the U.S. federal agency responsible for providing recommendations for the prevention of work-related injury and illness said that exposure to HF should be no more than "3 ppm [2.5 mg/m (3)] as limit-time-weighted average for up to a 10-hour workday and a 40-hour workweek, and a short-term exposure limit is 6 ppm [5 mg/m (3)]" (2012, November 16).

In terms of air pollution and water contamination caused by chemical leak, the Ministry of Environment, Daegu Regional Environmental Agency (DREA), and NIER announced that the atmosphere, including groundwater and soil around the accident, are not polluted by hydrofluoric acid (Ministry of Environment 2012, October 18; National Emergency Operations Center [NEOC] 2012, October 23). The Korean Federation for Environmental Movement and the Citizens' Institute for Environmental Studies argued that evacuated residents cannot trust the government announcement (YNA 2012, October 23).

The Korea Industrial Complex Corp. (KICC) reported that between 77 and 80 companies in the industrial zone were forced to shut down temporarily costing them about U.S. $15.9 million on production lost (Kyeonghyang 2012, October 8). According to Local Emergency Safety Operations Headquarter in Gumi, the estimated physical damages is around U.S. $1.7 million, and crops, vegetable, and fruit on more than 372 hectares (919 acres) of agricultural lands were withering within 200 meters of the explosion site (LESOH 2012, October 8). In addition, about 3,997 cows, goats and other livestock exhibiting symptoms being affected by the chemical leak (LESOH 2012, October 30).

The major events after the chemical spill are outlined in Table 7–1. The table highlights three important points related to emergency response: (1) It took close to a month for the city to be declared a disaster area. (2) Federal agencies took control of the response. (3) Media outlets were critical of the federal agencies' response efforts.

At the regional level, the North Kyeongsang provincial government committed U.S. $1 million to the city of Gumi and organized a task force team to support the local government administration (North Kyeongsang Government 2012, October 10). The city government of Gumi announced that it would extend the local tax payment due date for households affected by the disaster up to a maximum of 9 months and reduce their electricity fees by 50% in the villages of Bongsan–ri and Incheon–ri (LESOH 2012, October 12). According to the *Korean Times* (2012, October 22), "residents of the affected villages will receive a 30 to 50 percent discount for their monthly payments of national health and pension service up to 6 months. The discount will be offered to people who suffered from not only health problems but also damage to their houses, farmland or livestock." Public officials from the Ministry of Health and Welfare also announced that the national government would pay full medical coverage to the victims who received medical treatment since the industrial disaster occurred (YNA 2012, October 22). The National Emergency Management Agency (NEMA) (22 October 2012), announced that it would "cover medical costs for 264 firefighters who worked at the scene of the gas leak."

Despite the emergency aid and financial assistance provided by national, provincial, and local governments, the negotiation to compensate the victims and pay the damages from the chemical leak was not successful (YNA 2012, November 13). On October 15, 2012, the citizens exposed to the toxic gas held a press conference and argued that "the city government of Gumi did not respond to the leak and even neglected residents in the polluted area without any other treatments after 18 hours from the accident" (YNA 2012, October 15). The mayor of Gumi announced that "the citizen group is requiring excessive compensations for the damages such as agricultural lands and healthcare compared to other special disaster zones affected by the tropical typhoons" (LESOH 2012, November 12) and "delayed a municipal ordinance to compensate the victims" (YNA 2012, November 13).

In terms of legal action, "the citizen group are filing legal action against national and local governments and KICC demanding about U.S. $1 billion compensations for agricultural lands and healthcare" (Donga 2012, October 9). However, the National Emergency Operations Center (NEOC) and the Ministry of Environment (2012, October 23) reported that "the effects of the chemical leak on the agricultural lands, domestic animals, and soil exposed to the chemical spill could not considered as a crop production in 2013." The city of Gumi took legal action against the Hube Global Corporation, "demanding the right to indemnity" (YNA 2012, November 14).

Adaptive Governance Approach to the 2012 Gumi Chemical Spill

Through a critical assessment of the Gumi chemical spill, this case study proposes adaptive governance as a way for national and local governments to respond to challenges. Specifically, this section focuses on crisis management techniques that can be newly adopted by national agencies and local governments to develop the ability to change processes based on public learning and deliberative procedures.

Responsiveness

Adaptive governance is based on critical mechanisms that sustain the response structure under physical and environmental stress as the crisis management system adjusts to cope with shifting conditions (Andrew & Kendra, 2012: 523). It is important for local governments to adopt strategies to reinforce the effectiveness of the crisis management system (Scholz & Stiftel, 2005). The National Assembly's Environment and Labor Committee criticized the poor response of national agencies and the city government of Gumi (Newsis 2012, October 16). The chain of information flow from the 119 local emergency center to other organizations such as national, regional, and local agencies and local government was not accurately designated or coordinated by the crisis management system (Chosun 2012, October 19). The representative of the ruling Saenuri Party, Wan-young Lee, said that "the DREA had been alerted an hour and 20 minutes after the gas leak and questioned whether the delay has to do with the government's past decision to close a bureau dealing with chemicals" (YNA 2012, October 16).

According to NEMA (2011: 29), "the lead agency for responding to crises related to the toxic chemical substance is the Ministry of Environment, and the ministry is obligated to establish the national safety management basic plan, respond to the chemical spill, and recover its damages." Despite that, "the DREA under the Ministry of Environment unsuccessfully responded to the leak, and even issued a serious emergency warning more than 6 hours later. Because the DREA did not follow the crisis response manual for mitigating the secondary damages without any other consideration, the residents were not evacuated for more than 4 hours and were gravely affected" (YNA 2012, October 16). In addition, "the NIER is a professional agency obligated to analyze the toxic chemical substances and to suggest effective operations on the crisis, but the agency delayed to dispatch a special chemical analysis vehicle to the scene because the vehicle was not prepared for the potential crisis such as the chemical spill" (Chosun 2012, October 23). The crisis re-sponsed manual on toxic chemical substances (2012) states that "the cancellation of the serious emergency warning depends on the decision of the crisis evaluation committee in the ministry of environment." The DREA, however, canceled the warning only 5 hours after the spill (YNA 2012, October 16).

The lack of information and poor judgment of national agencies led to confusion over the appropriate decisions that should be taken by local agencies, which led to secondary damages to local communities. For example, a member of the National Assembly, Sangjung Shim, criticized the national government by highlighting "the wrong information provided by the NIER caused the confusion of the first responders and the wrong evacuation of residents." She also indicated that even though the chemical crisis response manual presents diverse ways to neutralize the toxic substance, the NIER and the DREA did not transmit the essential information to the local agencies and government (Sisanews 2012, October 17). The local representative, Myengseok Park, argued that "the city government did not provide any information [on] the toxic chemical [to] … local communities before the evacuation and even [evacuated] residents at the HF-exposed area without neutralizing the effects of HF on September 28" (Chosun 2012, October 19).

While similar HF accidents had actually occurred 3 years before in the same chemical plant, the city government of Gumi had categorized the firm as a good chemical management firm (Chosun 2012, October 19). The city government of Gumi state that "since the NIER offered the toxic chemical analysis results that the degree of the HF pollution within .31 miles from the accident was about 1 ppm under 30 ppm as the significant level, we allowed local residents to return to their home even though it was uncertain whether the area was safe from contamination" (LESOH 2012, October 4). NEMA also released an announcement about the reason why local firefighters responded to the chemical leak by using water, noting that "the key information guide for the chemical substance provided by the ministry of environment illustrates that the spilled HF gas should be diluted and dispersed by using abundant amounts of water" (NEMA 2012, October 10). These statements imply that the information flow during the crisis caused inappropriate responses, resulting in secondary damages to local communities.

The distrust of the affected community group on the city government delayed the compensation procedure. On 2 p.m. October 2, 2012, the citizen group met the mayor in their village affected by the chemical and demanded the evacuation plan coordinated by the government (LESOH 2012, October 4). However, the Ministry of Environment announced that the chemical investigation result on October 5 reported that the "groundwater within the accident area was safe to drink, and the effects of the HF spill did not influence the groundwater" (Ministry of Environment 2012, October 5). Based on the findings of the taskforce, the city government refused to evacuate. As a result, villagers could evacuate from the affected site on October 6 more than ten days after the event (LESOH 2012, October 7). The affected residents accused that "the NIER only tried to collect samples in the area .31 to .81 mile away from the accident, and failed to provide a timely evacuation in response to the chemical spill" (YNA 2012, October 7).

To resolve the problem connected to the chemical spill, on October 6, the national government sent a 26-member team consisting of public officials and experts to conduct an assessment on the severity of the crisis. Vice prime minister, Yook Dong-han, said that "the government will make detailed measures and standards to administer support, and plans to carry out another round of in-depth inspections into the region as early as possible" (YNA 2012, October). The national government also dispatched psychiatric experts to a youth center and a food waste disposal facility in Gumi to which some

50 residents evacuated (LESOH 2012, October 30) According to the NEOC's report (2012, October 26), a total of 12,243 residents received medical examinations. All the evacuated residents received consultations and "21 of them received medication for depression, sleep disorder and headache." Nevertheless, netizens lambasted "the government's belated response, city authorities' incompetence, and the mainstream media's silence on this critical issue. Twitter users have uploaded photos of affected farmlands" (YNA 2012, October).

Public and Scientific Learning

Adaptive governance plays an important role in establishing mechanisms to enhance learning processes through the crisis management system (Andrew & Kendra, 2012; Scholz & Stiftel, 2005). Since public information and scientific evidence are very limited and complicated due to the incompatibility of the crisis management system, adaptive governance presents guidance for how networks disseminate significant information and diverse experiences among local agencies beyond bureaucratic boundaries (Brunner & Lynch, 2010). In this case, there was limited public information about the chemical leak during the early stages of the accident. Information was mostly reported by online sources rather than by the government.

Lack of information from public agencies exacerbated the confusion regarding the nature of the disaster. For example, "Officials claim there was no explosion. They said, the acid leak was first contained [when firefighters] … deployed motorized sprinklers to neutralize the poisonous emissions, which caused a chemical reaction and created smoke that made it look like an explosion." Because of unfamiliarity with the chemical gas and a lack of public and scientific information, firefighters as the first responders responded to the accident without any information about the danger of HF, and thus 506 firefighters were injured during the initial response (27% of injured people) (YNA 2012, October 8; Chosun 2012, October 19). News media also reported that the firefighters did not wear chemical resistant suits and masks to protect themselves against the toxic chemical. Firefighters failed to use calcium hydroxide, the neutralizing agent for hydrofluoric acid, because they did not know they were supposed to until the professional chemical analyst from the NIER arrived about 8 hours after the initial leak.

The mechanism to share learning processes with other local agencies should be adopted to regional and local emergency management agencies, and the ability to learn from public and scientific information may be the fundamental element for adaptive governance. For instance, "During the parliamentary inspection meeting, a representative of the Democratic United Party accused that the government had been wrong in saying that there was no danger in the region even though one to five parts per million (ppm) of hydrofluoric acid were found in the air. The affected communities rejected the short-term compensation plan provided by the government and argued that "the government did not provide any information and evidence to convince them" (YNA 2012, October 13).

On 24 October 2012, the government finally decided to take action by disposing of crops and culling livestock from the affected region. A special team of on-site inspectors said that overall farming conditions were not a problem since soil and water pollution are below dangerous levels. As part of its precautionary measures, the government ordered the use of lime powder to detoxify the soil for farming. The Chief Director of Rural Development Administration said that "when the acid combines with lime in soil it becomes insoluble. The soil becomes acid-free. It's possible to farm this land next year." Despite the assurance, the affected communities were unsatisfied, frustrated, and angry about the lack of information provided by government agencies especially related to their property rights, livelihood, and when they can return to their homes.

Learning from the Crisis: Public and Policy Responses

The lack of hazard information exacerbated the confusion regarding the nature of incident management, indicating that LESOH as the principal EOC did not spontaneously coordinate the predetermined operations. For instance, LESOH claimed there was explosion when the chemical spill occurred, but the acid leak was first contained when firefighters deployed motorized sprinklers to neutralize the poisonous emissions, which caused a chemical reaction and created smoke that made it look like an explosion (YNA 2012, October 8). Because of inadequate communication and documentation, moreover, fire fighters as the first responder were committed to the accident without any information about the danger of the chemical gas, and thus 506 firefighters were injured during the initial response (27% of injured people) (Chosun

2012, October 19). News media also reported that the firefighters did not wear chemical resistant suits and masks to protect themselves against the toxic chemical. Nevertheless, LESOH carried out cleanup operations to keep residue from running into the Nakdong River, one of the country's four largest waterways, rather than concentrating on the role of the pivotal EOC (LESOH 2012, October 4).

Although local agencies' function and authority to response to natural disaster is clearly specified in the national statutes, disaster caused by large scale industrial accident is not obvious to local government agencies. The hierarchical structure as centralized decision making works well in a highly fragmented administrative system during a large scale disaster, but it has not been as effective in a poorly defined incident management. Local agencies await directives from the provincial and national governments. Yet, it was unclear as to why it took the national government close to two weeks to response to the crisis. From the citizen perspective, the cause of the chemical leak was dysfunctions of incident management system, and inefficient emergency response resulted in miscommunication among national and local agencies.

According to the indication in the inspection of the government office, On October 18, 2012, the Ministry of Public Administration and Safety (MOPAS) announced that 22 crisis management standard manuals will be improved in such a way to meet realistic needs of crisis response and recovery (Segye 2012, October 19). In addition, the Act for the chemical substance legislation and assessment will be also considered as the objective of a follow-up measures because the Act cannot cover small firms dealing the toxic chemical aids under 1 ton (Kookmin 2012, October 11). On October 23, 2012, the government approved a bill to conduct special inspections into companies that deal with dangerous chemicals. However, residents and nongovernmental organizations are urging the government to ensure there are more systematic ways to deal with the crisis. The recent chemical disaster in the Republic of Korea underscores the critical importance of preparing communities to cope with environmental emergencies for the protection of human health and nature.

Conclusion

Although these segmented functions need adequate communication and information flow, local agencies showed passive response activities and high dependency on national agencies' role such as hazard assessment (Jung & Park, 2016). As McConnell (2003) indicated, the principal agency's failure to assess the hazard resulted in failures of other functions of emergency response such as hazard operations, population protection, and incident management. Moreover, a lack of interorganizational communication was connected to other elements of incident management, implying that without adequate information flow among agencies, agency notification, mobilization of emergency facilities, and analysis and planning might not be performed effectively. Lastly, the principal EOC in the jurisdiction needed to have adequate authority to coordinate interorganizational activities. By monitoring and evaluating the coordinated operations crisis management can mitigate damages from the hazard as well as achieve successful emergency response.

On top of that, during the early stage of the emergency response, there was a lack of interagency communication reflecting a highly fragmented and hierarchical governance structure. The crisis was unexpected and small in scale in comparison to other industrial disasters, but it nevertheless threatened lives, livelihoods, and the economic viability of the region. Lack of interagency communication, dissemination of public information and risk communication as well as uncertainty related to the consequences of the incident affected how public agencies manage the crisis. The inconsistency of information related to the cause also put the national government in an unfavorable spotlight (Hankyoreh 2012, October 23). For example, the national government was blamed for "bringing residents back to the affected area even though the area was still contaminated" (Korea Herald 2012, October 10). There were reports that firefighters were unaware of the composition of the chemical and thus failed to use calcium hydroxide, the neutralizing agent for hydrofluoric acid.

The adaptive governance perspective highlights the problems or aspects that need to be resolved or improved. First, the hierarchical structure can impose inefficiency as decisions by one specialized agency may impose negative externalities on others (Jung & Song, 2015). It is to respond to disaster than to mitigate or prepare for the eventuality of a disaster. Second, the Gumi chemical spill crisis can be argued to have been precipitated by organizational failure and human errors. While the situation was grave, during the early stage of the emergency response, it was uncertain as to when public agencies should have taken charge and how they should have activated a systematic approach for managing the crisis. National, provincial, and local agencies were perceived by the public as being too slow and inadequately prepared to cope with emergencies, leading to frustration and anger. The crisis was exacerbated further by the media coverage about human suffering and environmental consequences. Since it may not be effective for the crisis management system to relying on a leading agency when responding to the initial crisis, the principal EOC consisting of diverse agencies in the hazard jurisdiction needs to have adequate authority that can secure appropriate information to make a decision to allocate resources and coordinate the first responding organizations.

This case study provides new insights into how crisis management based on the adaptive governance perspective can contribute to redesigning the current system, which focuses mainly on natural disasters in developing countries. Since the nationally centralized but segmented crisis management system cannot fully respond to accident-triggered crises such as chemical spills and gas explosions, designing the crisis management system as adaptive governance is important for responding to those hazards by using self-organized networks and deliberative mechanisms to mitigate the costs. Particularly, this case study encourages crisis managers to understand the adaptive governance perspective and identify existing challenges of crisis management. We also hope future researchers will investigate the challenges of emergency recovery and mitigation from the point of view of adaptive governance.

References

Andrew, S. A., & Kendra, J. M.(2012). An Adaptive Governance Approach to Disaster-Related Behavioural Health Services. *Disasters*, 36(3): 514-532. doi: 10.1111/j.1467-7717.2011.01262.x

British Broadcasting Corporation(2012, October 8). South Korea Designates Chemical Leak Area 'Disaster Zone'. *British Broadcasting Corporation*.

Brown, L.(2011). The Great Food Crisis of 2011. *Foreign Policy*, 3: 28.

Brunner, R. D., & Lynch, A. H.(2010). *Adaptive Governance and Climate Change.* Boston, MA: American Meterological Society Books.

Chosun(2012, October 19). Comprehensive Report for the Gumi Chemical Spill, *Chosun.*

______(2012, October 23). Lies of Ministry of Environment, *Chosun.*

CNN(2012, October 9). Toxic Leak in South Korea Sickens Thousands, Ruin Crops, *CNN.*

Gill, D. A., & Picou, J. S.(1998). Technological Disaster and Chronic Community Stress. *Society & Natural Resources,* 11(8): 795–815. doi: 10.1080/08941929809381119

Gunderson, L., & Light, S.(2006). Adaptive Management and Adaptive Governance in the Everglades Ecosystem. *Policy Sciences,* 39(4): 323–334. doi: 10.1007/s11077–006–9027–2

Ha, K.(2009). Emergency Management in Korea: Just Started, but Rapidly Evolving, in *The Comparative Emergency Management Book Project* edited by FEMA. Accessed on November 22, 2012: http://training.fema.gov/EMIWeb/edu.

Ha, K. & Ahn, J.(2009). Application of the Spider–Web Approach to Korean Emergency, *Journal of Homeland Security and Emergency Management.* Volume 6, Issue 1, Pages–, ISSN (Online) 1547–7355. doi: 10.2202/1547–7355.1676, November 2009.

HanKyoreh(2012, October 23). Damages in the Gumi Chemical Spill, *HanKyoreh.*

Herard, D.(2010). *The Hungarian Toxic Red Sludge Spill and Determining Public Accountability.* Disaster Risk Reduction Program: Florida International University.

Hermann, M. G., & Dayton, B. W.(2009). Transboundary Crises through the Eyes of Policymakers: Sense Making and Crisis Management. *Journal of Contingencies and Crisis Management,* 17(4): 233–241. doi: 10.1111/j.1468–5973.2009.00590.x

Jung, K. & Park, W.(2016). Tracing Interorganizational Information Networks during Emergency Responses: A Webometric Approach to the 2012 Gumi Chemical Spill. *Government Information Quarterly,* 33(1): 133–141. doi: 10.1016/j.giq.2015

Kookmin(2012, October 11). Toxic Chemical Aid Management by Small and Medium Enterprises, *Kookmin.*

Korean Herald(2012, October 10). The Chemical Spill was a Disaster by Public Agencies, *Korean Herald.*

Korean Medical Association(2012, October 10). *Press Release: The Effect of Hydrogen Fluoride on Human.* Seoul: Korean Medical Association.

Korean Times(2012, October 10). Camera Recording of Gumi Chemical Leak Unveiled *Korean Times.*

Lalonde, C.(2007). The Potential Contribution of the Field of Organizational Development to Crisis Management. *Journal of Contingencies and Crisis Management,* 15(2): 95–104. doi: 10.1111/j.1468–5973.2007.00508.x

Le Monde(2012, October 12). En Corée du Sud, un Drame Écologique Gêne le Pouvoir, *Le Monde.*

Lewis, G. B.(1991). Turnover and the Quiet Crisis in the Federal Civil Service. *Public*

Administration Review, 51(2): 145–155. doi: 10.2307/977108

Lindell, M. K., & Perry, R. W.(1992). *Behavioural Foundations of Community Emergency Planning*. Washington, D.C.: Hemisphere Publishing.

Lindell, M. K., Prater, C. S., & Perry, R. W.(2006). *Introduction to Emergency Management*. New York: Wiley.

Local Emergency and Safety Operations Headquarter(2012, November 12). Daily Report: the Gumi Chemical Spill (November 12), *The City Government of Gumi*.

______(2012, October 4). Daily Report: the Gumi Chemical Spill (October 4): *The City Government of Gumi*.

______(2012, October 7). Daily report: the Gumi Chemical Spill (October 7), *The City Government of Gumi*.

______(2012, October 12). Daily Report: the Gumi Chemical Spill (October 12), *The City Government of Gumi*.

Lutz, L. D., & Lindell, M. K.(2008). Incident Command System as a Response Model Within Emergency Operation Centers during Hurricane Rita. *Journal of Contingencies and Crisis Management*, 16(3): 122–134. doi: 10.1111/j.1468–5973.2008.00541.x

McEntire, D.(Ed.)(2007). *Disciplines, Disasters, and Emergency Management: the Convergence and Divergence of Concepts, Issues and Trends from the Research Literature*. Emmetsburg, MD: Federal Emergency Management Agency, Emergency Management Institute.

Ministry of Public Administration and Safety(2010). *Public Adninistration and Safety White Book*. Seoul, South Korea: Ministry of Public Administration and Safety.

National Diet of Japan(2012). *The Official Report of the Fukyshima Nuclear Accident Independent Investigation Commission*. Tokyo: National Diet of Japan.

National Emergency Management Agency(2011). *Chronological List of Disasters*. Seoul, South Korea: National Emergency Management Agency.

______(2012, October 10). Press Release: Resonses to the Gumi Chemical Spill Using Water. *National Emergency Management Agency*.

National Institute of Environmental Research(2012). *What is the Hydrogen Fluoride?* Seoul: National Institute of Environmental Research.

Neal, D. M., & Phillips, B. D.(1994). Effective Emergency Management: Reconsidering the Bureaucratic Approach. *Disasters*, 19(4): 327–337.

Newsis(2012, October 12). Comments from Vladimir Sakharov in the UNDP, *Newsis*.

______(2012, October 16). Criticism of National Assembly's Envrionment and Labor Committee, *Newsis*.

Ostrom, E.(1998). A Behavioral Approach to the Rational Choice Theory of Collective Action: Presidential Address, American Political Science Association, 1997. *The American Political Science Review*, 92(1): 1–22.

Pearson, C. M., & Clair, J. A.(1998). Reframing Crisis Management. *The Academy of*

Management Review, 23(1): 59－76. doi: 10.2307/259099

Perry, R. W., & Lindell, M. K.(1997). Principles for Managing Community Relocation as a Hazard Mitigation Measure. *Journal of Contingencies and Crisis Management*, 5(1): 49－59. doi: 10.1111/1468－5973.00036

Quarantelli, E. L.(1988). DISASTER CRISIS MANAGEMENT: A SUMMARY OF RESEARCH FINDINGS. *Journal of Management Studies*, 25(4): 373－385. doi: 10.1111/j.1467－6486.1988.tb00043.x

Quarantelli, E. L., & Dynes, R. R.(1977). Response to Social Crisis and Disaster. *Annual Review of Sociology*, 3(Article Type: Research－Article/Full Publication Date: 1977/ Copyright © 1977 Annual Reviews): 23－49. doi: 10.2307/2945929

Raw Story(2012, October 5). South Korea Probes Toxic Leak as Impact Worsens, *The Raw story*.

Schneider, S. K.(1992). Governmental Response to Disasters: The Conflict between Bureaucratic Procedures and Emergent Norms. *Public Administration Review*, 52(2): 135－145. doi: 10.2307/976467

Scholz, J. T., & Stiftel, B.(Eds.)(2005). *Adaptive Governance and Water Conflict*. Washington D.C.: Resources for the Future.

Segye(2012, October 19). Reexamination of 22 Crisis Management Standard Manuals, *Segye*.

Seoul Broadcasting System(2012, September 28). Limited Protective Action in the Gumi Chemicall Spill, *Seoul Broadcasting System*.

Sheoin, T.(2009). Wating for Another Bhopal. *Global Social Policy*, 9(3): 408－433.

Sisanews(2012, October 17). The Big Fault of Daegu Regional Environment Agency and the Ministry of Environment, *Sisanews*.

The U.S. National Institute for Occupatonal Safety and Health(2012, November 16). *Recommendations for the Prevention of Work－Related Injury and Illness*: The U.S. National Institute for Occupatonal Safety and Health.

Vihalemm, T., Kiisel, M., & Harro－Loit, H.(2012). Citizens' Response Patterns to Warning Messages. *Journal of Contingencies and Crisis Management*, 20(1): 13－25. doi: 10.1111/j.1468－5973.2011.00655.x

Waugh, W. L.(2006). Public Administration, Emergency Management, and Disaster Policy. In D. McEntire (Ed.), *Disciplines, Disasters, and Emergency Management: the Convergence and Divergence of Concepts, Issues and Trends from the Research Literature*, 604: 10－25. Emmetsburg, MD: Federal Emergency Management Agency, Emergency Management Institute.

Waugh, W. L., & Streib, G.(2006). Collaboration and Leadership for Effective Emergency Management. *Public Administration Review*, 66: 131－140. doi: 10.1111/j.1540－6210.2006.00673.x

Webb, G.(2004). Role Improvising During Crisis Situations. *International Journal of Emergency Management*, 2(1): 47－61.

Yardley, J.(2005, November 26). Spill in China Brings Danger, and Cover–Up, *New York Times.*

Yonhap News Agency(2012a, October 16). Environmental Agency Broke the Manual for Crisis Response, *Yonhap News Agency.*

______(2012b, October 4). Gov't Scurries to Contain Damage from Massive Gas Leak in Gumi, *Yonhap News Agency.*

______(2012, Novemebr 13). The Dispute Between Victims and Local Government Extended Over a Long Period, *Yonhap News Agency.*

______(2012, October 8). Serious Post Traumatic Stress Disorder of Fire Fighters, *Yonhap News Agency.*

______(2012, October 13). Distrust of Victims on the Inspection of the Gumi Chemical Spill, *Yonhap News Agency.*

______(2012, October 26). Over 12,243 Residents Affected by the Gumi Chemical Spill, *Yonhap News Agency.*

Teaching Note

Critical Assessment of the 2012 Gumi Chemical Spill: An Adaptive Governance Approach

Case Description

This case study follows the 2012 Gumi chemical spill, consequences for key stakeholders affiliated with public agencies, nonprofits, media, and affected communities. On September 27, 2012, a toxic chemical leak released hydrofluoric acid at Gumi's National Industrial Complex, located 124 miles southeast of Seoul, Korea. The accident occurred when two Hube Globe Chemical Corporation workers working on a tanker attempted to unload hydrofluoric acid into a storage tank. About 8 tons of hydrofluoric acid escaped into the atmosphere and spread across a 4-km radius, killing 5 workers, affecting 12,243 residents, and damaging 212 hectares of agricultural land and 3,944 individual animals that were injured or killed. By 22 October 2012, about 11,083 people had received treatment for nausea, chest pain, rashes, or sore eyes after inhaling fumes from the chemical leak. More than 300 residents including elderly people were evacuated to public-run facilities in Bongsan-ri, Incheon-ri, and Baekhyeon-ri.

Adaptive governance, as a tool for critical assessment of the 2012 Gumi chemical spill, is an emergent framework for the management of complex environmental crises derived from new or unanticipated situations. Designing the crisis management system as adaptive governance is based on self-organized communities to overcome the tragedy of the commons and on a consensus about deliberative mechanisms to mitigate the costs. The critical requirement of adaptive governance is the change from centralized decision making and technical rationality" to "decentralized decision making and procedural rationality.

Teaching Objectives

This case illustrates the complexity of crisis management and the challenges to coping with an unexpected event. The case itself and the analytic framework to identify key stakeholders can be utilized in undergraduate or graduate public management and organizational behavior courses. A technological disaster such as chemical spills and explosions in industrial zones is an appropriate example of crisis management as well as adaptive governance. That is, because such an event is embedded in social settings and environments such as industrial areas, it exacerbates the consequences and mess in crisis management. This case study raises key questions about how crisis management mattered in responding to the 2012 Gumi chemical spill, how the decisions made in crisis management impacted collaborations and overall response, and what challenges were discovered. This case study can also be used to facilitate discussions of the following topics: (1) crisis management in natural and technological disasters; (2) the adaptive governance approach to an unanticipated event; and (3) change from centralized technical rationality to decentralized procedural rationality.

Teaching Strategies

This teaching note includes "crisis management" as a conceptual background and "adaptive governance approach" as an analytic tool, which helps an instructor guide students' group discussion of the case. The instructor first presents a conceptual basis to define a crisis and the roles of various stakeholders in coping with an unanticipated event. Then, the instructor takes an adaptive governance approach that is an analytic tool to identify multiple stakeholders in the deliberative mechanisms that respond to an unexpected situation. Since crisis response manuals in general and response activities in the chemical spill specifically might not fully present an opportunity for responders to be adaptive to consequences of the event, the instructor should facilitate students to find both challenges and opportunities thorough the adaptive governance approach for (1) responsiveness, (2) public and scientific learning, and (3) the deliberation process. For instance, an instructor is able to assign one role among key stakeholders — for example, the Korean Ministry of Environment as the principal agency, the City government of Gumi as the crisis response coordinator, Gumi Fire and Police Station as first responders, and so forth — to each group. In their discussion, students in each group should identify each body's original role in crisis management before and after the chemical spill, and thus they can understand different roles in crisis management based on interorganizational collaboration for timely resource coordination.

Crisis Management: Finding the role of public organizations

The response to the chemical spill as a result of an industrial accident is defined here as an organizational crisis in which government agencies must respond to an incident that has a low probability of occurrence, but very large consequences on the economic viability of the affected community. In other words, the crisis is a high-impact event characterized by ambiguity of cause, effect, and means of resolution, as well as by a belief that decisions must be made swiftly. While public organizations generally play an important role in crisis and emergency management, they are relatively slow to improve their management systems. Nevertheless, there is a natural affinity between public organizations and crisis management. First, public organizations should plan, organize, manage, lead, coordinate, and evaluate crisis management. That is, all response activities are based on internal and external resources of public organization. Second, emergency management by a public organization may be in service of publicly mandated societal goals, mainly focusing on preparing for, responding to, and recovering from damage from disasters. Third, crisis management needs an understanding of social and political contexts, decision making, communication, leadership, analytical skills, budgeting, and human resource management.

However, public organizations may exacerbate a crisis when they as principal agents fail to identify that the principles of crisis management are different from the principles of disaster preparedness planning. In particular, public organizations within the crisis management system that only consider the possibility of natural disasters, which mostly follow a consistent sequence of crises at identifiable levels, cannot adequately respond to technological disasters, which impose disastrous consequences on human community as new types of conflict or challenge. It is also argued that the plans are often unfeasible because they are mostly symbolic or hypothetical rather than practicable, public organizations often fail to respond to unanticipated severe crises. This implies that public organizations that play an important role in crisis management should critically deal with the discordance between crisis preparedness plans and the nature of technological disasters.

This case study of the chemical spill in Gumi, South Korea, allowed us to rethink the failures of the command-control system as well as the need for the emergency response framework for effective crisis management. The chemical spill, which crippled the city of Gumi, contributes to the crisis management literature by demonstrating that the hierarchical traditional disaster response system adopted in South Korea, although successful in responding to natural disasters, was not as effective in responding to the chemical incident. The chemical spill was the first of its kind and, in the South Korean context, it was uncertain as to when the national government would take charge of the affected area and provide assistance to disaster victims. The national government was criticized for its poor response, particularly its failure to provide a timely warning to the populace about the chemical spill. The local government was criticized for failing to take precautionary actions and evacuate residents living in close proximity to the affected area. Public service announcements to warn citizens on what protective actions to take were extremely limited, causing confusion and mistrust in the first week. The key findings are summarized in Table 7-2.

Moreover, during the early stages of emergency response, there was a lack of inter-agency communication reflecting a highly fragmented and hierarchical governance structure. The crisis was unexpected and small in scale in comparison to other industrial disasters, but it nevertheless threatened lives, livelihoods, and the economic viability of the region for years to come. Failures in interagency communication, dissemination of public information, and risk communication as well as uncertainty related to the consequences of the incident affected crisis management. Inconsistent information related to the

Table 7-2. Emergency Response Functions, Principal Agency and Key Findings

Element		Principal Agency	Findings
Emergency Assessment			
	Threat detection and emergency classification	MOE, DREA	Delayed detection and inaccurate classification
	Hazard & environmental monitoring	MOE, DREA	Continuous monitoring, but inadequate
	Population monitoring and assessment	LESOH	N/A
	Damage assessment	LESOH	N/A
Hazard Operations			
	Hazard source control	LFS	High reliance on the manual and careless applications
	Building construction practices	LFS, LESOH	N/A
Population Protection			
	Population warning	LESOH	Delayed warning and inadequate hazard information
	Protective action selection and implement	LESOH	Delayed selection and a fail to implement
	Impact zone access control and security	LPS	Immediate treatment
	Hazard exposure control	MOE, DREA	Careless expose control
	Emergency medical care	LFS, LESOH	Relatively adequate initial care, but limited to the incident site
Incident Management			
	Agency notification and mobilization	LFS, LESOH	Inadequate information flow
	Mobilization of emergency facilities/equipment	LESOH	Segmented facilities
	Communication/ documentation	LESOH	Absence of the role for communication and documentation
	Analysis/planning	MOE, LESOH	Separated analysis/plan
	Internal direction and control	LESOH	Inadequate authority of the principal EOC

Source: Adopted to Lindell & Perry (1992; 1996).
Note: MOE (Ministry of Environment); DREA (Daegu Regional Environment Agency); LESOH (Local Emergency Safety Operations Headquarter); LFS (Local Fire Station); LPS (Local Police Station).

cause of the accident and bringing residents back to the affected area even though it was still contaminated caused the national government to receive a lot of bad press. There were reports that firefighters, who were unaware of the composition of the chemical, failed to use calcium hydroxide, the neutralizing agent for hydrofluoric acid delaying the response and recovery efforts.

Adaptive Governance Approach: Identifying challenges and opportunities

Adaptive governance is an emergent framework for the management of complicated issues derived from new or unanticipated situations. The design of the crisis management system as adaptive governance is based on the ability of self-organized communities to overcome the tragedy of the commons and on a consensus about deliberative mechanisms to mitigate the costs of collective actions. The critical requirement of adaptive governance is the change from centralized decision making and technical rationality to decentralized decision making and procedural rationality. The case study of the chemical spill in Gumi, South Korea, assesses the crisis management system in response to the leak in light of the challenges that national and local governments must resolve and suggests implications for equipping the crisis management system through deliberative mechanisms based on multiple stakeholders' consensus to be adaptive and resilient to unanticipated emergencies.

Responsiveness is considered a traditional approach to organizational structure, highlighting the notion that principal agencies such as the Ministry of Environment and the Ministry of Public Safety and Security perform coordinated responses. However, organizational structures in principal agencies might impose tremendous burdens on local governments if an unexpected event exceeds their response capacities without additional resource coordination. It is important that local governments adopt strategies to reinforce the effectiveness of the crisis management system. The National Assembly's Environment and Labor Committee criticized the poor response of national agencies and the city government of Gumi. That is, the chain of information flow from the 119 local emergency center to other organizations such as national, regional, and local agencies and local government was not accurately designated or coordinated by the crisis management system.

Public and Scientific Learning, or the ability to respond to an unanticipated event as a cohesive organizational structure, also dependson the cognitive capacity of individual emergency managers to process similar and overlapping representations of situational circumstances. Since crisis responses involve a constant state of fluctuation, limited capacity to process risk information cannot be determined at any point in time. Poorly articulated training materials affect the operational representation of individual perceptions and the understanding of task completion. Adaptive mechanisms to enhance public and scientific learning processes through crisis management manuals may be necessary but not sufficient for practical reasons. In order to minimize disconnection and confusion about the chemical spill, training in emergency management principles such as full-scale exercises should also be available for responders, as practiced at the provincial and local level. Hence, facilitating learning processes and local training should be emphasized and conducted by the regional and local agencies.

Learning from the Crisis: Public and Policy Responses requires a combination of expertise, representation, and commitment of those who are not yet an established part of the crisis response process. It depends on the level of stakeholders' involvement in the response processes, and disaster response manuals are directly influenced by the decisions of specialized authorities. Although public agencies' function and authority to respond to natural disaster is clearly specified in national statutes, the need to respond to a disaster caused by a large-scale industrial accident is not obvious or foreseen by local government agencies. The hierarchical structure as centralized decision making works well in a highly fragmented administrative system during a large-scale disaster, but it has not been as effective in a poorly defined emergency situation. For example, local agencies must await directives from the provincial and national governments. In the case of the Gumi disaster, it was unclear as to why it took the national government close to two weeks to respond to the crisis. From the citizen perspective, the cause of the chemical leak, corporate responsibility, and the government's slow response require explanation and public scrutiny.

Suggested Discussion Questions

The following questions can be used to facilitate students' group discussion of the case:

1. What are the differences between an accident and a crisis? Define the terms crisis and crisis management and note their relation to hazards and vulnerability.
2. What are the roles of public, private, and nonprofit sectors in crisis management? Define the responsibility of each sector in crisis management and note the needs for interorganizational collaboration (e.g., limited resources and dysfunctional information flow).
3. What steps must be taken by principal agencies as a control tower and first responders in the field in order to effectively respond to hazardous materials incidents such as the chemical spill and explosion?
4. What kind of challenges did each of key stakeholders have after the chemical spill? Corresponding to these challenges, what are the lessons and/or opportunities for first responders and principal agencies?
5. What resources are needed to enhance adaptive governance mechanisms such as responsiveness, public and scientific learning, and the deliberation process in the case of natural and/or technological disasters?

Potential Assignments

1. Select a disaster of your choice (e.g., typhoons, floods, wildfires, hazardous material spill, explosion, etc.). Create a timeline of crisis management focusing on response activities and identify the role of principal agencies and local first responders engaged in crisis responses.
2. You are an emergency manager who is in charge of crisis response coordination in a local government. A serious chemical spill is affecting your community, and many elderly citizens may be severely impacted. The principal agencies at the national and provincial levels are providing contradictory advice about the need to evacuate from a site and/or stay inside. Should you do anything about this? How can you secure timely information and rapid resource mobilization?

08
Chapter

Public Health Crisis in South Korea: Policy Failure or Social Distrust?

Dohyeong Kim

Introduction

There is a growing threat from emerging infectious diseases in South Korea, such as the recent outbreak of Middle East Respiratory Syndrome coronavirus (MERS−Cov or MERS) in 2015 which infected a total of 186 people and killed 36. Nevertheless, there has been little discussion on the fundamental questions as to what underlies public health crises and what needs to be restructured and reconsidered for more rapid and effective responses to future pandemics in South Korea. This case study provides a comprehensive review of all the relevant documents on the recent outbreaks of infectious diseases in South Korea such as SARS (Severe Acute Respiratory Syndrome) in 2003, H1N1 (also called swine flu) in 2009, and MERS in 2015, specifically highlighting three concerns raised during and after the crisis: government system failure, poor communication and social distrust.

Preventing outbreaks of emerging and unprecedented infectious diseases is difficult and becoming even more complicated considering the increase in the number of international travelers. However, keeping an outbreak under good control is possible depending on how effectively the responsible agency of the government responds to the initial incidents and communicates and collaborates with all stakeholders and the general public. South Korea's lessons from major outbreaks since 2000 have sparked debate on the following questions: What made the outbreak an embarrassing and conspicuous sign of incapability to control disease? Did the policymakers who were in charge make informed and timely decisions and react ideally to all outstanding problems? If not, was it due to policy failure, poor communication, social distrust, or a combination of all three? This case document overviews the background data and information on the recent outbreaks of infectious diseases in South Korea and then discusses various issues and concerns involved in these incidents.

Background

SARS in 2003

Severe Acute Respiratory Syndrome (SARS) is a viral respiratory infectious disease that was a serious global health concern throughout Asia in 2003. Since the first case of SARS was found in the Guangdong province of China, the disease spread rapidly to individuals in 37 countries around the world (Smith, 2006). During the pandemic period, China had 5,328 cases and Hong Kong had 1,755 cases, and their fatalities were 6.6% and 17% respectively (World Health Organization, 2009). Moreover, in Singapore and the Philippines, SARS fatality was as high as 14% (World Health Organization, 2009). In contrast to other Asian countries, South Korea had only three infected persons and no deaths, mainly because sufficient time and information were given to prepare an effective quarantine system that prevented the spread of the outbreak within the country (Gal & Jun, 2015). The Korean government's reaction to SARS was evaluated as a successful response by the World Health Organization.

In response to the SARS outbreak, a national surveillance system in South Korea was launched on March 16, 2003. The system reported the clinical, laboratory, and radiologic features of 3 probable cases of SARS diagnosed between April 22 and May 12, 2003. The first case was a 41-year-old man who was diagnosed as a probable case of SARS because he had fever, cough, travel history to China, and radiologic finding of pneumonic infiltration. The second was an 81-year-old American who came from the Philippines and was going to America via South Korea. He also had fever, cough, and radiologic finding of pneumonic infiltration. The third was a 28-year-old man who reported fever, cough, travel history to Taiwan, and pneumonic infiltration on chest X-ray. Their symptoms improved in 5~7 days after symptomatic treatment and the antibody test was negative in all patients (Lim et al., 2004).

The Korean government's responses against SARS during the outbreak were focused mostly on: (1) recognizing all the cases from other countries and the World Health Organization (WHO) recommendations, (2) issuing the national warning on March 16, 2003, (3) monitoring all the people (about 890,775) who came from SARS epidemic countries, and (4) conducting follow-up monitoring on them 5~10 days after immigration. Moreover, the government tracked down 226,774 people who had fever or any respiratory symptoms. Among them, three probable cases and 17 suspect cases were revealed and further investigated. However, no secondary infection or domestic occurrence was reported in South Korea (Lim et al., 2004).

H1N1 in 2009

In late March of 2009, an outbreak of influenza was detected in Mexico, which was eventually identified as H1N1 influenza A. In June 2009, the World Health Organization (WHO) raised its pandemic alert to the highest level and more than 214 countries reported confirmed cases of pandemic H1N1 influenza (World Health Organization, 2009). When the infection by H1N1 was associated with pneumonia, admission to an intensive care unit was necessary in 36.1% of all individuals and 10.4% required mechanical ventilation. Despite the administration of antiviral and antibacterial agents, the mortality rate of H1N1-assocated pneumonia was 7.2% (Choi et al., 2011).

In South Korea, the first case of H1N1 infection was found on May 2, 2009. Between May and August in 2009, about 750,000 cases of H1N1 were confirmed by laboratory tests. Influenza activity peaked in November 2009 but declined rapidly to below baseline levels in February 2010. According to the official report on the 2009 pandemic H1N1 in South Korea, 252 deaths were associated with the disease and its case-fatality rate was reported as 0.03% (Kim, 2016).

Following the WHO recommendations, the Korean government developed a plan for pandemic influenza preparedness and response in 2006. The Team of Training for Public Health Crisis was initially set up as one part of the Division of Epidemic Intelligence Service within the Korean Center for Disease Control and Prevention (KCDC). The main responsibility of the team was to prepare for a tabletop exercise for pandemic influenza in South Korea to simulate the casualties using a mathematical model, for the purpose of identifying the required medical resources (Chu, Lee, Choi, Youn, & Lee, 2011). In 2007, the team was separated from the division and became an independent division of KCDC. The division was requested to enhance the country's preparedness to secure medical resources, to provide manuals, and to train public health personnel in case of an emerging infectious disease causing public health crises. The division played a significant role in handling the H1N1 outbreak in 2009 and revised the pandemic influenza preparedness and response plan based on the experience. The revised version of the plan contains sections on international cooperation and newly adapted environments in South Korea (Lee, Oh, Park, Chu, & Son, 2013). Specifically, the government released a travel warning against visiting Mexico City and three other Mexican states, improved the level of quarantine and safety checks on travelers arriving from the United States and Mexico, and increased the scrutiny of inspection standards for imported pork from these countries. An emergency quarantine system in border areas was also in place, with a simple test of people with flu symptom at airports and ports (China, 2009; Suh et al., 2013).

MERS in 2015

The first case of MERS was reported in Saudi Arabia in 2012. Until May 2013, MERS had frequently been referred to as a SARS-like virus, but it is distinct from SARS or the common-cold coronavirus. Despite the 2014 outbreak in Saudi Arabia, only sporadic travel-associated importations occurred in countries outside the Middle East before the 2015 pandemic outbreak. Most global health experts gauged that MERS was a low risk for causing an epidemic and considered it unlikely to propagate enough to cause a massive outbreak (Suh et al., 2013).

However, a massive outbreak occurred in South Korea from May to July 2015, with the second greatest number of cases in the world after Saudi Arabia. In May 2015, a 68-year-old Korean man who returned from travel in the Middle East was diagnosed with MERS nine days after he initially sought medical attention. In contrast to the initial hope and underestimated risk by the government, it was expanded to a large-scale outbreak which ended up infecting a total of 186 people and killing 36 (case fatality rate 19%). Out of the confirmed cases, 111 were male and 75 were female, and most of them were in their 50s and 60s. 15.1% of the confirmed cases were first-generation cases infected by the index case, 67.2% were second generation cases, and 17.2% were third generation cases (Lim, 2015). 44% of the confirmed cases were admitted or treated in the same hospital with a confirmed case, 38% were family members, health care aides, or visitors, and 17% were medical staff (Ki, 2015). The government officially declared the end of the outbreak on December 23, 2015 (Kim et al., 2016), about six months after its onset. The outbreak had a severe negative impact on South Korea's economy, particularly due to over 100,000 cancelled foreigner visits and decreased exports. During the outbreak, many schools and businesses were temporarily shut down and almost all planned events and activities were cancelled.

After announcing the end of MERS, the government started to take follow-up measures and make plans not only for preparedness for infectious diseases but also for victims of MERS. For example, the government made a plan to increase the number of experts in the KCDC, to enhance quarantine and surveillance in airports (Kim et al., 2016) and to compensate medical institutions that suffered damages from the MERS outbreak in the amount of about 100 billion won (USD 84 million) (Lee, 2015). Moreover, as one of the plans for economic restoration, the government gave foreign travelers automatic MERS insurance plans that covered five million Korean won (USD 4,530) in healthcare compensation for foreign visitors if they were diagnosed with MERS within 20 days of entry and 100 million Korean won (USD 90,660) for any death from MERS (Lee, 2015).

Three Critical Issues

A review of background on three major outbreaks of infectious diseases in South Korea reveals several critical issues which could be debated further to understand fundamental problems underlying the public health crises, specifically government system failure, poor communication and social distrust. Most of the literature, including the media reports and journal articles, reported those three issues as keys to explain various social phenomena observed during the outbreaks in South Korea. Despite considerable efforts at prevention by the Korean government such as setting new regulations, raising budgets and re-structuring organizations, a substantial level of concern still exists among Koreans in terms of governmental and social preparedness for upcoming public health crises. An in-depth discussion and debate on these issues would help obtain a clear and broad picture of the problems and provide a valuable contribution to public health policy in South Korea. Each of the issues is discussed below based on the available literature, focusing on the recent MERS outbreak for which relatively more information has been reported.

Governmental System Failure

The Korean government's response to the SARS outbreak in 2013 was evaluated positively as proactive preparedness since the national emergency alert system was strictly enforced in accordance with the manual. Since the emergency alert system against SARS was issued on March 16, 2003, all travelers who entered South Korea through airports or ports were quarantined until the alert system ended on July 7. The Korean government assigned 70 soldiers from the Korean Army Medical Corp to the quarantine system and allocated an additional 10 heat monitoring sensors at airports to check all travelers. In addition, 242 local health centers took charge of tracking about 230,000 people who were travelling to and from the SARS-endemic countries. During the alert period, a total of about 620,000 people were quarantined, and around 2,200 people were isolated because they had contacted with SARS patients. Approximately 3,300 consultation calls were made through the emergency number 133. For all these proactive preparedness activities, the Korean government spent KRW 6.6 billion, valued as much as USD 5.51 million (People's Daily Online, 2003). As a result, only three SARS cases were finally confirmed in South Korea. The WHO complimented these efforts as the best proactive response and prevention against SARS (Ji, 2015).

In contrast to SARS, the Korean government's disease response system functioned in response to MERS relatively poorly due to the failure to prepare and use an adequate manual for MERS, which turned out to have different transmission patterns than SARS. As aforementioned, the first MERS case was imported to South Korea by a person who returned from a business trip to the Middle East area. When he had the symptoms of cough and fever, he visited a small clinic in his hometown of Asan, south of Seoul. He was initially diagnosed with simple flu or pneumonia in the clinic, but his case was finally confirmed as MERS nine days after he visited the hospital. An international Chinese newspaper, *Xinhuanet*, argued that the initial response to MERS in South Korea was to be blamed by citing the comment of a Korean infectious disease specialist at the Korea Medical Institute that "the biggest reason for MERS is that the patient zero was diagnosed too belatedly" (Yoo, 2015). One reason for their belated response was pointed out to be the absence of a manual guiding health professionals on how to handle a case of unprecedented infectious diseases such as MERS (Kim, 2015). If the doctor in the small clinic in Asan had had prior knowledge of MERS or had been able to refer to a relevant manual, the patient zero would have been immediately transferred to a larger hospital which is more experienced and capable of treating such patients. Another criticism was the lack of knowledge of the different transmission patterns between SARS and MERS because the responsive actions based on the manual prepared for SARS were not as effective or made the situation even worse. In fact, most specialists in the public health field argued that the government should be aware of recent pandemics in other countries and have a plan for preparedness and response against all outstanding diseases (Dennis et al., 2001; Osterholm, 2005; World Health Organization, 2009). Interestingly, one news article revealed that the Korean government had an internal report which highlighted the possibility of the disease in the country in 2012 but failed to prepare and provide an adequate manual to health facilities (Hong, 2015).

Another pervasive criticism of the government's failure to handle emergency incidents was around the absence of a "control tower" that should play a leading and responsible role during the response period. During the MERS crisis, it was argued that at least two control towers needed to be set up for national disease control, including an executive control tower for executing preventive measures against viral diseases and another for supporting the executive control tower. However, no effective control tower was in place in South Korea during the epidemic, particularly for the first few weeks of the outbreak — the "golden time," or most vital moment for disease control (Chung, 2015; Kim, 2015; McGrath, 2015). Some argued that either the Minister of

Health and Welfare or the head of the KCDC should take full responsibility (Seungki, 2015). When a country has a mass outbreak of infectious disease, a high level of confusion and conflict tend to be prevalent in society and even within governments. In this context, the "control tower" could play a critical role in clarifying confusion and coordinating conflict in the process of handling the crisis. Lee (2015) suggested an elastic collaboration system centered by a control tower for the Korean government. In this system, a control tower should keep a balance between rigidity and flexibility and coordinate actors from multiple public and private organizations. During the government intervention period for MERS in South Korea, however, a substantial level of confusion and conflict arose among actors because of the lack of such an elastic collaboration system.

Some argued that inadequate preparation or use of the manuals and the absence of a control tower occurred in the process of reorganizing an administration system. When a new regime begins, the governmental structure is typically reorganized in various degrees. For instance, in the reorganization process of the Lee Myung-bak administration in 2008, about 2,600 disaster management manuals created by the previous presidency (the Roh administration) were removed. In addition, the main responsibility for disaster management was delegated from the Blue House to 2,622 government ministries and agents. The National Security Council in the Blue House had played a role as a control tower before it was abolished in the process of government reorganization in 2008. This administrative reorganization made the government fail to set up an effective control tower which should be in full charge of handling disease outbreaks (McGrath 2015; Yoo, 2015).

The government's system failure was also rooted in its suboptimal organizational structure and capacity, particularly when it hindered a responsible agent from being responsive to an unprecedented disease outbreak. Although the KCDC, the main agency responsible for preventing and controlling infectious disease epidemics in South Korea, was developed by benchmarking the U.S. Centers for Disease Control and Prevention (CDC), it was criticized for its inefficiency and incapability in comparison to CDC, particularly during the MERS crisis such as less flexibility in handling emergent situations and a smaller labor force (Kim et al., 2015). Comparing the two organizational charts of the upper level governmental units including the CDC (Figure 8-1) and

KCDC (Figure 8−2), it seems evident that the director of the KCDC had less power and authority than the CDC director. The CDC is under the direct supervision of the secretary of the U.S. Department of Health and Human Services, while some institutional hierarchy intervenes between the KCDC and the Minister of Health and Welfare in South Korea. Moreover, the CDC director is directly appointed by the U.S. President, while the KCDC director is appointed by the Minister of Health and Welfare. Such bureaucratic hiera-rchy could result in an inefficient and untimely response to emergency incidents

Figure 8–1. Organizational Chart of the U.S. Department of Health and Human Services

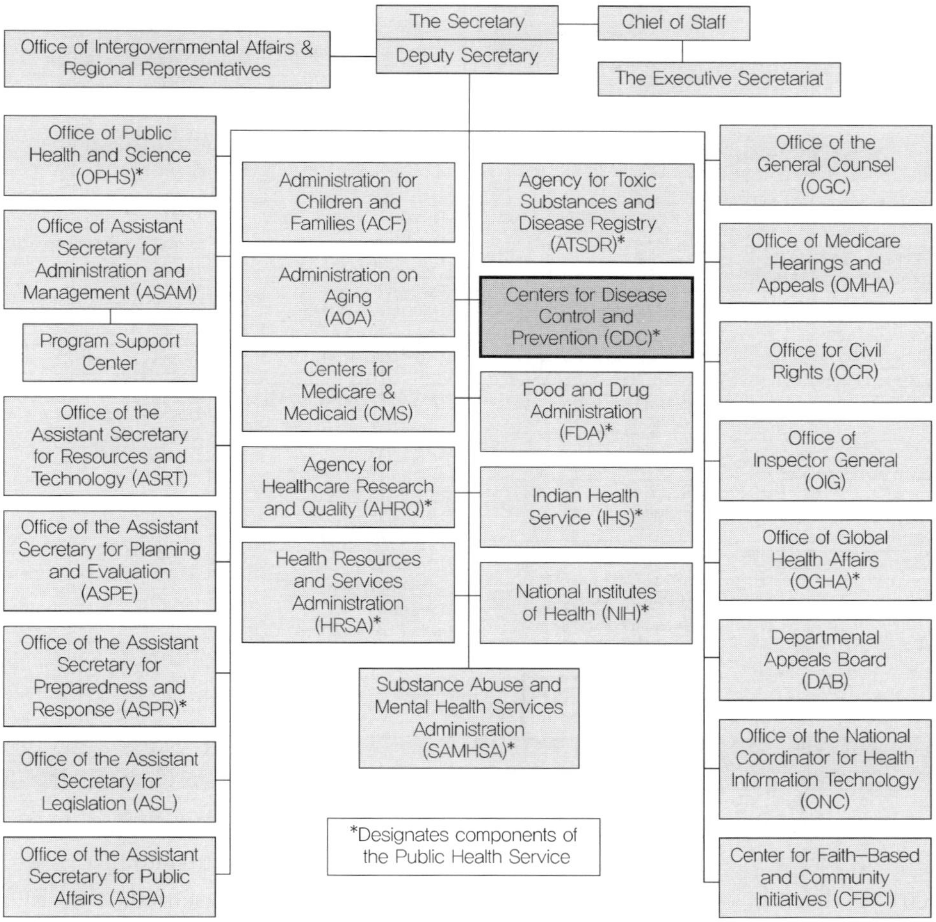

Source: http://www.netage.com/economics/gov/USHHS-chart-top.html

Figure 8–2. Organizational Chart of the Ministry of Health and Welfare in South Korea

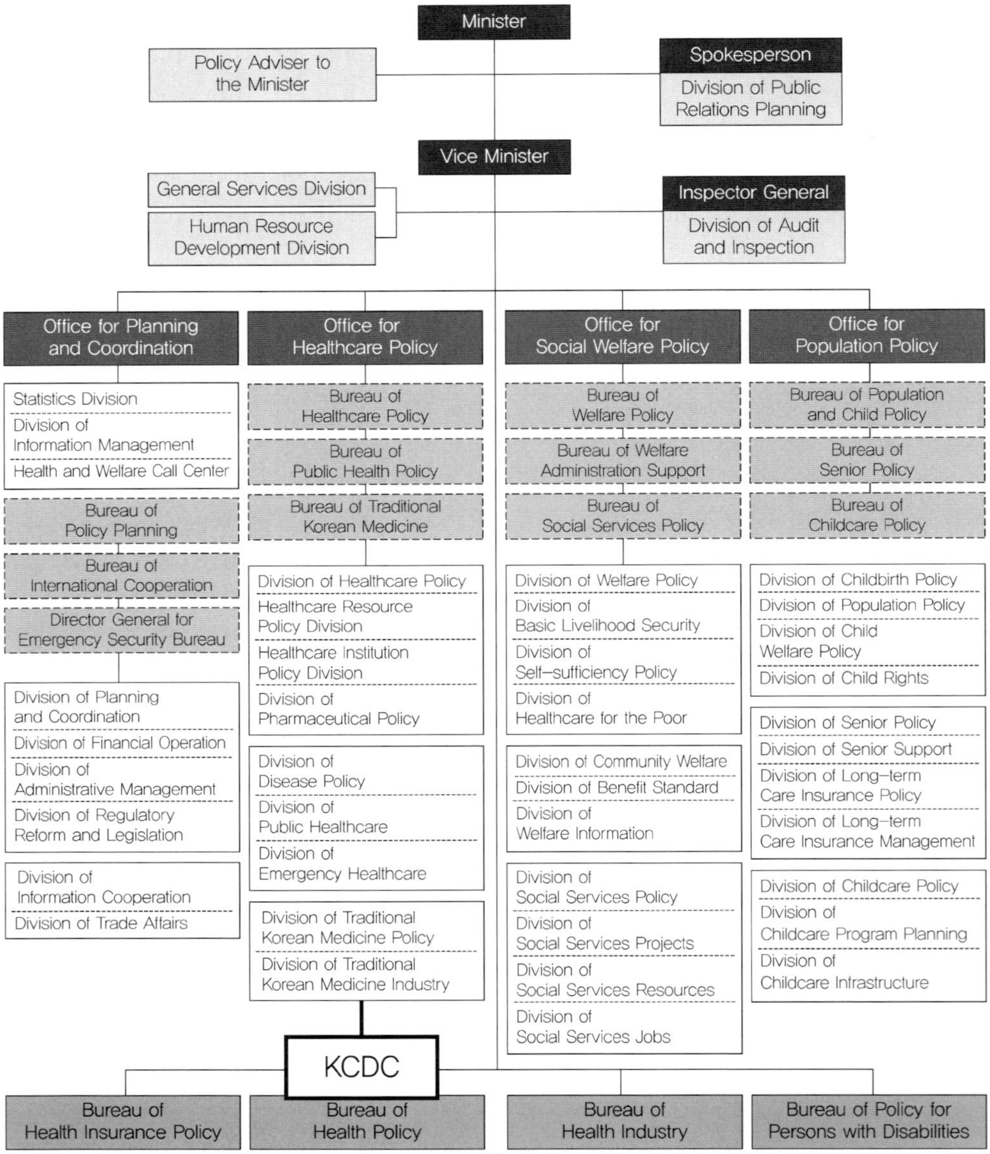

Source: http://www.mohw.go.kr/eng/sg/ssg0103mn.jsp?PAR_MENU_ID=1001&MENU_ID=100103

such as disease outbreak. In the MERS epidemic, for instance, the KCDC director had an excessive burden to report the progress of the outbreak not only to President Park but also to the Minister of Health and Welfare, which could hinder timely and effective decisions for handling the outbreak. A comparison of the organizational structures between KCDC and CDC could help understand the decision-making process during the outbreak between the two countries.

Moreover, the KCDC director did not have strong administrative authority for personnel and budget, and thus there were legal and practical constraints to hire more experts and workers during the MERS outbreak (Ryu, 2015). There was also a substantial difference in financial support from the government between these countries. While the CDC received USD 1.77 billion for Ebola preparedness and response after the Ebola outbreak in 2015,[1] the KCDC was granted only KRW 508 billion (USD 4.6 million) for MERS preparedness and response in 2016.[2] This comparison implies that the MERS crisis — which resulted in greater damage compared to SARS and H1N1 — stemmed from a governmental public health system failure in South Korea. All these comparisons between the KCDC and CDC are summarized in Table 8-1.

Table 8-1. Comparison between KCDC and CDC

	KCDC	CDC
Date of establishment	2004	1946
Upper echelon	Ministry of Health and Welfare	Department of Health and Human Services
Director's position and authority	Ministerial appointee (Chief Admin. C1 level) No budgetary & personnel rights[3]	Presidential appointee (Deputy Secretary level) Have budgetary & personnel rights
Budget (2014)	USD 510 million	USD 11.3 billion
Supplementary budgets after the Infectious Disease	USD 4.6 million	USD 1.77 billion
Workforce	425	15,000
International Office	2 (Geneva, Manila)	Around 50 countries

1) http://www.cdc.gov/budget/ebola/index.html

2) http://www.mers.go.kr/mers/html/jsp/Menu_I/mers03_12_04.jsp

3) The director of the KCDC is now a presidential appointee position with budget and personnel authority. After the MERS outbreak, the Korean government raised the position to a deputy secretary level. (from http://www.kpanews.co.kr/article/medipharm/show.asp?idx=166277&n_category=C)

In response to the expert advice on this concern pertaining to KCDC's limited resources, after the declaration of the end of MERS, the Korean government set aside a budget of KRW 78.6 billion (USD 70 million) for additional facilities for epidemic diseases such as negative pressure isolation rooms and quarantine facilities (Chung, 2015). However, the KCDC needs to be further expanded to include more experts and specialists who can serve as an advisory group on infectious disease and preventive medicine and a standing committee to assist policymakers at the control tower in making timely and appropriate decisions. In addition, the quality of regular staff and advisory personnel in the KCDC should be well maintained by strengthening their job security and offering consistent training opportunities. If discretionary authority is given to well-trained epidemiological experts, the response to an emergency incident is expected to be faster (Yoo, 2015).

On the contrary, despite severe criticism from most Korean media (including social media) during the MERS outbreak, in the press statement of a joint mission conducted by the WHO and the Ministry of Health and Welfare (MHW) in South Korea, the WHO evaluated that the South Korean government's efforts to prevent the spread of MERS, such as containment measures, contact tracing, monitoring, quarantine, and expanding laboratory testing, were relatively well completed (Harris & Clements-Hunt, 2015). The WHO said that the outbreak was not entirely due to by government's carelessness because MERS diagnosis is not easy and is particularly difficult in the early stage of an outbreak when awareness about it is low. WHO additionally argued that it is hard for a government to immediately recognize and suspect the first MERS case because early symptoms of MERS look like other influenza illnesses. Moreover, the patient, who later became the first case, did not report his travel history to the Middle East when he first sought treatment (Ahn, 2015).

Poor Communication

The WHO emphasized communication as one of the core capacities for successful implementation of plans that will avoid enormous damages from an outbreak (World Health Organization, 2005a). The five key points for outbreak communication highlighted by the WHO guidelines are: (1) building, maintaining or restoring trust; (2) announcing early; (3) being transparent; (4)

understanding the public; and (5) incorporating risk communication into preparedness planning (World Health Organization, 2005b). In addition, in the event of an outbreak, the role of risk communicators is to align the public's risk perception with the scientific view. They must have visibility and legitimacy of their messages, understand the political and social environments, and comprehend the specific cultural milieu (Fung, Tse, Chan, & Fu, 2015).

The Korean government was strongly criticized for its poor communication strategy because it did not immediately reveal the list of the hospitals where the confirmed patients of MERS were hospitalized. (Fung et al., 2015; Kim et al., 2016). The issue of revealing the list of hospitals in which the MERS patients were treated provided acute tension between the government and the public. During the couple of weeks while the government was hesitant to release the hospital list, a tremendous amount of wrong and unauthorized information, including a false list, was spread through the internet via social media. In fact, there was a controversy about whether or not the hospital information should be entirely open to the public. Proponents of releasing the list of hospitals in which patients were treated argued that it would help for people to track patients and result in fewer infections because of the public caution about the infection path. Opponents of releasing the information were concerned about the possibility of negative reputations for the hospital in the list and argued that it would result in a stigma (Fung et al., 2015). Others argued, however, that keeping the public away from the true information could aggravate rumors and fears, particularly if a high level of public distrust against the government's competence and honesty is prevalent. The government was very cautious in revealing the information of hospitals in order to avoid social panic.

Under public pressure, the government changed its policy and eventually publicized the list of hospitals in which MERS patients had been treated when the spread of false rumors about the hospitals was perceived to be out of control (Kim et al., 2016). On June 7, 2015, Deputy Economic Prime Minister and Minister of Strategy and Planning Choi Kyoung-hwan, who was acting as Prime Minister in South Korea, held an emergency press conference to announce the names of hospitals associated with MERS infections. This highlighted the lesson that the government's efforts at effective communication and collaboration would be critical even before the size of the infection becomes large.

The Korean government tried to provide information about MERS right after the confirmation of the first cases through press releases, regular press briefings, a 24-hour communication hotline, and the web portal site "MERS PORTAL" (www.mers.go.kr). However, according to the survey of public awareness about the government's risk communication concerning the MERS outbreak in South Korea, 53.9% of the respondents disagreed 10% strongly disagreed that the government appropriately communicated with the public. The white paper about MERS published in 2016 suggested several reasons behind the government's failure to communicate with the public (Kim et al., 2016). First of all, there was a shortage of public communication specialists in an emergency situation. For instance, only 5~6 staff members in the KCDC were in full charge of public communication. By comparison, the CDC has a special department and 500 communication specialists solely dedicated to communication in its Office of the Associate Director for Communication.

Another concern of poor communication in South Korea was related to the lack of accuracy and congruency among the information released by multiple governmental agencies. For example, the city government of Seoul criticized the MHW for not sharing information about the confirmed patients on June 4, 2014. The next day, MHW publicized that they would not release the information due to the confidentiality concern (Hu, 2015). Such tension and miscommunication between the central and local governments made people more confused and less trusting of public information and announcements from governmental sources. In addition, many criticisms were placed on insufficient communication and collaboration between public health facilities and private clinics/hospitals in response to the epidemic. It is argued that, during the MERS crisis, the level of public-private partnership along with effective communication was way below what was required by the official disaster management manuals (Kim, 2015). In the emergency situation, the collaborative optimal operation of all available health facilities, both public and private, under one command is critical in order to minimize the impact of the epidemic.

The H1N1 outbreak in 2009 had also revealed some problems of communication among the central and local governments, medical sectors, and the general public. During the outbreak, significant confusion and miscommunication occurred among medical staffs in the government-designated hospitals where the infected patients were treated regarding distribution of treatments and personal protection kits, availability of isolation rooms and guidelines for prescribing antiviral agents. The government's unprofessional way of communicating the core information with medical specialists and the public elevated the level of public distrust, which extended to even more serious communication issues, such as spreading unnecessary fear and anxiety among the general public. Excessive competition among the news media worsened the phenomenon. Since most people obtained information about H1N1 through media reports, over-reporting of the outcome and situation increased public anxiety and distrust toward the government (Kim, 2010).

Social Distrust

Both governmental system failure and poor communication have a negative impact on the level of social trust. Considering that one of the core missions of the government is to protect its people from enemies (Kettl, 2000) including not only physical entities but also invisible viruses, the government should take aggressive actions to fight against them. However, the mission cannot be completed without building a good level of social trust between the government and the general public (Tambo, Oljira, Oluwasogo, Khater, & Xiao-Nong, 2015). As discussed above, the Korean government did not seem to perform well in this context, including a belated disclosure of critical information and miscommunication among government organizations. For example, President Park Geun-hye was briefed on the incidence of MERS 6 days after the confirmation of the first case, and some senior officials and politicians were found to have been away from their offices or unaware of MERS for a while. Because of these inappropriate behaviors of senior public officials, the government was criticized by the public (Choe, 2015b). During this period, the public actually experienced social panic because the process of designating the hospitals was riddled with confusion and suspected falsehoods (Choi, 2015). In many respects, the government's decision to reveal information about the hospitals was forced by public opinion. This undetermined leadership raised social confusion and anxiety, which added to the already high level of social distrust.

Several impacts of social distrust occurred among Koreans while MERS was ongoing. It stimulated many internet users to create unconfirmed sources of information about MERS, mainly on social media such as Facebook, Twitter, and Kakaotalk, where people easily communicate and share information. In the situation that the government did not reveal the list of hospitals, people were afraid of infection, so they were more likely to rely on unauthorized and unidentified information sources and to spread such information to others (Hong & Jin, 2015). The entire society could then plunge into confusion, which caused political conflicts as well (Kim et al., 2016). Such political and administrative conflicts, such as inconsistent information between the central and local government, increased the level of social distrust and eventually evolved into social and political panic.

Social distrust within the society may cause "doctor shopping," which was also pointed out as the major source of the Korean version of the MERS outbreak. The WHO argued that the common practice of going from hospital to hospital seeking care helped spread MERS in South Korea. According to the joint advisory team of the WHO and MHW, the accessibility and affordability of health care in South Korea encouraged "doctor shopping," which reflects a social culture in which patients frequently consult specialists in several facilities before deciding on a first-choice facility (Ahn, 2015).

The level of social distrust toward the Korean government was directly measured by a telephone survey conducted in June 2015 during the MERS outbreak (Kim et al., 2016). The survey-based study found that while the level of risk-related perception of MERS was relatively low, the level of distrust toward the government was pretty high. This study insists that this high level of distrust brought about the low levels of compliance with a voluntary quarantine (Kim et al., 2016). Moreover, the people in South Korea believed that self-quarantine or voluntary quarantine program was ineffective to control the disease. Even worse, there was a public perception that any government-directed program increased the risk of MERS (Kim, 2015). A solid level of public trust toward the government during an emergency situation such as unexpected disease outbreak should increase the level of public compliance, and thus the government's programs for the purpose of preventing the spread of disease tend to achieve successful outcomes as intended (Wallerstein, 2006). As Kim et al. (2015) argued, if there had been strong social trust in South Korea, the Korean people would have been less afraid of MERS and would have more actively followed the government's policy directions for controlling the disease.

Social distrust can be caused not only by the government but also by the media. Some argued that the media can manufacture threats to the public health and the threats can evolve to historical and cultural myths of fear among people within a society. In this framework, the media may contribute to unwarranted public fear, intolerance, and distrust (Muzzatti, 2005). In the reality of MERS, after the official confirmation of the first patient, most of the news media used sensational headlines about MERS that exaggerated how dangerous and contagious it was. It seems evident that, although there is an opinion that South Korea did a great job during the spread of MERS (Butler, 2015), such irresponsible and uncontrolled messages from the media contributed to public fears of infection and as a result aggravated social distrust in Korean society that then resulted in social overreactions to the disease such as temporary shut-down of kindergartens and elementary schools in spite of minimal risk of community infection. A medical expert said that closing schools was medically wrong because most MERS patients were infected in health clinics (Choe, 2015a). It is known that social trust is one of important factors that could reduce the number of infected patients and prevent the severe spread of a disease (Rosenbrock, 1987). However, enhancing social trust takes a long time and needs society-wide collaborative efforts including the government, the media and the public.

Summary

In this case study document, we reviewed three major infectious diseases outbreaks in South Korea since 2000 (SARS, H1N1 and MERS) and discussed how the country addressed each of the epidemics, focusing on three sources of the public health crises: governmental system failure, poor communication and social distrust. The discussion on these issues provided by this document, along with relevant materials, facilitates a constructive debate which can provide a valuable contribution to the design of informed public health policy in South Korea.

Table 8-2 shows a summary of the comparisons among the three outbreaks discussed so far. Although a direct comparison among them is limited considering their intrinsic distinctions such as pathologic and epidemiologic characteristics, a comparative review of these experiences would facilitate a constructive discussion among policymakers, stakeholders and the public to improve the government's disease control and prevention system, facilitate an open and unbiased communication process and decrease the level of social distrust in South Korea. This case study can provide guidance for debates among policymakers, stakeholders, scholars and students pertaining to the issues, which can then generate wisdom for the Korean government and society on how to avoid repeating the same mistakes and challenges from the past epidemics when the next public health crisis comes.

Table 8-2. Comparison of Three Infectious Disease Outbreaks in South Korea

	SARS	H1N1	MERS
Time of the first case	September 2003	May 2009	May 2015
Cases	3	750,000	186
Death	0	252	36
Mortality	0%	0.03%	19.35%
Policy/System changes	KCDC founded	None	KCDC expanded and promoted
Communication process	Good	Poor between government and local hospitals	Poor between government & public; between central and local governments
Control tower	Prime Minister	Prime Minister	None
President's approval rating after the epidemic[4)]	29%	27%	33%
Isolated people	2,200	N/A (distributing antiviral agents)	1,364
Time quarantine started	Before the first case was confirmed	Before the first case was confirmed	2 weeks after the first case was confirmed

Questions for Discussion

- What were the key factors that caused nationwide social panic during the MERS crisis in South Korea in comparison with the two previous

4) http://weekly.khan.co.kr/khnm.html?mode=view&artid=201407141653231&code=113

outbreaks of SARS and H1N1?

- Was the Korean government's preparedness and response to SARS, H1N1 and MERS appropriate? Why or why not?
- Did the Korean government system including the main responsible agency (KCDC) have enough capacities and adequate organizational structure to control an unprecedented disease such as SARS or MERS in comparison to the U.S. CDC?
- Was the Korean government's information sharing strategy about diseases and patients suitable during the infectious disease outbreaks?
- What are the roles and responsibilities of the central government and local governments in handling a public health crisis?
- What is the mechanism of trust and distrust formation among the government, news media and people within their complex relationships and interactions?
- How could a high level of social distrust aggravate the public health crisis in a country (e.g., broken communication process, non-compliance with the government's direction, excessive untrustworthy information, etc.)?
- Which would be the most critical barrier to handling a public health crisis in the Korean context: government system failure, poor communication or social distrust? What about in your country or region?

References

Ahn, Y. J.(2015). 'Doctor Shopping' Helped Spread MERS, World Health Organization Says. *NBC NEWS*.

Butler, D.(2015). South Korean MERS Outbreak is Not a Global Threat. *Nature*. Retrieved from http://www.nature.com/news/south-korean-mers-outbreak-is-not-a-global-threat-1.17709. doi, 10.

China, R.(2009, April 26, 2009). FACTBOX-Asia Moves to Ward Off New Flu Virus, *Reuters*. Retrieved from http://www.reuters.com/article/idUST344175

Choe, S. H.(2015a, June 1, 2015). Fears of MERS Virus Prompt Broadening of Cautions in South Korea, *The New York Times*. Retrieved from http://www.nytimes.com/2015/06/04/world/asia/south-korea-mers-cases-lead-schools-to-close.html?_r=2

______(2015b, Jne 12, 2015). MERS Tarnishes Korean President's Image as Leader, *The New York Times*. Retrieved from http://www.nytimes.com/2015/06/13/world/mers-tarnishes-korean-presidents-image-as-leader.html?_r=0

Choi, H. J.(2015, June 8, 2015). Government Belatedly Changes Quarantine Policy "Disclose Names of All Hospitals," *The Kyunghyang Shinmum*. Retrieved from http://english.khan.co.kr/khan_art_view.html?artid=201506081916067&code=710100

Choi, W., Yim, J., Park, J., Kim, S., Na, M., Lee, W., … Kim, W.(2011). Clinical Characteristics and Outcomes of H1N1-Associated Pneumonia Among Adults in South Korea. *The International Journal of Tuberculosis and Lung Disease*, 15(2): 270-275.

Chu, C., Lee, J., Choi, D. H., Youn, S. K., & Lee, J. K.(2011). Sensitivity Analysis of the Parameters of Korea's Pandemic Influenza Preparedness Plan. *Osong Public Health and Research Perspectives*, 2(3): 210-215.

Chung, A. Y.(2015). Korea Yet to Recover from MERS Completely, *The Korea Times*. Retrieved from http://www.koreatimes.co.kr/www/news/nation/2015/12/116_194030.html

Dennis, D. T., Inglesby, T. V., Henderson, D. A., Bartlett, J. G., Ascher, M. S., Eitzen, E., … Layton, M.(2001). Tularemia as a Biological Weapon: Medical and Public Health Management. *Jama*, 285(21): 2763-2773.

Fung, I. C. H., Tse, Z. T. H., Chan, B. S. B., & Fu, K. W.(2015). Middle East Respiratory Syndrome in the Republic of Korea: Transparency and Communication are Key. *Western Pacific Surveillance and Response Journal: WPSAR*, 6(3): 1.

Gal, A., & Jun, K.(2015). Korea's MERS Outbreak Highlights SARS Lessons, *The Wall Street Journal*.

Harris, M., & Clements-Hunt, A.(2015). WHO Recommends Continuation of Strong Disease Control Measures to Bring MERS-CoV Outbreak in Republic of Korea to an End [Press release]

Hong, S. J., & Jin, M. J.(2015). MERS and Social Media Intersect, *Korea JoongAng Daily*. Retrieved from http://koreajoongangdaily.joins.com/news/article/article.aspx?aid=3005702

Hong, Y.(2015, June 17, 2016). Useless MERS's Guildlines NEWSTAPA. Retrieved from http://newstapa.org/26394

Hu, E.(2015). South Korea's MERS Crisis Exposes Public Distrust Of Leaders, *NPR*. Retrieved from http://www.npr.org/sections/goatsandsoda/2015/06/05/412118009/south-koreas-mers-crisis-exposes-public-distrust-of-leaders

Ji, Y.(2015). Difffent Responses between President Rho and Park, *Ohmynews*. Retrieved from http://www.ohmynews.com/NWS_Web/View/at_pg.aspx?CNTN_CD=A0002116048

Kettl, D. F.(2000). The Transformation of Governance: Globalization, Devolution, and the Role of Government. *Public Administration Review*, 60(6): 488-497.

Ki, M.(2015). 2015 MERS Outbreak in Korea: Hospital-to-Hospital Transmission. *Epidemiology and Health*, 37.

Kim, D. H.(2015). Structural Factors of the Middle East Respiratory Syndrome Coronavirus Outbreak as a Public Health Crisis in Korea and Future Response Strategies. *Journal of Preventive Medicine and Public Health*, 48(6): 265-270.

Kim, E., Liao, Q., Yu, E., Kim, J., Yoon, S., Lam, W., & Fielding, R.(2016). Middle East Respiratory Syndrome in South Korea during 2015: Risk-Related Perceptions and Quarantine Attitudes. *American Journal of Infection Control.*

Kim, J. Y.(2016). The 2009 H1N1 Pandemic Influenza in Korea. *Tuberculosis and Respiratory Diseases*, 79(2): 70-73.

Kim, N., Kim, T., Park, E., Song, E., Jun, J., Choi, S., … Kim, T.(2016). The 2015 MERS Outbreak in the Republic of Korea: Learning from MERS (White Paper).

Kim, N., Park, E., Jun, J., KIM, D., Jung, J., Kim, J., … Kim, D.(2015). A Study on Infectious Disease Prevention and Control Systems of Korea: Focused on the Middle East Respiratory Syndrome Coronavirus: *Korea Insitute for Health and Social Affairs.*

Kim, W.(2010). Pandemic Influenza(H1N1 2009): Experience and Lessons. *Infect Chemother*, 42(2): 61-63.

Kim, Y. W., Yoon, S. J., & Oh, I. H.(2013). The Economic Burden of the 2009 Pandemic H1N1 Influenza in Korea. *Scandinavian Journal of Infectious Diseases*, 45(5): 390-396.

Lee, B.(2015). Foreign Travellers to Get Automatic MERS Insurance from S. Korea Government. *the Hankyoreh*. Retrieved from http://english.hani.co.kr/arti/english_edition/e_international/697124.html

Lee, D.(2015). Government Administrative Control Tower in Crisis Management System: Definition, Issues, and Policy Implications. *Korean Journal of Policy Studies*, 30(3): 125-145.

Lee, E.(2015, Sept 25, 2015). Unclear Standards for Compensation, *Korea Joongang Daily*. Retrieved from http://koreajoongangdaily.joins.com/news/article/article.aspx?aid=3009647

Lee, H. Y., Oh, M. N., Park, Y. S., Chu, C., & Son, T. J.(2013). Public Health Crisis Preparedness and Response in Korea. *Osong Public Health and Research Perspectives*, 4(5): 278-284.

Lim, P. L.(2015). Middle East Respiratory Syndrome (MERS) in Asia: Lessons Gleaned from the South Korean Outbreak. *Transactions of The Royal Society of Tropical Medicine and Hygiene*, 109(9): 541-542.

Lim, S., Choi, H. S., Shin, H., Ahn, J. H., Baik, J. J., Choi, Y. H., & Lee, J. K.(2004). Three Cases of Severe Acute Respiratory Syndrome Imported into South Korea. *Korean Journal of Medicine*, 67(6): 655-661.

McGrath, B.(2015, 23 June). MERS Outbreak Exposes South Korean Government's Lack of Preparation, World Socialist Web Site. Retrieved from https://www.wsws.org/en/articles/articles/2015/06/23/mers-j23.html

Muzzatti, S. L.(2005). Bits of Falling Sky and Global Pandemics: Moral Panic and Severe Acute Respiratory Syndrome (SARS). *Illness, Crisis, & Loss*, 13(2): 117-128.

Osterholm, M. T.(2005). Preparing for the Next Pandemic. *New England Journal of Medicine*, 352(18): 1839-1842.

People's Daily Online(2003, May 7, 2003). S. Korea to Spend U.S. $5.5 Million on Preventing SARS Spread, People's Daily Online. Retrieved from http://en.people.cn/200305/07/eng20030507_116360.shtml

Rosenbrock, R.(1987). Some Social and Health Policy Requirements for the Prevention of AIDS. *Health Promotion International*, 2(2): 161–168.

Ryu, K. H.(2015, June 20, 2015). The Korea Centers for Disease Control and Prevention DongA. Retrieved from http://news.donga.com/List/Series_70030000000712/3/70030000000712/20150620/71971437/1

Seungki, Y.(2015, 20 August). News Analysis: What Lessons S. Korea Learn from MERS Outbreak, *Asia & Pacific Edition*. Retrieved from http://news.xinhuanet.com/english/2015–08/20/c_134537135.htm

Shankar, S.(2015). MERS Outbreak Hits Puth Korea Economy, GDP Growth at 6–Year Low, *International Business Times*. Retrieved from http://www.ibtimes.com/mers–outbreak–hits–south–korea–economy–gdp–growth–6–year–low–2021093

Smith, R. D.(2006). Responding to Global Infectious Disease Outbreaks: Lessons from SARS on the Role of Risk Perception, Communication and Management. *Social Science & Medicine*, 63(12): 3113–3123. doi: 10.1016/j.socscimed.2006.08.004

Suh, M., Kang, D. R., Lee, D. H., Choi, Y. J., Tchoe, B., Nam, C. M., … Youm, Y.(2013). Socioeconomic Burden of Influenza in the Republic of Korea, 2007~2010. *PloS one*, 8(12), e84121.

Tambo, E., Oljira, T., Oluwasogo, O. A., Khater, E. I., & Xiao–Nong, Z.(2015). Averting MERS–Cov Emerging Threat and Epidemics: the Importance of Community Alertness and Preparedness Policies and Programs. *Prevention and Infection Control.*

Wallerstein, N.(2006). What is the Evidence on Effectiveness of Empowerment to Improve Health?

World Health Organization(2005a). Risk Communication and the International Health Regu–lation. *World Health Organization.*

______(2005b). WHO Outbreak Communication Guidelines. Author.

______(2009). Pandemic H1N1 2009.

Yoo, S.(2015, 20 August). News Analysis: What Lessons S. Korea Learn from MERS Out–break, *Asia & Pacific Edition*. Retrieved from http://news.xinhuanet.com/english/2015–08/20/c_134537135.html

Teaching Note

Public Health Crisis in South Korea:

Policy Failure or Social Distrust?

Overview

This case study will help students to learn comprehensive policy analytic perspectives and discuss with others about critical public health issues. This case consists of a case study (as a separate document), a decision-forcing game (role play), and teaching resources to engage students in discussion about three recent outbreaks of infectious diseases in South Korea. The case, "Public Health Crisis in South Korea: Government Failure or Social Distrust?" can be used as a main resource to help students understand the background and debate around several controversial issues involved in this case, such as governmental system failure, poor communication, and social distrust. More in-depth discussions and further learning can be made in class with the complementary exercise and teaching resources provided in this teaching note such as teaching plans and objectives, debate questions, and role playing opportunity.

Case Summary

South Korea has experienced three large-scale infectious disease epidemics; SARS in 2003, H1N1 in 2009, and MERS in 2015. The central government of South Korea played an important role in responding to these public health crises, but was criticized for its belated response, weak quarantine process, lack of professional capacity and so on. Particularly in response to MERS, the government's way of communicating with the media and the public concerning the disease accelerated the spread of rumors and aggravated the degree of fear and distrust within the Korean society. The first half of this case illustrates these three epidemic experiences in a chronological order without any position argument so that students can gain some level of independent knowledge and perspectives about the case. The second half of the case introduces three relevant issues — government failure, poor communication and social distrust — in order to help students to critically think about the issues. While reviewing the case along with class discussions, students are expected to learn the roles of government in addressing disease epidemics and communicating with other social entities in emergency situations.

Positioning

This case study could be used in classroom for various undergraduate and graduate level courses in public administration, public policy and management, governance and leadership, particularly for a group of students who have special interests in public health policy and risk management.

Learning Objectives

This case is ideal for multiple discussions such as:

- Finding out key factors of nationwide social panic during the MERS crisis in South Korea in comparison with the two previous outbreaks of SARS and H1N1.
- Assessing whether the Korean government's preparedness and response to SARS, H1N1 and MERS was appropriate or not.
- Evaluating whether the Korean government system including the main responsible agency (KCDC) had enough capacities and adequate organizational structure to control the unprecedented disease in comparison to the U.S. CDC.
- Examining whether or not the government's strategy of information sharing about diseases and patients was suitable or not during the outbreaks.

- Identifying the roles and responsibilities of the central government and local governments in handling a public health crisis.
- Understanding the mechanism of trust and distrust formation among the government, news media, and people within their complex relationships and interactions.
- Considering how a high level of social distrust could aggravate the public health crisis in a country (e.g., broken communication process, non-compliance with the government's direction, excessive untrustworthy information, etc.)
- Debating which will be the most critical barrier to handling public health crises in the Korean context: government system failure, poor communication, or social distrust.

Class Preparation Assignments and Discussion Questions

In order for a more effective class discussion using the case, students should read the case thoroughly and use the information to deliberate the following questions in advance prior to class. The full list of reference should be made available to students as supporting materials so that they can refer to them whenever necessary. Alternatively, the list of general questions could be provided to students after reading the Background section, and then the issue-specific questions after reading the entire case document.

General Questions:

1. Among the three issues discussed in the case, which do you think is the most critical problem in handling public health crises in the Korean context? How about in your country or region?
2. How are those issues related to each other? Would a better understanding of these issues help policymakers to design a better strategy for the outbreak?
3. When a country with the limited capacity of public health facilities, staff, and other resources faces an unexpected disease outbreak, what issue should be prioritized to overcome?
4. Why did the effectiveness of the government response vary across the three different epidemics?

5. What kind of characteristics or circumstances lead to the different responses?

Issue-specific Questions:

Government Failure:

1. Do you think that the responsible agency in South Korea (KCDC) had limited administrative capacities to control the unexpected disease outbreak, compared to the U.S. CDC? If so, why? Please support your answer with evidence from the case document, including Figures 8-1 and Figures 8-2. Feel free to use any external resources.
2. Do you think the Korean government should reform and restructure the KCDC? If so, what plan would you suggest to improve its preparedness and responsiveness to any future outbreak? For instance, does the KCDC need larger staff/budget/resources? Should it remain small but assume a stronger authority? Which needs to be prioritized? You may suggest multiple alternatives for the KCDC and prioritize them. Refer to Table 8-1 in the case document.
3. During infectious disease outbreaks, what roles and responsibilities should the central (or federal) and local government have? What should function as a "control tower?" Based on the experiences in South Korea described in the case document, list a few imperative roles of the central and local government with supporting evidence.

Poor Communication:

1. As described in the subsection of "Poor Communication" in the case document, five guidelines of risk communication were suggested by WHO in 2005 as follows:
   (1) Building, maintaining or restoring trust
   (2) Announcing early
   (3) Being transparent
   (4) Understanding the public
   (5) Incorporating risk communication into preparedness planning

   In terms of risk communication, how well did the Korean central government do in response to the MERS case? If you were appointed as an evaluator from WHO, how would you evaluate their performances and

why?

2. The Korean government was hesitant to release the list of the hospitals where MERS patients were treated because they thought it would create unnecessary anxiety and social chaos. Do you find the justification reasonable? Why or why not?
3. Please read the following news article, which highlights a miscommunication between the central and local governments during the MERS crisis. It is found that the government agencies blamed each other for their reaction to the public. Which government agency do you think made a more reasonable and right decision on information sharing and crisis management?

Pulse by Maeil Business Newspaper print

Miscommunications between governments escalate civil unrest

2015.06.05 16:23:54 | 2015.06.05 16:56:59

While the government is struggling to counter the Middle East respiratory syndrome virus, miscommunications between central and regional governments are escalating the public unrest.

Seoul Mayor Park Won-soon late Thursday that a doctor confirmed to have contracted MERS came into direct and indirect contact with more than 1,500 Seoul residents, while criticizing health authorities are not sharing information with the city in a correct manner.

The announcement was immediately delivered to the public, raising speculation that the deadly virus has spread into the community. But the mayor is also under pressure because he made a hurried announcement even without discussion with the Ministry of Health and Welfare, fueling a public confusion.

On Friday, the presidential office said it is deeply concerned about rising public anxiety following the mayor's announcement because there are many discrepancies between the mayor's statement and the ministry's explanation and the interview with the doctor.

Health and Welfare Minister Moon Hyung-pyo said it is very regrettable that the Seoul Metropolitan Government made a unilateral announcement.

Meanwhile, the mayor protested the government's statement that the city is promoting public unrest despite the urgency of the matter and the current situation cannot be solved by the central government alone.

Source: http://pulsenews.co.kr/print.php?sc=30800001&year=2015&no=542249

Social Distrust:

1. The following picture illustrates something that happened in South Korea during the MERS outbreak; the people who attended a wedding ceremony for a young couple shielded their faces with white masks due to their fear of possible infection. Actually, respiratory disease experts insisted that MERS was not a human virus and could not easily spread between people, unlike SARS.[5] Why do you think the Korean people had such an extreme level of fear about MERS? Was it related to the government's clumsy response to the outbreak or an excessive level of social distrust in Korean society?

2. Among the government, news media, and the people, who do you think plays the most significant role in terms of building social trust or distrust in order to address future outbreaks more effectively? In fact, the government was blamed for a lack of transparency in terms of sharing patient and disease information during MERS, while the news media was criticized for exaggerating the seriousness of the disease during the outbreak. In addition, many people tend to have self-seeking behaviors such as NIMBY, doctor shopping, or creating and spreading rumors. Who holds key to restore the loss of social trust in South Korea? How about your country or region?

---

5) Butler, D. (2015). South Korean MERS Outbreak is Not a Global Threat. *Nature*. Retrieved from http://www.nature.com/news/south-korean-mers-outbreak-is-not-a-global-threat-1.17709.

Suggested Teaching Plan

This 90-minute teaching plan is one of the class examples which can be adopted by a class instructor or facilitator, including various group discussion sessions and decision-forcing game. This plan is designed for targeting upper-level undergraduate or graduate students who are interested in public policy, management and governance. The time allocation along with teaching materials suggested below should be modified based on class structure and student level.

Introduction (5 minutes)

An instructor/facilitator briefly introduces three recent infectious disease epidemics in South Korea (SARS, H1N1, and MERS) so that students can gain the basic knowledge on the diseases and start thinking about the impact of the public health crises on the country. The world map can be used to help students identify the geographic features of South Korea.

Small-group case review and discussions (15 minutes)

Small groups are formed with 4~5 students in each. Each group reviews the case materials along with discussion questions for about 7 minutes. Students can take notes with their thoughts and ideas while reviewing the case. During the remaining time (about 8 minutes), students in each group share their ideas based on discussion questions and summarize their consensus in preparation for a class-wide discussion session.

Class-wide discussion (10 minutes)

Each group takes turn in presenting their ideas and opinions to the entire class. This session provides students with the opportunity to observe how others view the same case differently, which helps students gain a comprehensive perspective of government's roles in addressing emergency situations and communicating relevant information with other stakeholders during the public health crisis. An instructor may need to summarize major lessons from the discussions before the break.

Short break (5~10 minutes)

Group formation for a decision–forcing game (5 minutes)

The entire class is divided into three groups, preferably with different members from the previous discussion session. Each group should designate a leader and a note taker. The other members in each group are assigned to play a role of staff members, cabinet members and assistants for their leaders. An instructor explains the rules of the game (role play) clearly to students.

Small–group preparation for a decision–forcing game (30 minutes)

Each group is assigned to a separate place so that each group cannot obtain any information from others. Students are encouraged to have internet access to seek out more information about the case, even beyond the information and resources provided by the case document. During this session, an instructor may visit each group meeting in order to check if students are on the right track.

Decision–forcing game (15 minutes~5 minutes for each group)

Based on the small–group discussions, each group presents their final positions on the issue to other groups. Throughout the game, students are expected to utilize what they have learned from the case materials and previous discussion sessions. An instructor should record and summarize all of their positions in order to moderate the final wrapping–up discussion. The detailed plan for a decision–forcing game is described below.

Wrapping–up (10 minutes)

Based on all the previous discussions and role–play exercises, the entire class is encouraged to reach some agreements and conclusions on the outstanding issues. For a wrap–up discussion, an instructor may show students the following figure that illustrates a conceptual framework among the three players in the decision–forcing game and their bi–directional interrelation through communication and trust. Students can discuss which link tends to be hampered during the public health crisis and what policy could be used to restore the broken link. This framework can help students to acquire a broad picture of the case along with take–home lessons and facilitate them to reach the final conclusion. A possible conclusion could be a collective strategic plan for how to restore the loss of public trust in Korean society by streamlining the communication process between the Blue House and KCDC.

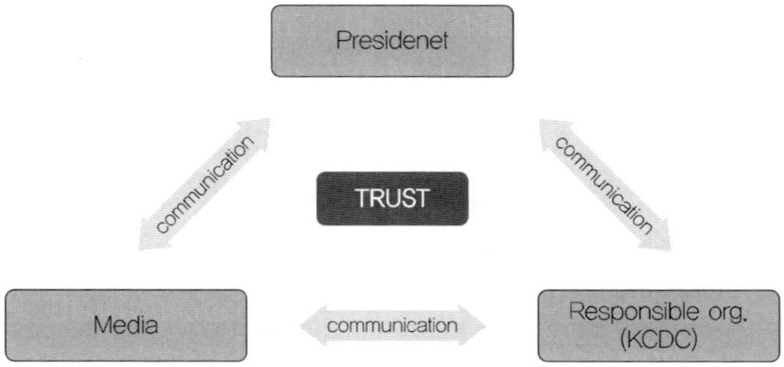

Decision Forcing Game:

This is a role playing exercise in which students interact in a simulated pandemic situation. The class is divided into three groups and each group assign a specific role to each student such as a protagonist (a decision maker) and other members of the given organizations. Different information will be provided to different groups in order to see how they interact to each other in the case of asymmetric information. Students should be given sufficient time to discuss the issue and outline their position within each group. Only the information made available each group should be used to support their conclusions. Once the entire class gathers, each group presents their decisions and positions on various outstanding issues which South Korea could face during the simulated pandemic emergency.

Each group assumes a role of representing three major players during the epidemic situation in South Korea, including the Blue House, KCDC, and a major news media company. The following scenario is one of the examples an instructor could provide to each group of students, but an instructor may add additional information if necessary. The information provided to each group should not be shared prior to the entire group session.

Group A: Blue House—the president and Cabinet members

Assume that you are the president of South Korea and are briefed that the first confirmed patient of the new infectious disease named WARS (West Africa Respiratory Syndrome) was found in a local hospital. Unfortunately, the patient was transferred through several hospitals before he was confirmed positive and isolated. The news media have begun to report this news and the fear has grown among the public. You, as the President, convene the members of your Cabinet, and discuss whether or not the list of the hospitals which the confirmed patient visited should be open to the public. Proponents argue that the public should be aware of the list so that they can protect themselves based on accurate information. It is also argued that the release of the hospital information should help rebuilding social trust in South Korea which has been seriously impaired by several inappropriate responses in the past. Meanwhile, the opponents insist that this information sharing can cause unnecessary anxiety among the public and even social chaos and the situation should be handled while maintaining some level of confidentiality.

As you find in the case document, South Korea has experienced several infectious disease pandemics in the past. In this situation, you, as the chair of Cabinet meeting and the president, have to make a strategic decision on sharing the hospital information with the public. What would be your decision to handle this case effectively and enhance the level of social trust? Please specify your rationale underlying your decision and discuss with other players who may have different information and opinions.

Group B: News media—the editor and staff members

Assume that you are the editor in one of major news media company in South Korea. You received an astounding news from one of credible information sources this morning that the first confirmed patient of the new infectious disease named WARS was found in a local hospital, and the patient was transferred through several hospitals before he was confirmed positive and isolated. You found this situation very similar as MERS in 2015 in which the news media was accused of irresponsible news reporting. The media is facing the dilemmatic situation where they are in between the public's right of knowledge and the government's request of embargo on the news. You have also received a lot of requests from your subscribers to reveal the list of infected hospitals.

In this situation, what would be your decision on revealing the information via the news media? If you hesitate to do so, you may lose many supporters and subscribers.

On the contrary, if you decide to report the news, you may lose your credibility as the hospital information may be incorrect and unconfirmed. Please specify your rationale underlying your decision and discuss with other players who may have different information and opinions.

Group C: KCDC–the director and senior officials

Assume that you are the newly–appointed director of KCDC after the 2015 MERS outbreak. Since then, the KCDC director has more administrative power and discretionary capability during the epidemic. Unfortunately, the first patient of the new infectious disease named WARS (West Africa Respiratory Syndrome) was found in a local hospital, but the patient was transferred through several hospitals before he was confirmed positive and isolated. Your office officially confirmed this case and reported the incident to the Blue House but found they seemed to be hesitant to reveal the information to the media/public mainly due to political reason. Some staff members argue that you must take an independent role of handling this case transparently as a main control tower and make a discretionary decision to disclose the list of infected hospitals for the benefits of the public.

What would be your strategic position in this scenario as a leader of the main government agency responsible for public health issues? You may need to take a risk of ruining your career if disclosing the information without full coordination with the Blue House, but at the same time, your office may be criticized by the media and the public if the epidemic spread rapidly to a large scale due to their hesitation of sharing critical information with the public. If you believe that the information should be disclosed and open to the public, would you take a discretionary action to reveal the information or try to persuade the Blue House? Please specify your rationale underlying your decision and discuss with other players who may have different information and opinions.

Index

Editor

Sujae Yoon (Korea Institute of Public Administration)

Authors

Hee Soun Jang (University of North Texas)
Kyujin Jung (Korea University)
Dohyeong Kim (University of Texas at Dallas)
Taehee Kim (Seoul National University of Science & Technology)
Younhee Kim (Pennsylvania State University, Harrisburg)
M. Jae Moon (Yonsei University)
Eunju Rho (University of Akron)
Chul-Young Roh (Lehman College)